THE
CHALLENGE
OF THE
EAST

THE
CHALLENGE
OF THE
EAST

BY SHERWOOD EDDY

ASIA IN REVOLUTION—
INDIA, CHINA, JAPAN,
KOREA, PHILIPPINES,
TURKEY, PALESTINE

GROSSET & DUNLAP
Publishers   *New York*
by arrangement with Farrar & Rinehart

CONTENTS

FOREWORD

The continent of Asia is in the midst of a vast revolution. The countries with which we shall deal—India, China, Japan, Korea, the Philippines, Turkey and Palestine—are danger zones wherever there are vast contending forces in the midst of international complications which involve other nations. Unquestionably the situation in these countries constitutes an unmistakable challenge to the Western world today.

In *The Challenge of Russia,* we endeavored objectively to estimate the values and dangers of the situation in that country, as *The Challenge of the East* does in the seven countries in Asia with which we are here concerned. In the regular course of his work the writer has been compelled to cross Asia and to go around the world twice in the last three years, in journeys which will have occupied the greater part of his time from June, 1929, to May, 1932. In addition to this the major portion of his life for the last thirty-five years has been spent in Asia. Beginning in 1896 fifteen years were spent among the students of the Indian Empire. Then, for the greater part of the next two decades, his work brought him in continuous contact, not only with alert students and awakening youth, but with the political, industrial, social and religious leaders in the Far and Near East, and in northern and southern Asia.

Everywhere there are signs that we are in the midst of one of the great transitional epochs of all history. Probably greater changes have taken place since the World War, and still greater transformations are likely to occur during the next few decades, than during any equal period of history. As men look back upon this era it may appear in perspective as great, or even greater, than the Renaissance, the Reformation, or the French Revolution.

We stood on the spot called "The Three Emperors' Corner," at the junction of the former empires or kingdoms of Russia, Prussia and Austria, where the three monarchs of the Romanoffs, Hohenzollerns and Hapsburgs met to make their compact against Napoleon. In place of these empires and monarchies a dozen republics have risen on the post-war map of Europe. We have witnessed seven revolutions within two years in Latin America, and the phenomenon is apparently increasing. We are probably entering upon a century of revolutionary movements that may appear as a "milky way" of revolutions.

In our journey around the world there appeared signs everywhere of the unrest which always marks such an era of transition—economic, political, intellectual. There was evidence of world-wide industrial depression with widespread unemployment, with workers everywhere, however inarticulate or helpless, demanding greater security of life and greater social justice, that millions should not be suddenly thrown out of employment through no fault of their own, to beg, or starve or walk the streets as spectres of fear, or to be driven desperate to contemplate revolution as a last resort. Often, based upon this economic situation, there existed widespread political unrest with a growing demand on the part of practically every dependent, conquered or exploited people for what Woodrow Wilson termed self-determination, or liberty in some form. And everywhere there was the inevitable intellectual unrest characterizing such a period of transition.

As we try to focus and unify the picture of all Asia, we shall find that we are facing not disjointed countries in an isolated Orient, but half of a new world at a boiling point of history. Nothing could be more false today than to say regarding East and West that "never the twain shall meet." They are meeting. They have met; and it will be with profound consequences to both. The ultimate effects will not all be on one side. The impact of the West has awakened the East. But it does not yet appear what will be the final contri-

bution of the East to the West. The vast continent of Asia
that was the cradle of the race, the birthplace of civilization,
the mother of all of the great religions of the world, and of
many of its philosophies, is now in the travail of a great rebirth and is entering upon a new creative epoch. Our planet
is yet young, our civilization is only adolescent, and the ancient
East is in process of renewing its youth.

Probably no human mind can fully grasp the import of the
volcanic age in which we are now living. Not only does the
East present a challenge to the West. Beyond the art of man
in any little moving or talking picture which we can artificially
produce, we see in Asia today an amazing panorama of political, social and economic experimentation in all the aspects of
its life. The colossal continent is now affording texts for the
study of the world's experiments, successes, failures and needs.
We could wish that Hegel might rewrite his *Philosophy of
History* in the light of this new Orient. When H. G. Wells'
great, great-grandson writes some future *Outline of History,*
he will doubtless find that both Russia and the East will have
had a powerful part to play in the reshaping of our volcanically
unsettled world. And it is against this world background that
we shall study the new Asia.

Students or youth of the post-war period cannot fully appreciate the magnitude of the changes that are now taking place.
If we contrast the world today with the world of forty years
ago when the writer graduated from college, or thirty-five
years ago, when he first went out to the Orient, the difference
is striking.

We saw Lord Curzon, as Viceroy, who was just arriving
in India as the last typical imperialist in a land that then
seemed changeless and caste-ridden. In China the corrupt
Manchus, the last of eighteen long dynasties, were on the
throne. The wily "Old Buddha," or Dowager Empress, was
even then preparing for the final spasm of revolt against the
resistless impact of the West in the Boxer Uprising. Every
Chinese, whether student or coolie, wore the queue, the age-
long symbol of loyalty to a petrified civilization binding him
to the past. The apparently irresistible advance of foreign

imperialism four centuries after the arrival of the truculent Portuguese in Macao, had fastened the unequal and unjust treaties of seventeen foreign nations upon helpless China, and "dogs and Chinese" were forbidden entrance to the favored parks of the foreigners on China's own soil.

Japan had thrown aside her feudal bows and arrows and was learning rapidly from the West, quietly and in obscurity, with no hint of her later victories over China and Russia. When Dr. Davis, of the Doshisha College, walked down the streets of Kyoto, the ancient capital, salt was sprinkled upon the ground where he had walked, to purify the city of his polluting presence. Notice boards forbidding any Japanese subject to embrace the hated and dreaded foreign religion on pain of death had only recently been removed from the roads.

Korea was still "the hermit nation" and "without doubt the worst governed state in Asia." Its parasitic, predatory aristocracy and corrupt officials were systematically robbing the common people, cowed by impaled human heads by the roadside. In stagnant, thriftless isolation, sunk in the superstition of shamanism, apart from a few liberal thinkers who were imprisoned by the corrupt King, the people lived their miserable lives untroubled by even the faintest dream of justice, liberty or "independence," terms which are now on the lips of everyone.

The Philippines were still under the corrupt and autocratic rule of ancient Spain. In 1896 Rizal, the patriot-martyr of the Filipinos, was shot by a Spanish firing squad. Under the reaction and vengeance of the friars, Filipino priests and patriotic laymen were being placed on trial or tortured to death, while mass deportations and colonies of political exiles from Spain had resulted in the policy of the Archbishop for "fire, sword and wholesale executions," to quench the growing aspirations of the Filipinos.

Turkey, under "Abdul the Damned," the worst and among the last of a long line of sultans, was suffering from periodic massacres and widespread degeneration, degradation and corruption.

In Palestine, the writer had found traveling alone dangerous under the rule of Turkey. Peace in the Christian shrines was preserved only by the bayonets of Turkish soldiers. The Arabs, in their black goats' hair tents, were living on a more backward and primitive cultural level than was to be found six thousand years before in Ur of the Chaldees, Abraham's birthplace. There was no dream either of "Arab independence," or of a realized Jewish National Home for the most persecuted race in the world.

What a change in outlook we face in the East today. As Upton Close well says: "All Asia has flared into revolt against the dominant white man. The revolt takes three main phases. It is against the white man's political rule, the imposition of his culture and religion, and, most deep seated of all, his arrogant assumption of social superiority." And the peoples of the East are in revolt, not only negatively against a stifling foreign imperialism, but positively for the realization of a new life of their own. In every awakened land of Asia, as indeed in all the world, men are now demanding and will inevitably and increasingly demand, *basic economic justice to provide decent living conditions for all, which shall make possible liberty for spiritual self-realization, both personal and national.*

There is something elemental, human and universal about this two-fold demand for basic economic justice and political liberty. These were the essential demands in the American Revolution of 1776, the French Revolution in 1789, and the Russian Revolution in 1917, though in the latter liberty was for one class and was conditioned by a temporary dictatorship, but the goal was a classless society. And just these demands for justice and liberty are imperatively made in all the seven countries of the East which we are now considering.

Everywhere there is the demand for freedom in the East—in India, the Philippines and Korea; in Egypt, Iraq and Palestine; from independent Japan to the free Republic of Turkey, and China with its insistence on the abrogation of every unequal treaty. The demand is unmistakable and persistent. The din of it is in our ears. Typical of the whole movement, while visiting the Philippines, we heard of a very small boy who, when asked to describe a cow, replied: "The cow is an animal with four legs, one at each corner. The cow gives milk, but as for me, give me—liberty, or give me death!"

To us this is, of course, very amusing. The little boy is just a joke. He is only reciting what our American educators have been teaching the youth of these islands for three decades. But this little boy is speaking not only for the Filipino people but for all of awakening Asia. He takes himself, as they all do, as seriously as did Patrick Henry, whose demands at the time were heard with the same irritation or amused contempt with which we in America now hear of that "bandit" rebel, Sandino.

At long perspective and at safe distance Macaulay could count the day of India's awakening as "the proudest day in English history," but when it actually comes it seems to many like insolent and ungrateful effrontery. Moreover, as in adolescence, the aspiration for independence often comes before the ability for or the experience of it. This brings inevitable conflict between the older and younger generations, and between the indigenous nationalism and the foreign imperialism.

Contrasted with that of a short generation ago, we face a new and challenging world in Asia today. In ancient India a changeless, caste- and custom-ridden people are in the midst of a volcanic upheaval, under the explosive power of a new nationalism. Separated in race, religion, language and caste, how can such a divided and subdivided subcontinent ever be united, with its nine contending religions, two hundred and twenty-two languages and dialects, and its more than three thousand castes and subcastes? "India is not and can never be a nation," we have been constantly told. But at the moment of writing they *are* being united under a great leadership, perhaps the most unique and significant in the world today. It is not improbable that as large a proportion of the people of India give their sympathy and allegiance to Mr. Gandhi today, as did the American colonists to George Washington in 1776. President John Adams estimated that one-third of the colonists were not in sympathy with the American Revolution at that time and opposed it at every stage; perhaps a third were indifferent, while a third actively and sacrificially supported it. It is probable that more than a third of the population of India supports Mr. Gandhi, while ninty-nine per cent of the Christian population of the Philippines is practically unanimous for independence. Even Carmi Thompson admitted that "the entire voting population is for independence." A great experiment is being tried in India, as another, the poles apart in method, is being tried in Russia; the one in individual freedom, the other in social control. Both are significant because liberty and justice are both imperative. And both may be valuable and instructive in the means used, although one may be in danger of the extreme of anarchy and the other of tyranny.

China, in the throes of a civil war which has threatened the life of the nation ever since the founding of the Republic in 1911, seems to be sinking in chaos. It has indeed reached almost the lowest point it has known in modern history and is undoubtedly the neediest nation in the world today. Yet the situation is far from hopeless. It is a familiar thought that the West passed through a series of four or five revolutions spread over as many centuries while China, unprepared, has to suffer them all at once. It is like a patient attacked by five major diseases at one time. Such an affliction would kill almost any nation but China. But she seems to be not only indestructible, but to have a marvelous power of survival and of perennial renewal. This immobilized solidarity, petrified by ancestor worship, intact for more than four millennia, is at last disintegrating under the crushing revolutionary forces of the modern world. Her farmers of forty centuries have now to face the challenge of high speed industrialism.

China, the oldest enduring civilization, which has witnessed the fall of all her early contemporaries, is staggering under the burden of five contemporary revolutions at once—an economic and industrial revolution, a political upheaval, an intellectual renaissance, a social transformation and a moral and religious reformation. The religious Reformation of the sixteenth century plunged Europe into civil war; it had political, military and social consequences. The same is true in China today. The old humanism of Confucianism, Taoism and Buddhism, priceless as was their contribution to classic China, is breaking down under the strain of modern life. Some force from outside must integrate and reconstruct China if she is to be saved. Christianity and Communism are both bidding for that place. The former, after more than a century of preparation, working through a body that once numbered some ten thousand foreign missionaries, and a vast network of schools, colleges and indigenous churches, seeks to reconstruct China by evolutionary, educational and ordered progress. The latter proposes a swift, destructive revolution under a ruthless dictatorship.

China is more immediately and widely threatened with Communism than any country in the world today. There is repeated concrete evidence that wherever it is locally established in China, it assumes forms more destructive and cruel, with greater loss of life than took place in Russia, even in the most destructive phases of the Soviet revolution. Only a generation ago in the Taiping Rebellion over twenty millions perished and it would not be at all impossible to have something approaching this repeated, if an Oriental, Tartar, Communist dictatorship is established in China. The Asiatic Stalin with his whole political machine would be behind them. Communists are today working feverishly in China, Germany and Poland. Should these fall under the dictatorship, there would be one solid U. S. S. R. as a group of federated republics, whose policy would be determined by the centralized dictatorship of Stalin and the inner nine of the Political Bureau in Moscow, to face a divided and warring capitalist world. China is the spearhead of the Communist advance in the East today, and all Western nations are involved there with their interests in life and property.

East and West, the old world and the new, meet in China today, as in each of the seven countries in Asia that we shall consider. We are witnessing simultaneously the disintegration of an old order and the creation and reintegration of the new. The process of destruction and disintegration is much more palpable, evident and dramatic than the silent and hidden growth of the new life within. But, while the destruction is more challenging, the constructive phase will ultimately be more promising and potent.

The achievements of modern Japan are epitomized and embodied in the person of that grand old man, Viscount Shibusawa. A boy of fourteen, when Commodore Perry's fleet forced open the unwilling doors of isolated, medieval Japan in 1854, he has seen this great people build a new social order and an invincible modern nation within his own lifetime. Lacking almost every condition of economic success, without adequate soil on her volcanic islands of lava and sand, deficient in all the basic raw materials of coal, iron and oil, with little capital and an impoverished people, facing frequent earthquakes, the last of which cost her a loss of three and a half billion dollars, and in a single day greater destruction of life and property than the whole Russo-Japanese war, Japan as a truly great nation has irresistibly forged to the front.

In thirty-five years Japan's foreign trade has increased 1740 per cent, to an annual total of approximately two billion dollars. She has multiplied her cotton spindles thirteenfold, her production of raw silk ninefold, and the value of her manufactured goods has increased three and a half billion dollars a year. Building her first tiny steamer as late as 1898, in two decades she has launched three million tons of shipping with the third largest merchant marine, and the third strongest navy in the world. During the same period she has increased her voters from half a million to thirteen million, with universal manhood suffrage. She has become an almost literate nation, claiming 99.47 per cent of her boys and 99.38 per cent of her girls of school going age in school. With a population of 64,000,000 on her beautiful but impoverished islands, increasing about a million a year, and with already 90,000,000 in her empire, Japan may be the first nation after Russia to adopt a modern and enlightened policy on birth control.

The Philippines and Korea, under the tutelage of the United States and Japan respectively, have been rapidly reformed and economically improved, and are both now demanding their political independence. Under three decades of American rule, the Philippines have made more advance in most departments of life than under the three hundred and seventy-seven years of Spanish rule. The population has increased from six to thirteen millions. The islands have been completely self-supporting and have increased their trade approximately more than tenfold in the last two decades. More than a third of all the children are already in school and sixty per cent of the population is now literate, under a better system of education than was found in many of our western states a generation ago. They already have a larger percentage of children in high schools than has England, France, Italy or Spain. They devote 28 per cent of their entire budget to education, a larger proportion than almost any other country in the world.

It should be remembered that the United States is not dealing with the Philippines merely as a private ward or as an isolated instance, but as one of the most advanced portions of the East. Our policy will have its effect on the whole of awakening Asia. In the developing conflict and under the growing demand for independence, the United States will soon have to throw its weight on the side of a repressive foreign imperialism or of the new nationalism.

Korea desires her independence from Japan as do the Philippines from the United States, or as does India from Great Britain. It would surprise many an American to find that in a great many respects Korea has made as brilliant a material advance under two decades of Japanese tutelage as have the Philippine Islands after three decades of American rule. A generation ago Korea's misgoverned and corrupt cities were in darkness; today they are lighted by electricity, with imposing modern buildings, wide streets, growing trade and multiplying signs of progress. Her once bare hills are newly afforested and her agriculture is being aided with the purpose of placing it upon a scientific basis. During the two decades of Japanese rule the trade of Korea has increased over thirteenfold to a total of $400,000,000, a greater total and proportion of growth than in the Philippines during the same period. The entire production of the peninsula has multiplied fivefold, its exports twentyfold and the output of industries twenty-threefold in the last twenty years. Once isolated as the "Land of the Morning Calm," Korea now finds herself on the longest railway in the world, stretching from Tokyo to Paris.

The new Republic of Turkey in the Near East is today sending a thrill of hope throughout Asia as did Japan from the Far East two decades ago. After thirty centuries of warfare about her straits, and thirteen centuries of strife between Moslem and Christian, and between the "Sick Man of Europe" and the ruthless imperialism of the Western Powers, we are witnessing at last the rebirth of Turkey in the greatest era of progress she has ever known. In place of the old sultanate and caliphate, we see a new spirit of nationalism in the new Parliament and the new Republic. On a single day, December 1, 1928, Turkey dared to change her very alphabet from the classic Arabic of the past to the modern Roman used in the West. A new national system of education has been organized and Turkey now has the ambition of becoming a literate nation within a decade.

Palestine, once an ancient battleground and meeting point of three continents, Asia, Africa and Europe; the point where the three great monotheisms of the world today meet in conflict, Judaism, Christianity and Islam, a "Holy Land" of all three religions, is at the same time perforce the battleground between an old and a new social order, a civilization of the East and of the West, and the point of strife between Arab and Jewish nationalism. An Arab majority is now claiming its "promised" independence for helping to win the War, while at the same time a Jewish minority demands the fulfillment of the Balfour Declaration, Palestine as a National Home for the Jewish people of the world, after centuries of prejudice, pogroms and persecutions. We shall find that although it is "the least of all lands," the entire world has a stake in Palestine, and world public opinion, expressed informally and through the League of Nations, may have the deciding voice in finding a way for the fulfillment of the legitimate aspirations of both peoples. It will require all the skill and sympathetic understanding of the British, who hold a mandate for Palestine under the League, to do elemental justice and

afford equal opportunity for both races in this conflict. But
as we contrast the sodden and corrupt misgovernment of this
country under the degenerate Turkish Empire two decades
ago, perhaps no equal area in all Asia has seen a more startling
transformation than this. The Jews have invested over $50,-
000,000 in their projects, many of which exhibit an almost
epic quality of heroism and sacrifice. Modern Zionism has
revived the spirit of Israel which existed among the Babylonian exiles in captivity, and the scattered Jews of the dis-
persion, after the destruction of the Temple by the Romans
in 70 A. D.

It bids fair to realize the dream of Theodor Herzl of forty
years ago as a modern prophet of hope for the national rebirth
of this long-persecuted people with a renaissance of Jewish
life, literature and culture, not as a mere geographical country,
but as a symbol of a people's resurrection. Under an impartial British administration, it may in time achieve not only
political democracy, but a genuine social awakening on the
part of the impoverished and degraded Arab fellaheen. Not
in their own aristocratic effendi, but in this new spirit of the
East, that is stirring everywhere, awakening fresh hopes over
whole masses of mankind, does their hope lie.

We desire to write objectively and impartially concerning
these seven countries and the continent of Asia as a whole.
We find ourselves in conscious sympathy both with the aspirations of the people of India and with the baffling problems
which confront the British in that country. We have unshaken
confidence in the character of the Chinese people and of their
great future, but also an appreciation of the difficulties which
now confront the foreigner there and of the necessity of dealing with the abysmal evils of China upon a basis of sympathetic realism rather than of sentimental romanticism.

We have a growing admiration and sympathy for the truly
great Japanese people and their remarkable achievements.
While we eagerly admit their brilliant accomplishments not
only in Japan, but in Korea, we are also in full sympathy with
the natural and inevitable aspirations of the Korean people for
early autonomy and ultimate independence. Although the

latter is not seriously entertained in Japan at present both peoples can proceed upon a basis of a growing autonomy—local, provincial and finally central; legal, political and cultural.

We view with satisfaction the achievements of the United States in the Philippines in so rapidly preparing a people for self-government, but also share with the Filipinos their hope of having their own government under some plan which will avert economic bankruptcy which immediate and unconditional independence would probably cause. We appreciate the brilliant achievements of the new Turkey, yet hope that the dangers of an undoubted dictatorship there may be steadily lessened. We feel the need of a genuine awakening and ultimate democracy for the Arab majority in Palestine, but sympathize also with the imperative need of a moral and spiritual homeland for the whole Jewish people and the successful colonization of the maximum number of Jews that can be settled in Palestine, without endangering the economic progress of the Arab majority in that land of slender resources.

If the writer has any bias or any personal equation against which the reader should be on his guard, it is a natural sympathy with the under dog, in favor, wherever possible, of the new nationalism against the old foreign imperialism. Yet we repeat that we must write with realism rather than sentimental idealism. There are certain facts which must be told today, however painful or humiliating they may be to the nationals of the various countries concerned, especially at a time when all the peoples above concerned are super-sensitive concerning their own defects.

There is an element of the saving of "face" in almost every country in Asia today. On its better side, face may mean honor, self-respect, dignity, propriety, the avoidance at all costs of a devastating inferiority complex. On its worse side it may stand for unreality and even hypocrisy, as when China today, with wounded dignity, points out the evils of the opium trade of foreign nations which are exploiting her, but without admitting the beam in her own eye of her own opium traffic, which is tenfold greater and more shameful than the activities of all the foreign nations in China combined. But no evils in Asia or the world are any more disgraceful than the shame of America's misgoverned cities, or the type of life that has been represented by Al Capone and the crime, racketeering and bootlegging of American gangland. If he has been no less patriotic for always being unsparing in exposing the social evils of America, the writer hopes he will not be counted unsympathetic when candor compels him to give a faithful and realistic presentation of actual conditions in all the countries in Asia, in this period of violent transition when things are far from ideal anywhere.

The writer is indebted to many friends in the various countries who have read portions of the manuscript and offered suggestions. He is especially indebted to his late friend, K. T. Paul, and to H. A. Popley in India, to Frank Lenz of China, to certain Korean and Japanese friends who have criticized the chapter on Korea, although after every effort to be fair he fears that the present chapter will satisfy neither; to Hon. Camilo Osias, Resident Commissioner in Washington, for suggestions on the chapter on the Philippines, and especially to Mrs. Betty Parker Wilks and Miss Jessica M. Moreland for reading the proofs in the writer's absence and for invaluable collaboration.

LONDON, July 4, 1931.

THE
CHALLENGE
OF THE
EAST

CHAPTER I

India is in revolution. She is in the midst of the first non-violent revolution of history on a large scale. And neither Great Britain nor the world has realized it, except for a few discerning spirits. The new type of revolution has so differed from that of the seven years of warfare of the tiny armies of the American colonies, or the brutal forces of destruction released in the French and Russian revolutions, that men have failed to grasp its deep significance. It was an epochal event when 3,000,000 colonists fought for and founded the first democratic republic of its type. It may be of even greater significance if, under the spiritual dominance of a single statesman-saint, the leaders and masses of 330,000,000 can be awakened to nationhood, forged into unity, though the most divided people on earth, led through a supreme conflict and trial of strength with the strongest empire in the world, and finally win a new constitution in political liberty, almost without bloodshed or violence, after ten thousand years of the most monotonous history of warfare and violent revolutions in the world.

Two men have led the two great revolutions of the twentieth century—Lenin and Gandhi. The one with clenched fist, standing on a gun-carriage in Petrograd, called for a revolution of blood and iron on the part of the workers of the world, and forged a dictatorship, a tyranny and a terror to carry out his demands of social justice. The other sits cross-legged upon the floor in the posture of Buddha, turning his spinning wheel—a wheel of fate, of freedom for one-fifth of the human race, or reconciliation between Orient and Occident by the appeal to reason rather than the age-long appeal to force.

There is vivid drama in this battle of "soul-force" between this wisp of a man, single-handed, and the vast British Empire and in principle against the whole machine civilization of the modern world. We see him as a timid boy, the product of caste-ridden Hinduism, married at the age of twelve, afraid even to sleep in the dark. We see him sinking into his seat in confusion as a young barrister at his first case in court, unable to open his lips, and in discouragement resolving to abandon the legal profession. We see him next in South Africa defending the cause of the liberation of his fellow Indians under indignity and injustice, losing himself, as he is mobbed, beaten and jailed, rising in a new courage, to become probably the most fearless man of his day. Submitting to scorn and violence, arrested and imprisoned again and again, he heartened and organized the weak until they shamed the strong, when ten thousand fellow Indians went proudly to prison with him. With the patience and courage of the terrible meek, tempered through twenty years of strife, he at last won freedom in principle for his despised and despoiled race in South Africa.

We see him back in India after the War, turning finally against the foreign Government after "the massacre of Amritsar", when hundreds of his unarmed fellow-countrymen were shot down by General Dyer, who was finally justified in his action by the resolution of the House of Lords and rewarded with a jeweled sword and a purse of $130,000. [1]

We see him next facing a British Judge before his first Indian sentence to six years' imprisonment, following his earlier campaign of non-violence, with the eyes of all India upon him as they draw the parallel of Christ before Pilate, as Gandhi thus pleads guilty: "I should know the consequences of every one of my acts. I knew that I was playing with fire. I ran the risk, and if I was set free I would still do the same. I wanted to avoid violence. Non-violence is the first article of my faith.

---

[1] Although the action of General Dyer was condemned by the minority report of the tardy Hunter Commission as having "caused great disservice to British rule in India," and by the House of Commons, it was condoned by the House of Lords whose action was published throughout the Indian press.

It is also the last article of my faith.   But I had either to
submit to a system which I consider has done irreparable harm
to my country, or incur the risk of the mad fury of my people
bursting forth. . . .   I am here therefore to invite and submit
to the highest penalty that can be inflicted upon me for what
in law is a deliberate crime and what appears to me to be the
highest duty of a citizen." [1]

We see him in prison—in his last of many imprisonments—
spending four hours a day, apparently impotent at his spinning
wheel, yet in spirit everywhere directing the whole campaign,
first against the salt tax, then the boycott of the Government
opium and liquor shops and of foreign trade, and finally in
Bardoli against the land tax.   The campaign grows in volume
in Bombay, in Bengal, in the Punjab.   Some fifty or sixty
thousand of his followers—Nationalists, Hindus, Moslems,
Sikhs and Christians, men and women, go boldly to prison
with him.   The hospitals in the troubled districts are filled with
the wounded and sometimes tortured prisoners.   The processions in protest march on in their white homespun caps.   The
brave Sikh ex-soldiers, wearing their sacred swords which,
under the leadership of Gandhi, they have vowed not to touch,
come marching on only to be clubbed into insensibility by the
foreign-led police force.

We see him once again with the leaders of the seventy
million Moslems reaching out a hand of reconciliation across
the abyss of the age-long religious, racial and political divisions that separate the two communities—Hindu and Moham-

[1] We may contrast with Mr. Gandhi's attitude that of his jailer, Sir
George Lloyd, when Governor of Bombay, who thought that his cause was
lost when they had him in prison: "Just a thin, spindly, shrimp of a fellow
was Gandhi!   But he swayed three hundred and nineteen million people and
held them at his beck and call.   He didn't care for material things.   He
preached nothing but the ideals and morals of India.   You can't govern a
country with ideals!   Still, that was where he got his grip upon the people.
He was their god . . . He gave us a scare!   His program filled our jails.
You can't go on arresting people forever, you know—not when there are
319,000,000 of them.   And if they had taken his next step and refused to
pay taxes!   God knows where we should have been!   Gandhi's was the
most colossal experiment in world history; and *it came within an inch of
succeeding*.   But he couldn't controls men's passions.   They became violent
and he called off his program.   You know the rest.   We jailed him."

medan. "He has long been the best known politician on the
planet; since Lenin died, he may be said to be the one who
has brought about the vastest and profoundest changes. Many,
in widely diverse lands, consider him the greatest man of his
generation. . . . His humanity, too, is one of the profoundest things this world has seen. He has pity and love for every
race, and most of all for the poor and oppressed. He is without fear or care of self. He is humorous, kindly, obstinate,
brave . . . He has definitely shifted the course of a people's
way—of the way of many peoples." Thus Edward Thompson of Oxford describes him. [1] Even his three Mohammedan
opponents each characterized him to Bishop McConnell as,
in the moral and spiritual sphere, "incomparably the greatest
man now living."

A new experiment is being tried on our planet today. To
grasp its significance we should think of Mr. Gandhi, not as
a strange, Oriental, ascetic, mystic saint or crank, but as the
embodiment of a principle—an eternal principle perhaps.
Here is a man who dares to apply the Sermon on the Mount
in politics, who dares to stake his very life and the freedom
and life of his nation on the conviction that love is "creation's
final law."

Can one weak man win freedom for 330,000,000 people,
nearly one-fifth of the human race, without striking a blow,
without boasting, without violence and without hate, empty-
handed, armed with no weapon but love? If he can he has
discovered something new upon this planet, something of
which George Washington never even faintly dreamed, something that will profoundly affect human history. If he can,
then the meek may begin to inherit the earth.

On March 12, 1930, barefooted, possessing nothing but the
one white cotton cloth upon his back, which he had made himself and was ready to give to any beggar who needed it more
than he, this little man with eighty-one of his followers and
friends started on his march to the sea. The project seemed
ludicrous. He proposed to take a handful of salt water and

---

[1] *The Reconstruction of India,* by Edward Thompson, pp. 130-136.

give it to the starving poor.   The gesture seemed so harmless, so futile.

Like the Stamp Act in the American Colonies in 1776 and the slogan "no taxation without representation," the salt tax in India, with its burden upon the poor, whether economic or psychological, had become a matter of principle, a burning issue, a test case.   India held that it was not by right rich Britain's monopoly.   It was God's sea and God's salt for God's poor.   Gandhi would with non-violence break this law, upheld by the unanimous moral sentiment of the people.

When he, with his seemingly impoverished and feeble followers, started for the sea to take his handful of salt, the man in the street in England laughed.   But England laughs no more. Within a year Gandhi had almost won without striking a blow!

In less than a year he emerged at three o'clock in the morning, after his final interview with Lord Irwin, from the archway of the Viceroy's palace in Delhi to walk six miles alone in a driving rain, and to throw himself down upon a bed of straw upon the floor, to snatch a few moments of rest before his morning hour of prayer.   But he had won the major portion of his claims, and Britain had yielded the people's right forever to make salt from the sea; their right to boycott the opium shops of the Government monopoly, that this unwanted poison drug should not be sold to the women and children of India; their right to boycott the importation of foreign cloth, a single item which if fully enforced would cause Great Britain an annual loss of over two hundred million dollars; and the right of the Nationalists to sixteen seats at the second Round Table Conference to draw up a final constitution for India.   But Mr. Gandhi will not take these sixteen seats.   He will take but one.   If he goes at all he will go alone to the Conference.   He is strong enough to stand alone.

We felt sorry for Woodrow Wilson going almost alone to Paris, to meet defeat, as one by one he surrendered or retreated on almost all of his fourteen points, beaten almost every time that Lloyd George and Clemenceau of the Big Four combined against him, and saving only his beloved League out of the

wreck. But we shall not feel sorry if Mr. Gandhi goes alone
to the Conference.

Following the ancient Indian practice of "sitting *dharna*,"
where an aggrieved person "sat fasting until death or redress
released him," Mr. Gandhi, as Professor Thompson points
out, has been sitting at the British Empire's threshold for
thirty years. Indeed he is waiting today at the whole world's
doorstep. Thus sits the humble Spinner of Sabarmati quietly
demanding both social justice for the impoverished masses,
in the poorest country on earth, and freedom for the most
populous conquered country in the world, challenging Britain's
right to rule, without the consent of the governed, three-quarters of her Empire, and boldly arraigning our whole materialistic, capitalistic, competitive civilization with its endless
injustice, exploitation and war. Here, in issues that are more
far-reaching than the mere form of government of India itself,
is the compelling voice of the East.

The character of the non-violent resistance of the Gandhi
Nationalists is related by many eye-witnesses. The following
account by the American newspaper correspondent, Negley
Farson, printed in the *Chicago Daily News* and *The Christian
Century* of July 2, 1930, gives a vivid picture of India in
revolution.

"Bearded Sikhs—several with blood dripping from their
mouths,—refusing to move or even to draw their 'karpans' or
sacred swords to defend themselves from a shower of lathi
blows. Hindu women and girls dressed in orange robes of
sacrifice flinging themselves on the bridles of horses and im-
ploring mounted police not to strike male congress volunteers.
Stretcher bearers waiting beside little islands of prostrate, un-
flinching, immovable Satyagrahis, who had flung themselves
on the ground, grouped about by their women upholding the
flag of swaraj.

"These were the scenes Saturday where the six-day deadlock between police and Mahatma Gandhi's followers broke
out in a bewildering, brutal and stupid spectacle. The trouble arose over a magistrate's order prohibiting a parade of
congress volunteers before Motilal Nehru, president of the

congress party, who came here to Bombay to lead and stiffen the civil disobedience campaign. Nehru, let it be said, has the reputation of being non-violent himself. Nehru was going to take the salute of this monster congress volunteer review. When he learned that the police had prohibited it, also that blood would be let, he persisted. Therefore, as the leader of one side, Nehru permitted it to come off. In fact he must have wanted it. After watching brutality that made me physically ill, martyrlike courage so sublime it wrung my heart—I asked a bleeding volunteer if that were not so.

" 'Yes,' he cried fanatically, 'we wanted it! We wanted it! We want to show the whole world what the British are doing to us!' Which gives you one reason why apparently decent English police sergeants were forced to beat non-resisting men. They were resisting—but in a manner peculiar to India itself.

"The scene opened at 6 o'clock outside the esplanade. At the police station facing the park some hundreds of yellow-turbaned, blue-clad, bare-legged Mahratti policemen were leaning on their dreaded bamboo lathis under the command of a score of English police sergeants. At 6:45, marching in good formation down the tree-lined boulevard, came the first detachment of volunteers. This was the ambulance unit, mostly boys and young doctors dressed in khaki, with Red Cross badges on their arms. They marched past the waiting police without a glance to the south side of the playing field, where they parked their ambulances and brought out their stretchers. It was gruesomely like nurses and orderlies preparing an operating theater.

"At 7 o'clock began to come processions of white robed volunteers bearing red, green and white banners, singing 'We Will Take Swaraj—India, Our Motherland.' At the head of each walked a detachment of women and girls dressed in orange robes, many garlanded with jasmine. As they passed the silent police leaning on their lathis the faces of the marchers tightened, but, set in the resolve of martyrdom, they marched steadily on and actually lined up behind the stretchers which were waiting to bear them wounded and bleeding off the field.

"Dark-faced Mahratti policemen in their sinister yellow turbans marched along in columns led by English sergeants across the field toward the waiting crowd. As they neared it the police went faster. The Hindus, who might be willing to die but dread physical pain, watched them approach with frightened eyes. Then the police broke into a charge.

"Crash! Whack! Whack! Whack! . . . At last the crowd broke. Only the orange clad women were left standing beside the prostrate figures of crumpled men. Congress volunteer ambulances clanging bells, stretcher bearers running helter skelter across the field. Whack! Whack! Whack!— one's anger flamed at the sound of those lathi blows.

"Then came a band of fifty Sikhs and the most amazing scene I have ever witnessed. The Sikhs, as you know, are of a fierce, fighting brotherhood. These Sikhs were Akalis of a fanatic religious sect. They wore the karpan, or sacred sword, and with them were fifteen of their young girls and women. Coming from all districts as representatives of the fighting Punjab, these splendid looking Sikhs swore they would not draw their karpans to defend themselves—they would not leave the field—and, be it noted, they did not! 'Never, never, never!' they cried to the terrific delight of their Hindu brothers in swaraj. 'We will never retreat. We will die, we will die.'

"I cannot describe it—but such fanaticism made one feel sick. The police felt so, too, and hesitated before hitting the Sikhs. They asked their women to leave the field. 'No,' said the women, 'we will die with our men.' It was terrible. Mounted Indian policemen, who had been galloping across the field whacking heads indiscriminately, came to a perfect stymie when they faced the little cluster of blue Akali turbans on the slender Sikh men. 'The Sikhs are brave men—how can we hit them?' It was not fear, but sheer respect. But the police, determined to try to clear the field, at last rushed around the Sikh women and began to hit the men. I stood within five feet of the Sikh leader as he took the lathi blows. He was a short, heavy muscled man, like one of the old Greek gods. "The blows came—he stood straight. His turban was knocked off. The long black hair was bared with the round topknot. He closed his eyes as the blows fell—until at last he swayed and fell to the ground. No other Sikhs had tried to shield him, but now, shouting their defiance and their determination to die rather than move, they wiped away the blood streaming from his mouth. Hysterical Hindus rushed to him bearing cakes of ice to rub the contusions over his brown eyes. The Sikh gave me a bloody smile—and stood up for more. And then the police threw up their hands. 'You can't go on hitting a blighter when he stands up to you like that.' For two hours these unbelievable scenes went on.

"The Sikhs had told the police that if the police left first they would leave too. The police did, and at 9 o'clock the survivors of the Sikhs, not one of whom was not covered with blood stains and with some part or another of his clothes torn, led the triumphant procession of Gandhi's non-violent congress followers down the streets. The injured in the hospitals must number several hundred, some seriously hurt from the wounds of lathi blows. No police were touched."

The India which is now in turmoil is not so much a single country as a vast subcontinent. More than any other country in the world, it is divided and subdivided by race, religion, language and caste. It is the great religious arena of the world with its nine principal faiths. The nearly one-fifth of the human race resident in India is divided between some 222 different languages and 2300 castes and subcastes. [1] Yet in the face of seemingly insurmountable obstacles a growing nucleus

---

[1] Statistics differ widely in India. In this chapter where possible we have followed *The Statistical Abstract for British India*, the *Census Reports*, and the annuals issued by the Government of India's Director of Public Information. The census is taken once every ten years. In 1921 the population of all India was 318,942,480. In the census of 1931, if India maintains her past average increase of 4.1 per cent a decade, it will be a little over 330,000,000, at which, roughly, we shall reckon the present population. The Census of 1921 recorded 188 distinct languages. Sir George Greerson in his *Linguistic Survey of India* recognizes 179 languages and 544 dialects.

of the people of India is now being forged into a new national
unity.

To grasp India in imagination, one must stand at the summit of the vast Himalayan range and look out across the
level river-plains of the north and the dry table-land of the
south. The Himalayas, sweeping across the northern boun-
dary for 1500 miles, form a vast watershed, the backbone of
the world, where the line of perpetual snow rises from 16,000
to over 29,000 feet, and the whole of Switzerland could be
lost in its largest valley. In the northern river-plains the
density of population rises in some districts to over 900 per
square mile, but over most of India the poor and primitive
cultivation furnishes but scant sustenance for this over-
crowded and underfed mass of humanity. Roughly nine-
tenths of the population is rural, living in 687,000 villages,
while only eleven per cent are in towns of over 5,000. About
three-fourths live by agriculture and only four per cent are
employed in factories. Of the total population seven per cent
are literate and ninety-three per cent are still illiterate. Up
to the present time there have been only about seven and a half
million voters, while some two hundred and forty millions
in British India are as yet unenfranchised.

The area of India is a little more than half that of the
United States, while it has nearly three times its population,
and a hundred times that of the thirteen colonies at the time
of the American Revolution. In less than a quarter of the
area of Russia is crowded more than twice Russia's population, but like the latter they vary in race, language and degrees of civilization. In spite of the handicap of its climate,
India has produced the one great tropical civilization. It has
been preeminently the home of religions, and with Judea it has
been one of the great spiritual teachers of mankind. Today,
after seven centuries of alien rule, the leaders of her people
are rising with a new passion for civil liberty and political
self-government.

The importance of India to the British Empire can hardly
be exaggerated. From the earliest times its lucrative trade
enormously enriched in turn each nation that dealt with it.

To this day, India constitutes the greatest market in the world for British goods. [1] In the matter of numbers alone, if from the 450,000,000 of the British Empire we subtract the 330,-000,000 in India, it leaves only some 120,000,000, or about the population of the United States, scattered over the six continents. In other words, the population of India alone is about three-fourths that of the British Empire. [2]

The British view of India is thus stated by the Marquess of Zetland: "Not uniformity but an overpowering and bewilder-ing diversity of race, of language, of social custom and tra-dition, of outlook and of culture is the outstanding character-istic of the Indian peoples. . . . It is well to bear in mind that the peoples that live in British India, apart from the native States, number some 250,000,000 souls; that they speak more than 220 languages belonging to six different families of speech; that of these 250,000,000, 229,000,000 are illiterate; that they comprise adherents of innumerable sects of no fewer than nine distinct religions; that they represent every phase of civilization from the Stone Age to the twentieth century; that no one of the 163 million Hindus may marry anyone of the 60 million Moslems; and finally, that the 163 million Hindus themselves are separated by an exclusive and fissiparous sys-tem of caste into innumerable water-tight compartments whose members are cut off from one another by an elaborate system of social institutions and religious taboos." [3]

To understand the present political situation in India we must recognize the significance of the diverse elements that compose it: 1. There is first of all *the dominant figure of Gandhi.* He seems to be the incarnate soul of India, who

---

[1] In 1920 the value of imports from Great Britain was roughly $900,000,000. In 1927 it had fallen to $425,000,000.

[2] Herbert Adams Gibbons in his *New Map of Asia* maintains that in the nineteenth and twentieth centuries Britain's foreign policy was largely governed by considerations for the safety of India. From the time when Britain fought Napoleon until she was involved in Turkey, Persia and Palestine; from her fear of Afghanistan and Russia in the north, and of the Berlin to Bagdad railway in the Near East, Britain's eye has always been upon India, where lies the bulk of her empire.

[3] *The Empire Review,* October, 1930. India and Self-Government.

gathers into himself the needs and aspirations of both the intellectuals and the masses and becomes their mouthpiece. He alone can measurably unite the Congress or lead the common people. Gentle as a little child, yet he is as hard to move as a mountain, once his mind is made up. He is the center and pivot of the whole situation in India today. And he is quietly, unalterably determined that his country shall be free.

2. There is the *Indian National Congress,* organized in 1885, which up to 1907 remained friendly to the government. It is a voluntary organization representing the politically minded leaders, now nationalist and extremist, most of the conservative "liberals" and Moslems having withdrawn. In addition to the more than 2000 voting delegates, and from fifteen to thirty thousand in attendance at the Congress, there are throughout the country perhaps a hundred thousand men educated in English who can be counted upon for political and social leadership in their various communities.

3. The third and chief element in the situation is the *plodding, poverty-stricken masses,* more than nine-tenths of whom are illiterate and who are not, until aroused on some vital issue, naturally politically minded. Among these masses must be mentioned the depressed classes. There are 43,000,-000 of these untouchable outcastes and members of the depressed classes who for centuries have been denied the most elemental rights of social justice on the part of the high caste Hindus. These backward classes have now formed their own organizations all over India, and are pressing for direct representation and the removal of their political and social disabilities.

4. There are *seventy million Moslems,* constituting one-fifth of the population. Though backward in education, they come of a fighting race, and are mindful of their ancient glory during the Great Mogul Empire. Differing radically in conviction and custom from the Hindus, who outnumber them more than three to one, they are brought into constant conflict with them over religious and economic questions. This conflict is fomented by the artificial and fatal system of communal voting, devised by the government, which inevitably

creates strife and pits one community against another. Though far from united, the majority of their educated leaders desire Dominion Status, or some form of self-government for India that shall safeguard their interests in all provinces and assure them, if possible, one-third of the seats in the National Assembly. Many of them believe that they can unite with Hindus in self-government, protecting the legitimate interests of each community, as have the French and English in Canada. The Moslem League was organized just before the War, and was supposed to do for Moslems what the National Congress did for Hindus. They have usually been less nationalistic than the Hindus, standing first of all for the protection of their own religious community. This cleavage between the Hindu and the Moslem represents the deepest division and danger in India.

5. *The Indian States* cover roughly one-third of the total area and comprise one-fifth of India's population. [1] There are 562 such States, 108 of which enjoy a measure of independence, though all are under the "Paramount Power" of the British. The progressive States in the South, Mysore, Trancore and Cochin, which have a constitutional government, and Baroda in the North, in matters of education, social legislation and economic activity are in many respects in advance of British India. Unfortunately the majority of the States are patriarchal, quasi-feudal in character, medieval in spirit and autocratic in administration. The princes are frequently extravagant and irresponsible. The backwardness, the poverty, the oppression of the people under corrupt government, courts and police, are in many States notorious. The steady pressure of the Paramount Power, through the British Resident or representative, makes for better government, but a foreign government dares not go too far in insisting on reforms.

The writer visited one State where the interests of its ruler seem to be chiefly drink, drugs, women and "graft." He had

---

[1] Their total area is 598,138 square miles and their population 68,652,974. The "Paramount Power" is the Crown acting through the Secretary of State for India and the Governor General in Council.

four wives and approximately a hundred concubines. In the past his sale of public offices, his stooping to the most petty bribery and wholesale robbery of his people have been disgraceful. His misrule has so sucessfully crushed the majority of the inhabitants that the only hope of the situation seems to be in the influence of the Government of British India. In recent years, under pressure from the Paramount Power a few of the more flagrant abuses have been remedied, but this is deeply resented by many of the princes, who regard the people and possessions of the States as their private property. These States are a problem for the future. If they are left out of any reform scheme they may honeycomb India with a whole group of disloyal "Irelands." If they are brought in, they may form a possible reactionary and divisive element. Mr. Gandhi does not want to see a large proportion of the seats in the National Assembly appointed by these rich and reactionary princes, who might endeavor to block all advance legislation for the benefit of the impoverished masses.

6. There are several smaller parties or elements in the political situation which should be noted. *The Liberal Party,* once known as the Moderates, was the right wing of the Nationalist Party. It has always stood for constitutional methods. In 1919 the Liberals left the Congress when it refused to accept the Montague-Chelmsford Reforms. Though in sympathy with him personally, they have been against the non-cooperation and civil disobedience campaigns of Mr. Gandhi. They stand for early Dominion Status.

The Non-Brahmin Party was organized to stimulate the political and social development of the non-Brahmin masses of South India, where a small minority of Brahmins had long practically controlled the appointments of the government. They have demanded equality in all social and religious matters and championed the rights of the Panchamas or outcastes. Later they became known as the Justice Party. From 1919 to 1926 they swept many of the elections in the Madras Presidency for the Council, remaining in power and doing much to break down caste exclusions.

The Sikh League was formed for the defense of their own interests in the Punjab. Their people number some three and a half millions. They have thrown in their weight with the Gandhi movement.

The Youth Leagues of India are for the most part patriotic, but inexperienced, irresponsible and radical, demanding complete independence, by any means, violent or non-violent. In any national struggle a few individuals will doubtless resort to crimes of violence. They will use the only weapons that they know. Many of them do not look to the non-violent Gandhi for leadership. With them may be reckoned the left wing of organized labor in the Trade Union Movement. Among certain railway and cotton mill workers, especially in Western India, Communist organizers have been at work, and under-paid, ignorant laborers, in a country as desperately poor as India, are likely to furnish fruitful soil for Russian propaganda. Youth, Communist labor, and a few intellectuals constitute the extreme left wing of the Nationalist movement.

To grasp the present situation in India it is especially important that we should understand the viewpoint both of the British rulers and of the Indian Nationalists. Let us attempt to examine the case in favor of British rule in India, and then the case of the Nationalists against it.

The British Case

For any unprejudiced observer a strong case can be made for the benefits of British rule in the past, and for India's continuance within the Empire for her own good. The writer desires personally to testify, after fifteen years' residence in India and repeated visits since, that on the whole, together with the Philippines, *he knows of no finer instance in history of the government of one people by another*. From the time of Warren Hastings and Lord Macaulay to Lord Irwin, he knows of no civil service in the world more distinguished and with a more sustained record for high integrity, and efficient, disinterested service. Over a great host of men, might well be inscribed the sentiment that is on the grave at Lucknow: "Here lies Henry Lawrence, who tried to do his duty."

Basically, England has provided the *Pax Britannica* where, after thirteen centuries of wars and invasions that repeatedly destroyed the political and economic fabric of the land, Britain has enabled a united India to know the blessings of external security and internal peace, under an honest and efficient administration. Had this not been so it would never have been possible for a small group of 165,000 British, only half of whom are officials and soldiers, peaceably to govern so long the 330,000,000 of India.

British justice has protected and sought to improve the condition of the forty-three million untouchable outcastes and depressed classes of India, in contrast to the treatment of the majority of the extravagant and irresponsible Indian princes, the exploitation of the landlords and of the majority of the high caste people of India, in accordance with the drastic prescriptions of the sacred *Laws of Manu*. In 1829 the British abolished suttee, or widow burning. Before the Mutiny British officers fought against violent and cruel crime, against dacoity, human sacrifice, thuggee, female infanticide and other deep-seated evils. This was the heroic age of British tradition in India.

The greatest road builders since the Romans, the British have extended their broad highways and 40,000 miles of railways across this vast subcontinent. India's mileage, which is still rapidly advancing, is double that of the United Kingdom and greater than any country in Europe. The management is in striking contrast to the pathetic inefficiency and corruption of many of the railways built or managed by the Chinese, or looted by their military commanders.

India has a splendid system of irrigation and the British can point to 28,000,000 acres irrigated by the Government.[1] Contrasted with China, where millions have perished in perennial famines, the Government has mitigated the ravages of famine and provided in the past a famine insurance that has enabled them to cope with this recurring menace in the

---

[1] The capital cost of the Government irrigation works was some $375,-000,000 and the value of the annual harvests which they insure is $570,000,000.

frequent failure of the monsoon rains. With all its faults, the land revenue system, contrasted with pre-British days, has helped the cultivators to face periods of economic distress. When the British annexed the Punjab a generation ago, the selling value of the land was only $1.25 an acre, and it is even less than this in some mismanaged Indian states today. Under British security and irrigation, land in the Punjab and elsewhere has increased over three hundred times in value. The average burden of taxation per capita, exclusive of the land revenue, is only $1.85 a year, and including the land revenue only $2.05.[1] India's whole budget, Central and Provincial together, is approximately only $800,000,000. If we take the average income per annum of the Indian family as $150, we may figure the taxation per family at $7.50, compared to taxation in the Philippines of $15, in Japan $45, in the United States $180 and Great Britain $332 per family. The land tax averages only thirty-two cents an acre.

In contrast to many of the Indian Princes, who hoard or squander their wealth, the British have invested five billion dollars in productive industries, railways, etc., which have for the most part benefited India as well as Britain.[2] Under Great Britain, India's trade has increased more than seven fold in seventy years.[3] Contrasted with China, the Government can point to an educational system with a total of some twelve millions in all institutions in 1931. Under the aegis of British justice there has developed an enormous amount of medical relief, philanthropy, social welfare work, foreign missions and missionary education that would require a whole volume to describe.

Best of all, and in spite of all its manifold faults, the stimulus and impact of Western culture as a whole, in its economic, administrative, social, religious and human contacts has, however painfully, produced a ferment of new ideas, a renaissance of new life, an awakening of national consciousness and an

[1] *Statistical Abstract of British India*, 1928, p. 220.
[2] Shah and Khambatta, *Wealth and Taxable Capacity of India*, pp. 215-221. K. T. Paul, *British Connection With India*, pp. 209–216.
[3] It rose from some $200.000,000 in 1858 to over $2,000,000,000 in 1930.

aspiration for a democratic government of their own. This is something new in India's long history. Contrasted favorably with the colonies and possessions of several of the other imperialistic powers, under Britain this vast subcontinent, containing nearly a fifth of the world's population, divided in race, religion, language and caste, has been forged into a new national unity.

Our space does not permit a fuller statement of the case for British rule in India, for it seems even more important to try to understand the viewpoint of the Indian Nationalists at this critical juncture, even though at some points we would have to disagree with them.

The Indian Nationalist Case

In reply to the claims of Great Britain the Indian Nationalist would state his case somewhat as follows: "We admit many of the material benefits of British rule. Some of our number would even say that no foreign Government could be better. Yet we must point out that imperialism inevitably exploits the weak and that we have been continually exploited in the interests of Britain. We believe with England's former Prime Minister that 'good government is no substitute for self-government.' The British writer, Sir John Seely, in his book, *The Expansion of England,* shows that India during the eighteenth and nineteenth centuries was regarded primarily as an instrument in the expansion of Britain. He says: 'Subjection for a long time to a foreign yoke is one of the most potent causes of national deterioration.'

"We Indians have benefited in many ways materially under British rule, but we have been morally undermined by the process. Even materially we have suffered at many points. Take for illustration our cotton trade. India was the home of the cotton plant, and until the 18th century supplied Europe with her cotton goods. Britain allowed Lancashire to kill this profitable Indian cottage industry, but long failed to have any adequate modern factories built in India to take its place. England imposed a tax of 75 per cent upon our cotton goods to protect her own, yet for decades allowed India no protection again the dumping of Britain's cheap, machine-made fabrics. [1]   Our cotton industry was almost destroyed and we were left with nothing but agriculture to sustain 178,000,000 cultivators with only an acre of arable land per capita for the whole population, with frequent failure of crops, in the poorest country in the world.   Cotton is only one of our industries that has been sacrificed.   Neither Indian agriculture nor industry has been adequately developed for the economic progress of India.

"We also object to the 'drain' of some $150,000,000 a year from India to England in salaries, pensions and interest on foreign loans.   It is true that the latter has been in productive investments in railways, etc., but we maintain that more of this money could have been found in India itself.   It is undeniable that India is left poor and that Britain has been enormously enriched.[2]

"In a land of extreme poverty where millions have not enough to eat, where the average income per capita is only $27.75 a year, or less than eight cents a day, Britain has imposed the highest paid civil service in the world.   The Viceroy receives more than the President of the United States; the cabinet members, the judges, the Governors and the whole foreign service are more highly paid than men in similar positions in America.   For the costly Viceroy's palace and Government buildings of New Delhi the wasteful extravagance of $55,000,000 has been imposed upon her.

"The cost of the Army has been a sore point with India, consuming 62.5 per cent of the entire central revenues of the

---

[1] Ramsay MacDonald after visiting India wrote: "We did our best to kill the cotton industry in India by prohibiting the import of Indian printed calicoes into England in 1721, and India would now pay us back and would keep us out altogether."   *Awakening of India*, p. 86.

[2] Vera Anstey in the *Economic Development of India* and Sir Theodore Morrison's *Economic Transition in India* show that the bulk of these "home charges" are in interest on the productive debt, and annuities on railways and irrigation works that have been of immense benefit to India, and that the balance of financial advantage has lain with India.   Indians claim, however, that they should not make payments on account of the expense of conquering India, nor on the debentures of the East India Company that, according to Lord Macaulay, so pillaged India in the early years.

country, thereby depleting all the other services including education.[1] Lajpat Rai says: 'The beauty of the English conquest of India lies in the fact that from the first to the last not one single penny was spent by the British on the conquest. India was conquered by the British with Indian money and largely with Indian blood.' The cost of all the wars in India and of some of the foreign expeditions has been borne by impoverished India. India has to provide some $228,000,000 a year for military services and a small, expensive army of less than 250,000 men. Australia and South Africa spend on defense only 2.4 per cent of their total revenue, Canada 2.9, New Zealand 3.9, the Irish Free State 7.2 per cent of their revenues and India 31.5 per cent of her Central and Provincial budgets together.

"Britain has imperially governed India with no adequate training for self-government, as though she intended to stay forever. For over a century from 1801 to 1901 'not one Indian occupied a seat in the Supreme, or Presidency, or Provincial Executive Councils nor in the Secretary of States' Council in England.' Romsesh Chandra Dutt was the only Indian permitted to rise to the charge of a division in the entire nineteenth century. As late as 1913 the British still held 2,153 out of 2,501 posts carrying a salary of over 800 rupees a month, or $3,500 or more a year. Lord Curzon, Lord Cromer and almost all their fellow countrymen held 'an inflexible belief in the permanence of British rule.' Typical of all Tory diehards, Winston Churchill said in 1929: 'The idea that India is a nation or could ever be fashioned into a nation is known to be a delusion by everyone acquainted with the facts.'

"You say that there are nearly twelve millions in the schools of India but you neglect to mention that only one-fifth of the children are in school, that 93 per cent of the population is still illiterate, and that this foreign system of education is the

---

[1] See *The Simon Report,* Vol. I, pp. 93, 362. Vol. II, p. 216. There are some 60,000 British and 150,000 Indian troops and 34,000 reservists. There have been 72 expeditions in 72 years against the independent tribes over the border.

most academic and utterly divorced from practical life in all the world. It is turning out thousands of graduates every year, half of whom cannot find adequate employment and join the ranks in revolt against the present intolerable bureaucratic system. One advertisement for a clerk at $3.25 a week brought in six hundred applications from these unemployed. Why cannot British India do as well by education as the Indian States of Baroda, Travancore and Mysore?

"We protest also against the policy of a foreign rule which by its communal electorates has artificially fomented divisions and strife between the 230,000,000 Hindus and 70,000,000 Mohammedans. Your whole policy has been to divide and rule. A score of British writers agree with Lord Elphinstone, former Governor of Bombay, in his policy: '*Divide et impera* was the old Roman motto and it should be ours.' You will note that it is in British India but seldom in the Indian States under our own rulers that Hindu-Musalman rioting occurs. This is very significant.

"But more than all, we protest against the racial discrimination of an insufferable Anglo-Saxon superiority so galling, so humiliating that it leaves a lasting inferiority complex and the bitter determination to throw off this almost universally hated foreign yoke. We do not deny the *Pax Britannica* and many material benefits of foreign rule, yet we deeply feel that India has been steadily exploited for the sake of Britain and the Empire."

Thus the Indian Nationalist states his case.

India's case may be summed up in the words of Mr. Gandhi, in whom the long inarticulate masses of India at last have found a voice:

"TO EVERY ENGLISHMAN IN INDIA"

"Dear Friend,

"In my humble opinion, no Indian has co-operated with the British Government more than I have for an unbroken period of twenty-nine years of public life in the face of circumstances that might well have turned any other man into a rebel. . . . It was free and voluntary cooperation based on the belief that the sum total of the activity of the British Government was for the benefit of India. I put my life in peril four times for the sake of the Empire. . . . I did all this in the full belief that acts such as mine must gain for my country an equal status in the Empire. So late as last December I pleaded hard for a trustful cooperation. . . . But the treachery of Mr. Lloyd George . . . and the condonation of the Punjab atrocities have completely shattered my faith in the good intentions of the Government and the nation which is supporting it. . . . See what this Empire means to India: Exploitation of India's resources for the benefit of Great Britain. An ever-increasing military expenditure, and a civil service the most expensive in the world. Extravagant working of every department in utter disregard of India's poverty. Disarmament and consequent emasculation of a whole nation. . . . Traffic in intoxicating liquors and drugs for the purpose of sustaining a top-heavy administration. Progressively repressive legislation in order to suppress an ever-growing agitation seeking to give expression to a nation's agony. Degrading treatment of Indians residing in your dominions . . .

"Bravery on the battlefield is thus impossible for us. Bravery of the soul still remains open to us. I know you will respond to that also. I am engaged in evolving that bravery. Non-cooperation means nothing less than training in self-sacrifice. . . . My religion forbids me to bear any ill-will towards you. . . . I expect to conquer you only by my suffering. . . . You are in search of a remedy to suppress this rising ebullition of national feeling. I venture to suggest to you that the only way to suppress it is to remove the causes. . . . But this you cannot do unless you consider every Indian to be in reality your equal and brother. . . . The other solution, namely repression, is open to you. I prophesy that it will fail." [1]

The writer returned to India for ten weeks at the close of 1929 and the beginning of 1930. After an absence of five years the most striking change observable was the widespread demand for complete self-determination and the growing distrust of the British Government. As the Calcutta *Statesman* wrote: "It is the loss of faith in Britain which of late years has poisoned life in India." After interviewing some fifty Indian leaders of all shades of opinion in all parts of the country, whether Hindu, Moslem, Sikh or Christian, we did not find a single one who wanted to continue under the exist-

[1] *Freedom's Battle*, Mahatma Gandhi, pp. 286-291.

ing relationship to Great Britain.[1] Some desired early Dominion Status similar to that enjoyed by Canada, others
demanded complete independence like that of the United
States. Within a few months over half of these fifty leaders
whom we had interviewed were in prison. On the best available authority, there were during 1930 at least 27,600 political
prisoners. Indians felt deep indignation that Britain could
rule only by keeping the best brains and character of India
in jail.

To understand the situation in India it should be remembered that the National Congress meeting at Madras in 1927
had adopted a resolution in favor of complete independence.
The following year at the Calcutta Congress, against Mr.
Nehru's plea for independence, Gandhi by his personal influence carried a resolution by 1350 to 973 votes in favor of
India's proposed constitution on the basis of Dominion Status.[2]
Mr. Gandhi's important resolution is memorable in that it
formed the basis for the action of the Lahore Congress in
1929 and all that followed:

"This Congress will adopt the constitution (for Dominion
Status) *if it is accepted in its entirety by the British Parliament on or before December 31st, 1929, but in the event of its
non-acceptance by that date the Congress will organise a campaign of non-violent non-cooperation by advising the country
to refuse taxation and in such other manner as may be decided
upon."*

Such was the situation when we landed in India in October,
1929. Although our visit had no political object whatever, we
tried, as in every other country, sympathetically to understand
what we could of the whole situation—political, social and
religious. We spent a memorable hour with the poet Tagore
in his home. We were entertained for two days as guests in
the home of Pandit Jawaharlal Nehru in his palatial residence

[1] A conservative Christian like the late K. T. Paul wrote: "No Indian
desires the continuance of the connection on the present basis." *The British
Connection with India*, p. 189.

[2] The Constitution was contained in the "Nehru Report" agreed upon and
adopted at the All Parties Conference.

in Allahabad. He is a fine featured Brahman of Kashmir, with a highly intelligent, sensitive, sad face, a perfect gentleman of English training at Harrow and Cambridge. His father was one of the ablest lawyers and politicians in India, formerly leader of the Swarajist party in the National Assembly, whose income from his private law practice had approximated $200,000 a year. Yet we found young Nehru clad in the coarse home-spun that is the badge of Indian nationalists today. Representative of the left wing of the party standing for full independence, leader of the organized radical youth movement and to some extent of the Trade Union movement of industrial workers, he has been three times in prison. He is a man of high honor, of sensitive conscience, holding very much the same attitude to the British Empire as did Thomas Jefferson or Benjamin Franklin in 1776. He has been a loyal follower of Mr. Gandhi and is the man most likely to succeed him as a political leader, but he has not the consistent and abiding conviction in the efficacy of non-violence which Mr. Gandhi has.

Following our visit with Mr. Nehru we met the Viceroy, Lord Irwin, who generously gave us an hour and a half of his time before starting on his southern tour. We were deeply impressed by him. Without the genius of that last great imperialist, the haughty Lord Curzon, Lord Irwin has won perhaps a greater measure of confidence, even during the period of most intense hatred and bitterness, than any Viceroy during the present generation. The son of Lord Halifax, that devout high churchman, Lord Irwin is first and foremost a simple, straightforward man and a humble, genuine Christian. The transparent sincerity of his religious faith has impressed all India, which respects a devout religious man of any faith. Indeed, it is not too much to say that he too is a saint of the Western type, as Gandhi is of the Eastern. It was due chiefly to these two men that the titanic revolution in India was kept prevailingly on a non-violent plane of almost continuous conference and concilation. It is as unjust to blame Lord Irwin or Ramsay MacDonald for occasional acts of police brutality, as it is to hold Mr. Gandhi responsible for occasional crimes of

violence by young men who were really in principle followers
of Lenin and had never professed allegiance to Gandhi's program of non-violence.   China changed governments almost
overnight by a military coup in 1911, whereas the revolution
in India has been long drawn out, yet maintained on a prevailingly non-violent basis chiefly because of these two men—
Gandhi and Irwin.

Tall, homely, we found in Lord Irwin some qualities
strongly reminiscent of Abraham Lincoln.   It is fortunate that
he and not Curzon was "the voice of England in the East"
during India's revolution.   It was fortunate for India that the
leaders on both sides of the struggle were such men as Ramsay
MacDonald, Wedgewood Benn, and Lord Irwin on the one
side; and Gandhi, Motilal and Jawaharlal Nehru on the other
side.   Several of these men would have gladly sacrificed their
lives to solve India's problem without bloodshed.

During our interview with Lord Irwin, while Kirby Page
and I were lunching with him, we mentioned our coming visit
with Mr. Gandhi in his home.   The Viceroy asked if we would
take a message to Mr. Gandhi for him and let him have
Gandhi's reply.   Recognizing that the two peoples were drifting apart, he was apparently losing no opportunity to come to
an understanding with the Indian leaders.   In his study Lord
Irwin read his carefully prepared statement which we took
down in writing and later read to Mr. Gandhi.

After listening to the Viceroy's message, Gandhi gave us
his reply, which was in substance as follows: "To be told that
India is an equal, as a beloved child in the home which has not
yet reached the age of responsibility and of its political majority, is not enough.   We are offered Dominion Status 'in the
fulness of time,' but this is an ominous phrase which leaves
our future and our fate solely to Britain's imperialistic decision, which we have found far from disinterested in the past.
Our position is clear and unmistakable.   It is stated in our
resolution of last year at the Calcutta Congress.   Unless our
demand for Dominion Status is accepted 'on or before December 31st, 1929,' that is, before the close of the coming Lahore
meeting, the National Congress, after vainly pleading for

Dominion Status for forty years, will be compelled to declare
for complete independence and to 'organize a campaign of
non-violent non-cooperation.'   And it will undoubtedly vote
for complete independence."

After thinking over Mr. Gandhi's reply, we said to him the
next day: "Mr. Gandhi, your reply seems to us in one way
very terrible.   There is a chance of agreement in the proposed
Round Table Conference.   You have in Lord Irwin the most
trusted Viceroy of our generation.   In Ramsay MacDonald,
from India's point of view, you have the best Prime Minister;
in Wedgewood Benn the best Secretary of State since Mr.
Montague.   You have the first official offer of ultimate Dominion Status, and in the Round Table Conference the first
opportunity of obtaining it by agreement.   Why then, without
even attending the Conference, do you launch a campaign
which you and no man living can keep non-violent, however
peaceful your intentions?"

He was sitting on the floor at his spinning wheel with the
light of the afternoon sun falling upon him.   He looked up
and said: "The answer is incredibly simple.   For years I have
been dealing with the British.   I do not think they will grant
us a Constitution based on Dominion Status at the coming
Round Table Conference.   They will not and indeed they
cannot in the present political situation in Great Britain.   If
I am wrong, if Ramsay MacDonald would ask Lord Irwin to
tell me privately, if they do not want to say it publicly, 'We
seriously intend to grant India the Constitution of a self-
governing Dominion and we intend to begin to make the
transfer of power to an autonomous India from the coming
Round Table Conference, though that transfer will inevitably
involve a period of some years.   We really intend to do this
and are willing to stake the political life of the Labor Government upon its fulfilment.'   If Mr. MacDonald would give this
assurance through the Viceroy, we would not only attend the
Conference, but I personally would face our National Congress
single-handed, and we would guarantee to meet the British
half way and to do everything to cooperate with them whole-
heartedly.   But you will find they will make no such guarantee.

And if they do not, we are already on record as being compelled to fall back upon the Calcutta resolution for complete independence."

We delivered this message to Lord Irwin, to Ramsay Mac-Donald and Wedgewood Benn long before the Lahore Congress, with Mr. Gandhi's clear statement that if they received no assurance from the Government, they would have to declare for independence and launch the non-cooperation campaign, but it was evident no such guarantee could be given.

Prior to the final break of the Nationalists with the Government and before his march to the sea, Mr. Gandhi wrote to the Viceroy: "In common with many of my countrymen I had hugged the fond hope that the proposed Round Table Conference might furnish a solution, but when you said plainly that you could not give any assurance that you or the British Cabinet would pledge yourselves to support the scheme of full Dominion Status, the Round Table Conference could not possibly furnish the solution for which vocal India is consciously, and the dumb millions unconsciously, thirsting." [1]

It was thus evident that Mr. Gandhi all along preferred what he called "substantial self-government" or Dominion Status within the Empire to independence, if it could be obtained on terms of honor and equality. But all self-respecting Indians are unwilling to continue indefinitely under a system of tutelage, on a status of racial inferiority, both in India and throughout the Empire, under what they regard as prejudiced foreigners seven thousand miles away as the sole judges of the time of their fitness for self-government. Left to them that time will never come. Britain's prestige as arbiter and umpire is gone.

In spite of the regrettable mutual distrust on both sides, it is the writer's conviction that India will be better off and can more safely make her great experiment in self-government within the Empire than on a basis of complete independence. On the latter basis, India has not half the ground of unity or hope of success of an independent China, united as the latter is in one race, with one written language, and one cultural

---

[1] *India and the Simon Report* by C. F. Andrews, p. 177.

tradition. It would seem that the "steel frame" of the Empire will help to hold together this building of loose bricks of diverse elements. Sudden independence, apart from some impossible historical miracle, would probably mean chaos, corruption and civil war such as India knew in the past for many centuries. It is no reflection upon India that this is so.

As the whole political situation in India centers so largely in Mr. Gandhi we must endeavor sympathetically to understand him, although this is almost an impossible task for the Western mind.

Gandhi was born on October 2, 1869, at Porbandar, north of Bombay. His father and grandfather had each held the office of Prime Minister in this little Indian State. He was married according to Hindu custom at the age of twelve, and at nineteen went to England for three years to study law. At twenty-four he went to South Africa on his first important law case. Instead of returning as he had intended in a few months, he gave the next twenty years of his life to fighting the battle for freedom for 150,000 of his fellow Indian subjects in semi-slavery in South Africa. It was there that he developed his technique of non-violence. Tolstoi counted his activity there "the most important of all the work now being done in the world."

It was after his first campaign, which lasted from 1918 to 1921, and just before the beginning of his last campaign that we spent ten days with Mr. Gandhi; three days in his home, in the Ashram or social settlement where he lives with a hundred and fifty of his followers, and some seven days with him in the Lahore National Congress, during Christmas week 1929.

We found that we differed with him at a score of points, political, social and religious, such as his asceticism, and on some of his religious attitudes as a Hindu. For he will undoubtedly remain a Hindu until the day of his death. But he was the one *Mahatma* or "great soul" we had ever known. Of four Christlike personalities the writer has known during a lifetime, Mr. Gandhi stands first and alone—first in utter integrity, in courage, in dauntless faith, in love or sympathy with suffering humanity, and in boundless self-sacrifice for his

cause. As we talked with him for hours, for he gave us most
lavishly of his crowded time, it seemed as though we were
speaking with Gautama Buddha twenty-five centuries ago in
India; or with Francis of Assisi, suddenly stepped out of the
thirteenth century; or, as a trained lawyer, speaking the language of political independence, yet always in the spirit of the
gentle St. Francis, as if we were talking with Thomas Jefferson. Indeed he seemed to combine these three contradictory
men in one—Gautama Buddha, Francis of Assisi and Thomas
Jefferson.

We had just met Einstein in Germany, a man with perhaps
a greater brain, but we had never met anyone who for hours
talked more solid sense than Gandhi.   Bishop McConnell
points out that although Gandhi is the first to confess any
fault or mistake, which he may call "a Himalayan blunder,"
yet he "almost never does a foolish thing."   To the West the
idea of turning the other cheek to the wrongdoer has always
seemed to be foolishness. It was Gandhi who translated the
idea of resistance to evil with good, and to violence with non-
violence into practical politics, who made non-violent resistance a working force in a nation's life, who made his fellow
countrymen think of their struggle for freedom in terms of
spiritual force, and forged pacifism into an effective tool
against war. The West seems to think that a man must either
be a saint and somewhat impractical, or shrewd and somewhat
crooked. Gandhi is both a saint and shrewd; he combines the
wisdom of the serpent and the harmlessness of the dove.

On the day we arrived in his city we were met at the train
by an Indian employer, and a labor leader who, under Gandhi's
influence, had renounced his comfortable circumstances to
identify himself with the cause of the unorganized and exploited mill hands in the seventy mills of Gandhi's city.   At
meal time we sat on the floor with the hundred and fifty
inmates of the Ashram. Seated next to us was another employer who had already given away about half a million
dollars, or half his wealth, and was devoting all his time to
Gandhi's crusades. On all sides we saw the remarkable influ-

ence of Gandhi, both in the changed lives in the Ashram itself and throughout India.

Our day in the Ashram began with morning prayer at four A. M. lasting for half an hour. Out under the stars of the Indian sky, on the river bank, sitting in the clean sand, it is a moving experience to hear the prayers and hymns of this reverent religious worship. After a bath, exercise and study comes the early breakfast; all sitting upon the floor eating their simple fare. Gandhi slips in last and sits with the children. His three daily meals consist of one bowl of the curds of goat's milk with an equal amount of fruit. He eats no bread or vegetables in his present frail state, and he never ate meat in his life, save with guilty conscience as a Hindu school boy. After breakfast his day is occupied by correspondence and endless interviews, including some bodily labor, consisting for him of at least an hour at his spinning wheel while he continues his interviews. This spinning is for him almost a sacrament. He longs that the impoverished farmers, with a third of their time spent in enforced idleness, shall recapture the lost cotton trade which he believes Britain killed with a seventy per cent duty on Indian fabrics. If they can make their own homespun in idle hours they can save the annual drain of $200,000,000 for foreign cotton goods and other imports from abroad. To him this spinning spells for the farmer bread, character and final freedom from an enervating foreign rule.

Several scenes were imprinted upon our memory in the days spent with Gandhi. We saw him first on our arrival at his Ashram on his "day of silence" which lasts from Sunday at 7 P. M. to Monday evening at the same hour. This period he spends in thought, in prayer, in meditation, or in writing before the work of the coming busy week. He smiled when he saw us and sent us a kindly little note saying he would see us when he broke his silence that evening. He appeared at first to be an almost toothless old man, thin, emaciated, with large ears and almost shaven head, his body half clad in a coarse homespun cotton cloth. His physical presence, like that of Socrates or the Apostle Paul, seemed weak and unprepossessing. Yet after the first few moments with him we never saw again those homely features. We were gazing into the depths of a great soul that seemed to shine through his whole face and figure. He moved about in the world before us but he seemed to live in God.

The second scene was after the hour of his evening prayer. Nothing keeps him from his periods of prayer at four in the morning and at 7 :30 in the evening. Sitting on his cot in the open air by the river bank—for he sleeps out under the stars— for an hour he answered our questions about God, about prayer and the things of the spirit. We were surprised to find running through his life a vein of pure rationalism or of agnosticism, not unlike that of Thomas Jefferson. Once he doubted everything; once he was an atheist. But others had found this experience of religion; he said he had resolved to make the world's faith in God his own. He had found it now. God was the great reality of his life. Another thing that impressed us, along with his rationality and common sense, was his humanity. He smiles much, he laughs heartily occasionally, he has a keen sense of humor and spends half an hour each afternoon when at home playing and romping with the children.

We remember him again as we sat beside him at meal time. There was just a touch of St. Francis about him here. The old monks once sewed a piece of fox fur beneath his coarse mantle to keep St. Francis warm, and he insisted upon their sewing a piece outside as well, that all might see that he had this little luxury. So too has Gandhi a passion for reality. He appeared to have just one tooth in his upper jaw. It would probably be difficult to negotiate even his curds of goat's milk and fruit with this equipment. We noticed that Bapuji—the dear Little Father, which is the name used affectionately in the home, for the word Mahatma would be foreign to the whole atmosphere of equal brotherhood and familiar affection —Bapuji would take from a bowl an artificial set of teeth to manage the scientific mastication of his breakfast. If he were to retain them during the day he would look younger and better than he really does. He would be using artificial or *"false"* teeth and then false something else. So we noticed that he left his artificial dentistry for its strictly scientific use at the next meal, and went on his way a smiling, toothless old man.

On the occasion of his last great fast of twenty-one days, when the Hindus and Mohammedans had been killing each other in riots until it almost broke his heart, sleepless, in agony of mind, he finally resolved to do what the Orient alone would understand and what would be effective only there. He would fast for three weeks; he would not touch a morsel of food for twenty-one days. India trembled and pleaded in protest against the fast. He had recently had an operation for appendicitis and was a mere shadow of a man. On the twelfth day the doctor said that his pulse was failing and that he would surely die if he did not take food. He only smiled and said: "Have faith in God. You have forgotten the power of prayer." He was stronger on the twenty-first day than he had been on the twelfth, having done his full work every day.

When he broke his fast he called upon his Hindu brother to read his favorite passage of scripture, he asked his Mohammedan brother to lead in prayer to the one God and father of all; then he asked his Christian friend, C. F. Andrews, to sing his favorite hymn, "When I Survey the Wondrous Cross." Then he was carried out, too weak to walk.

Two scenes we recall vividly from the Lahore Congress. One evening his enemy had risen to speak, ostensibly to flatter him, but in reality endeavoring to win the majority from allegiance to Gandhi. The latter was to reply, and then the vote was to be taken. At half past seven, while his enemy was still speaking, came his hour for worship. We saw him slip quietly off the back of the platform, and followed him across to his tent for his unfailing hour of prayer. We tried to recall any other politician in the world today, say for instance in our American Senate, or any other statesman in history, who at the crisis of the debate would count prayer a really more dynamic, a more practical and efficacious way of working than taking part in that debate. But we could think of none.

We saw him for the last time when some 15,000 were gathered in the great tent at the National Congress. He had been sitting quietly out of sight at the back of the platform, always engaged in his handspinning. The time had arrived when he must present his epoch-making resolution. We were sitting on the ground some ten feet away from him. He remained seated, as he is unable to speak standing, and with the microphone held close to his lips, he quietly made his resolution, first of sympathy for the Viceroy, in the attempt which had just been made upon his life, and then for independence for India.

Before leaving we went to say goodbye to Bapuji. He was on his way to give a last message to the Congress. Outside the tent a great crowd had gathered in the hope of seeing him as he passed, for, owing to the newspaper, railway, telegraph and modern means of communication, he is undoubtedly more widely known and followed by more millions during his own lifetime than any religious leader of the past. It was impossible for him to move because of the pressing crowd. The young Volunteers in uniform formed a kind of football wedge to drive a way through so that he could move. Every eye was fixed upon this frail figure. We saw the upturned faces of his people lit with an affection like a shaft of sunlight. We saw mothers hold up their children that they might see him as he passed. We saw educated men close their eyes in prayer, or stoop to touch the hem of his garment, or to kiss those aged feet, or to gather the dust from his sandals and then kiss their hands.

We saw his sad face for the last time as he disappeared in the great tent, to take up what then seemed the almost hopeless struggle for freedom. But why hopeless? He moved, as calm as Buddha, in the unbroken peace of an inward spiritual Nirvana, and on that battle-scarred old face, which bore the marks of mobs and imprisonment, of fasting, of failure and of heart-break, we saw a light—"the light that never was on land or sea."

Two areas remain to be dealt with if we are to understand the non-violent revolution in India and the present situation there. On the one hand, are the basic economic, social and religious facts which condition India's life and make the drafting or execution of a democratic constitution for this vast subcontinent a matter of such titanic difficulty. Doubtless it is the most difficult task ever faced in the whole history of constitutional government. On the other hand, there is the background of India's past history which alone can interpret the present. This may be omitted by the busy reader or by those to whom it is already familiar.

Economic Conditions

Once Burma is separated, as recommended by the Simon Report, India is a country basically poor in raw materials. Her whole expenditure on government, central and provincial together, is only about $800,000,000 which is utterly inadequate for the development of education and social services that she requires. Her poverty is bound up with the social and political situation. Especially in India, economic factors cannot be considered in isolation, apart from their social and religious causes, or their political results. "The economic condition of the people is the crux of Indian politics."[1] Why should her soil be rich and yet her people poor? Why should her ancient civilization be so advanced yet her present outlook be so medieval? The basic economic fact about India is her abysmal poverty. Material does not exist for exact statistics but the chief reliable estimates of the average *per capita* income for various years in rupees and dollars has been as follows:[1]

	Year	Per Capita Income in Rupees	Dollars
Dadabhai Naoroji	1870	20	$6.66
Lord Cromer	1882	27	9.00
Lord Curzon	1906	30	10.00
Findlay Shirras	1911	50	16.66
Census Bombay Presidency, rural	1921	75	25.00
Shah and Khambatta[2]	1922	74	27.00

[1] Vera Anstey, *Economic Development of India,* to which we are deeply indebted throughout this section.

[2] Modern Review, October 1929, *Indian Poverty* by R. K. Das. Budget studies in districts show an average *per capita* income of rupees 44 in the

We may roughly calculate the average *per capita* income today at about twenty-seven dollars a year, or a little less than seven and a half cents a day.

This poverty is due in part to the fragmentation of land and the concentration of an excessive population upon the soil which is cultivated by most primitive methods. The 230 millions who live by agriculture cultivate but 226 million acres of land, or less than one acre for each person,[1] and far less than the fifteen acres estimated by several authorities as the minimum from which a family can earn a decent livelihood, under present methods of cultivation. There are 125 million landless craftsmen and casual laborers.[2] When the monsoon fails as it so often does their condition becomes precarious, or one of terrible privation. Multitudes exist upon less than the "jail standard" of seven cents a day per prisoner. Casual agricultural labor is paid from 10 to 16 cents a day for a man and from 6 to 8 cents for a woman.[3]

If we seek to trace the causes that lie at the base of India's poverty—economic, social, religious and political—we shall find in these the chief handicaps of India, which probably constitute the most formidable problems which confront the builders of any nation today.

Of the physical and economic causes of India's poverty we may note the following:

1. *The tropical climate,* whether in the scorching furnace of the northern summer, or the steaming hothouse of the East Coast, makes for lassitude, enervation and resignation. The frequent failure of the monsoon and its threat of hunger or famine crushes hope and initiative.

2. *Primitive agriculture* in a population bound by custom, conservatism and tradition, where new ideas come up against the blank wall of illiteracy, superstition and prejudice. Manure is consumed as fuel instead of being used as a fertilizer. Scientific seed selection and plant husbandry are rarely practiced.

---

[1] *Statistical Abstract for British India,* 1928, pp. 36, 337.
[2] G. T. Garratt, *An Indian Commentary,* pp. 48, 58, 69.
[3] *Census Report,* 1926, Vol. I, p. 275.

Deccan, 52 in Bengal, 72 in Madras, 100 in the Punjab. See H. H. Mann, *Land and Labor in a Deccan Village,* 1917; J. C. Jack, *Economic Life of a Bengal District,* 1906–10; Gilbert Slater, *Some South Indian Villages,* 1918; M. L. Darling, *The Punjab Peasant in Prosperity and Debt,* 1925.

The "sacred cow" has caused the economic waste of some 600
million dollars annually, or about four times the income from
all the land revenue.[1] Inferior, diseased and aged cattle consume the inadequate fodder supply and the breeds degenerate.
As Bishop McConnell writes: "The cobras in India are in
actual effects on human living less deadly than the cows, for
the expensiveness and uselessness of cows by the million, which
are not well enough nourished to serve as milk producers,
means that babies die that cows may live."

3. *Undeveloped industry* is a further cause of poverty. The
decline of the former cottage industries and handicrafts was
not promptly followed by the introduction of modern factories.
Cotton and jute mills have recently increased, the enterprising
Tata iron and steel works and hydroelectric power have been
developed, coal and petroleum have been profitably produced.
Nevertheless with abundant raw materials, natural resources,
cheap labor supply and good markets, India is industrially backward. The cotton industry of Lancashire has been developed
rather than that of India. Little more than a million and a
half, or not half of one per cent of the population, are employed in factories.[2]

4. *Unemployment*. The 107 million cultivators and actual
workers in agriculture are unemployed or under-employed for
almost half the year. Even if we calculate only three months'
unemployment for the peasants it would be the equivalent of
some 27 million workers idle for the entire year. Unemployment is greater at all times in India and China than in any other
countries. Even at a wage of five cents a day the economic loss
would be some twelve times the total yearly appropriations for
education, public health, agricultural and industrial improvements.[3] No wonder Mr. Gandhi is heroically striving to utilize
the idle time of the peasants to recapture the cottage industry
of homespun to offset the annual expenditure of $200,000,000
for foreign cloth.[4]

5. *Uneconomic customs, classes and structure of society.*

---

[1] *Proceedings of the Board of Agriculture,* Jan. 21, 1924. At least 14
million of India's 151 million head of cattle are an economic liability rather
than an asset.
[2] *Statistical Abstract,* 1928, p. 668. Only 1,518,391 are in factories.
[3] *Statistical Abstract,* 1926, p. 138.
[4] *Statistical Abstract,* 1926, p. 463.

the past crushes the present. Individualism and initiative are subordinated to the domination of the community. Untouchables form a tremendous economic handicap to India.[1]

2. *Debt* is an increasing cause rather than a result of poverty. Rates of interest often range from 36 per cent to more than double that proportion. The money lender who alone usually keeps the account often holds the debtor in his power and all debt tends to become permanent. In the Punjab one-fourth of those paying income tax are money lenders.[2] In several provinces the majority of the cultivators are in debt. Many are born in debt, live in debt, die in debt and bequeath this inheritance to their children. Most of the total indebtedness of the people, estimated at over two billion dollars, is economically unproductive.[3] A new hope of deliverance is seen in the effective Cooperative Societies now including over three and a half million members. There are still more than nine out of ten cultivators outside the cooperative movement, while nearly all the families of Russia are included in their societies, except the disfranchised.

3. *Litigation,* like gambling in China, furnishes a costly indoor sport for a population that has a lack of healthy interests. It is estimated that not less than 350 million dollars is consumed in India's two million civil suits annually, employing a hundred thousand lawyers and legal agents.[4]

4. *Ignorance and illiteracy* are contributory causes of poverty. In spite of the fact that there are some twelve millions in educational institutions in India, with 93 per cent of the population illiterate, less than twenty million men and three million women can read and write. No school is to be found in over half a million of the smaller Indian villages with a population of less than 500. That is, three-fourths of the 687 thousand villages are without any school whatsoever. The

---

[1] "The table of social precedence attached to the Cochin Census Report shows that while a Nayor can pollute a man of a higher caste only by touching him, people of the Kammalan group, including masons, blacksmiths, carpenters and workers in leather, pollute at a distance of 24 feet, toddy drawers at 30 feet, Pulayan cultivators at 48 feet, while in the case of the Pariahs who eat beef the range of pollution is no less than 64 feet." H. H. Risley, *Census Report,* 1911.

[2] *Indian Cooperative Studies,* R. B. Ewbank, p. 212.

[3] *An Indian Commentary,* G. T. Garratt, p. 39.

[4] Ibid. p. 74.

quality of the education has been far too academic and literary. Perhaps no national system of education is more divorced from the practical concerns of actual life than is that of India.

5. *Drink and drugs* are an economic drain. The excise revenue from these sources is nearly 60 million dollars.[1] Mothers often feed opium to their children. The Government deserves full credit for the curtailment of its foreign opium trade. The drink evil is not as bad as it is in the West but it is growing. In the Madras Presidency, for instance, there has been a steady increase in the consumption of foreign liquors, country spirits, beer, toddy, opium and other drugs. Professor Thompson says: "Opium has been a damnable story, a dirty, indefensible business." [2]

6. *The status of women* is an economic as well as a social handicap. Count Okuma attributed the rapid advance of Japan largely to the new freedom and education given to women, saying that no country could far advance under a double standard that left its mothers to train the rising generation in ignorance. The Hindu *Laws of Manu* thus prescribed for woman: "Let her be in subjection to her father in her childhood, to her husband in her youth, to her sons when her husband has died; let a woman never enjoy independence." [3] Even today "the legal position of a woman in India is decidedly inferior to that of a man." The early age at which Hinduism imposes betrothal, marriage and motherhood upon India's women means enfeebled mothers, weakened infants and an appalling child mortality.[4] Following irrevocable betrothal in childhood, the death of the little fiancé may leave the girl a widow for life and prohibit remarriage. There is an enormous total of 27 million widows in India.[5] The system of *purdah* and the seclu-

---

[1] *Statistical Abstract,* 1926, p. 195.

[2] *Reconstruction of India,* p. 252.

[3] *Village Schools in India,* Mason Olcott, p. 48.

[4] In Bombay 97 per cent of the workers' families live in single rooms with an average of four inmates to each, while in London the average is 1.78 per room. The infant mortality rises as high as 66 per cent of registered births and even higher in some other cities. *India in 1927-28,* p. 52. *Statistical Abstract,* 1926, p. 23.

[5] The Sarda Act, although not as yet enforced and sustained by public opinion, has raised the legal age of marriage for girls to fourteen years and for boys to eighteen, against the indignant protest of the orthodox religious leaders. The author of the act pointed out that there were 331,793 widows under 15 years, 97,596 under 10. 12.016 under 5. and 612 Hindu widows who

sion of both Hindu and Mohammedan women is an added handicap.

7. *An uncontrolled birth rate* is an ominous economic factor. According to the best Indian authorities, the "optimum" population has long since been passed, so that India *under existing conditions* can only sustain about one-half of its present population at a level of decency and comfort.[1] The population of India tends to increase at an uneconomic rate. The brilliant irrigation schemes of the Punjab instead of bringing prosperity have brought a multiplication of population to consume the food supply.[2] An unrestricted flood of babies in India and China raises a population problem that will soon become insistent. The writer called recently at the home of a prominent Indian official who had thirteen small children, a year apart in age, and one wife already dead. He was an enthusiastic convert to the modern reform of birth control.[3]

8. *Orthodox religion wherever it is a reactionary force* affects economic and all other aspects of life. The greatest thing about India has been her spiritual heritage, her age-long quest for the divine. From Gautama to Gandhi and Tagore, India has produced an unbroken line of spiritual saints and seers. Her emphasis upon the reality of the life of the spirit may yet greatly enrich the West with its too material and mechanistic absorption. Many modern books, like Professor Radha Krishnan's *Hindu View of Life,* describe the better and brighter side of vital religion which has been India's chief glory. But unfortunately the orthodox wing of some of the older religions

---

[1] M. L. Darling, *The Punjab Peasant in Prosperity and Debt,* pp. 253–287.

According to V. B. G. Sapre in his *Essentials of Indian Economics,* pp. 126, 195, an average of about 20 acres of "dry" land and five of "wet" cultivation is needed to support a family. This would displace half the existing population. R. K. Das maintains that one-third the present population would be the "optimum" for India. *Modern Review,* Oct., 1929.

[2] The Lyallpur Colony between 1891 and 1911 increased from 60,000 to 1,000,000.

[3] Sir Vepa Ramesam of the High Court, Madras, is leading the *Neo-Malthusian League* with several hundred members. Although not burdened with the medieval laws of the United States in this matter, they will face an even greater obstacle in iron-bound social custom and orthodox religious reaction.

---

were babies not yet a year old, yet who were forbidden to remarry. Prostitutes are frequently recruited from the class of widows to whom normal life is denied. *India in 1927-28,* p. 52. *Statistical Abstract,* 1926, p. 23.

has become socially petrified and reactionary. For example, the successful agitation against the erection of a weir over the Ganges at Hardwar prevented the irrigation of a wide district and deprived thousands of farmers of water.[1] But this is only one typical instance of many where all progress, all scientific innovation, all new methods have been persistently blocked under the tyranny of custom and religious sanction. Such religion engenders a fatalistic attitude where the highest aim is not to triumph over life but to escape from it. Rigid traditionalism, conservatism and orthodox conformity become the ideal rather than progress. Thus the joint family becomes "a nursery for parasites and an extinguisher on individual enterprise." Individual submission is insisted upon rather than initiative and achievement. These at once forbid all change for the better, as well as the reform of social evils, and the destruction of obnoxious pests which do much economic damage. It is therefore not surprising that, although it takes different forms in various countries, an anti-religious movement has developed in Russia, in Turkey, in China, and to a less extent in India, the home of religions.

9. *Lack of cooperation* between the Government and the governed, between communities, castes and religions, is a final source of weakness. In the Indian States, save in a few cases, there has been little tendency of the rulers to cooperate with their people. In British India the Government is under suspicion no matter what aid it offers to the peasants through its agricultural colleges or otherwise. This is, of course, accentuated by racial prejudice. But the mere substitution of an Indian for a foreign government will not automatically solve India's problems, nor will a written constitution based upon Dominion Status, nor a declaration of independence. Sooner or later Indians will have to learn the lesson that no one can save them nor defeat them but themselves. They will have to work out their own salvation. Even a brief review of the obstacles and causes of India's basic poverty already noted will convince almost anyone that no country faces greater obstacles than does India. *But they are not insurmountable*. Medieval Europe faced many similar conditions, yet its various countries have for the most part successfully achieved nationhood in

---

[1] Round Table, June, 1925, p. 527, quoted by Vera Anstey, *Economic Development of India*, p. 53.

spite of them. Nationalism has almost accomplished miracles in the past and may do so again. Where the pessimist sees a difficulty in every opportunity, the optimist will see an opportunity in every difficulty. If India is to achieve any real freedom it will be along the path of realism, cooperation and unity. And in that path, despite terrific odds, she has already set her feet. With the achievement of independence or Dominion Status her difficulties will have only just begun. But it will be psychologically impossible for India adequately to tackle her social problems and set her own house in order until in principle her political problem has been solved. One natural and inevitable result of the present racial and political tension is India's sullen, defiant defense of disagreeable facts, or even the denial of their existence. But sooner or later facts such as we have just presented will have to be faced realistically as they have long been recognized by Mr. Gandhi, the editor of the Social Reformer and other leaders.

India's Past

Recent excavations reveal an early civilization in northern India dating back to about 3500 B.C. Successive invasions entered India for several thousand years. In turn came the white-skinned Aryans who settled India, the conquering Greeks under Alexander the Great in 326 B.C., then the Scythian hordes, followed by nearly a thousand years of Moslem invasions, culminating in the Great Mogul Empire in 1526.

Then came a long line of European explorers, adventurers and conquerors. The Portuguese in the fifteenth century were followed by the Dutch, Danish and French in the sixteenth and seventeenth. The British East India Company was established under Queen Elizabeth in 1600. They acquired a local foothold in three successive trading stations in Madras, Calcutta and Bombay. Clive's brilliant victory over the Nawab of Bengal in 1757 by force and intrigue laid the foundations of British rule in India a hundred and seventy-five years ago. This rule was consolidated by Warren Hastings as Governor General, the first of thirty great administrative organizers and Viceroys that were to follow. From Warren Hastings onward we can trace a gradual quickening of conscience and a growing sense of responsibility on the part of the best of British statesmen and rulers.[1] This has been accompanied by the gradual awakening of a new national consciousness in India itself and a growing desire for free institutions and self-government. This awakening may be traced to such causes and successive events as, in 1835, Macaulay's famous educational minute which made the English language the basis of Indian education,[2] in 1857 the Mutiny with its dream of independence, in 1858 the Proclamation of Queen Victoria, in 1905 Japan's victory over Russia which sent a thrill of hope throughout Asia, and Lord Curzon's autocratic partition of Bengal, which soon raised the demand in India for "home rule" and "home production."

Three advance steps in democracy have been taken in recent years in India. In 1909 the Morley-Minto Reforms; in 1919 the Montagu-Chelmsford Constitution and its plan of dyarchy; and on October 31, 1929, the Announcement of Lord Irwin promising ultimate Dominion Status for India, leading to the Round Table Conference and the drawing up of a new Constitution. The entire national movement is largely the result of the total impact of Western culture upon India, in education, literature, the press, and the awakening of the political, social and religious life of the people. It produced throughout the Orient a renaissance of national life and aspiration. A whole volume could be written to show the effects of the impact of the East upon the West. Following the unrest in India of the first decade of the twentieth century Britain responded with the above mentioned three concessions.

---

[1] According to Lord Macaulay India was often looted by the agents of the East India Company. Up to the time of Warren Hastings the system of Government was "corrupt and full of abuses." Clive said: "When I think of the marvelous riches of that country and the comparatively small part which I took away, I am astonished at my own moderation." The Calcutta *Statesman* of April 9, 1925, observed: "We came as traders and adventurers wishing to make money. We were against our will drawn into politics and wars . . . In the end we found a higher purpose than our own. We then began to talk about our moral mission."

[2] Macaulay said: "It may be that the public mind of India may expand under our system until it has outgrown that system; that by good government we may educate our subjects into a capacity for better government that having become instructed in European knowledge they may, in some future age, demand European institutions. Whether such a day will ever come, I know not. But never will I attempt to avert or retard it. Whenever it comes, it will be the proudest day in English history." Speech by Macaulay in the House of Commons, July, 1833.

Three Experiments in Democracy

1. *The Morley-Minto Reforms* of 1909 marked the first advance. Lord Morley, then Secretary of State for India, knew from his Irish experience that mere repression provided no permanent remedy for unrest. His proposed reforms were embodied in the Indian Councils Act of 1909.[1] The reforms were a courageous and sincere effort to adjust the Government to the awakening national consciousness. The principle of election was legally admitted. The new councils could now discuss the budget and propose resolutions. Indians could criticize and express their views but the element of responsibility was entirely lacking. Ultimate decisions always rested with the Government and the principle of autocracy, though modified, was still maintained. Lord Morley admitted that the reforms were not intended to lead "directly or indirectly to the establishment of a parliamentary system in India," and he expressed his distrust for "natives in positions of high responsibility." He did not believe in applying the democratic principle to the East, where he compared it to a fur coat in a tropical climate.

For a time the proposals were well received and somewhat relieved the tension of political unrest, but they were unsatisfying. Moreover it is probable that a fatal mistake was made in introducing the principle of communal or economic rather than geographical representation for the elected members. This developed later into bitter division and strife between communal castes, leagues and religions, instead of teaching national responsibility and true public service.[2]

2. *The Montagu-Chelmsford Reforms.* The epoch-making announcement of Mr. Montagu in the House of Commons in August, 1917, provided for "increasing the association of Indians in every branch of the administration, and *the gradual development of self-governing institutions, with a view to the progressive realisation of responsible government in India as an integral part of the British Empire.*" This was to be

---

[1] This provided that the provincial legislative councils were to be enlarged by an elected majority of non-officials, though in the National Assembly the British officials were still to remain in the majority.

[2] "The initiation of this principle in India was the greatest blunder which the British have ever committed." *An Indian Commentary*, p. 159, by G. T. Garratt, Indian Civil Service, Retired.

achieved by successive stages and the first of these was to be the trial for a decade of the principle of dyarchy, or a dual government in the provinces. The "reserved" subjects were still controlled chiefly by the British Civil Service, responsible through the Governor to the Secretary of State and Parliament. The "transferred" subjects were under the care of Indian members responsible to an elected assembly and the electorate.[1]

The Montagu-Chelmsford Reforms, with all the defects of dyarchy, were a bold advance and had they been made a year earlier after the Armistice, in recognition of India's splendid contribution to the winning of the War, they would have met with an enthusiastic response and the full cooperation of nearly all parties. As it was, however, they came after the terrible bitterness aroused by the Rowlatt Act and by "the tragedy of Amritsar" so that the National Congress, now dominated by the extreme national party, wholly condemned the plan and demanded full provincial autonomy at once. On the whole, however, except for two suspensions, the reforms functioned regularly and with moderate success.[2] The outstanding weakness of the plan was that it gave the ministers responsibility without power, and the Legislatures power without responsibility. It tended toward an executive divided and competitive partly on racial lines. The representatives of the reserved subjects, chiefly foreigners, held the purse for what they considered the real concerns, while there were left inadequate appropriations and limited powers for Indian Ministers responsible for education and constructive reforms.

Even before the end of the decade of tentative trial of the plan of dyarchy, growing opposition to the contradictions of the system led to the appointment of a Commission to propose to Parliament a plan for a new Constitution for India.[3] It was

---

[1] The new Constitution enfranchised less than seven and a half million of the two hundred and forty-seven million inhabitants of British India. The "reserved" subjects were law and order, finance, police, jails and labor. The "transferred" subjects were education, local self-government, medical relief, sanitation and agriculture.

[2] Except for two periods of suspension in Bengal and the Central provinces when Legislatures refused to vote the Ministers' salaries, the system has been in operation in the nine major provinces since 1921.

[3] The Simon Commission was charged with "inquiring into the working of the systems of government . . . as to whether and to what extent it is desirable to establish the principle of responsible government."

supposed in India that such a Statutory Commission would follow the lines of the various Royal Commissions that had visited India from time to time composed of, say, four Indians and four Englishmen, with a British president. To appoint a Commission to propose the future Constitution of India without a single Indian representative was interpreted as a direct "insult to India," and it immediately united men of all parties against the plan.[1] When Sir John Simon and the Commission reached Bombay in 1928 they were received with black flags as a sign of mourning, business was suspended, the Stock Exchange closed and the Indian newspapers stopped publication. Such scenes were also reported in other cities. Too late an effort at conciliation was made by the appointment of an "Indian Central Committee" from the Indian legislature to sit with the Simon Commission, though not on equal terms.

3. *Lord Irwin's Statement on Indian Reforms* on October 31, 1929, followed by the Round Table Conference. The tension had increased for a year following the arrival of the Simon Commission when Lord Irwin made his great effort to stem the ebbing tide of confidence in the British Government by returning to England and securing permission to make his long-awaited announcement on Indian reforms. This announcement promised a Round Table Conference between the British Government, representatives of British India and the autonomous Indian States, and Dominion Status as the goal of India's constitutional progress.[2] The Viceroy's statement

---

[1] Dr. Ansari, the president of the National Congress, thus voiced the nationalist position: "No sane or self-respecting Indian can ever admit the claim of Great Britain to be the sole judge of the measure and time of India's political advance. . . . We can have no part or lot in a Commission which has been appointed in direct defiance of the declared will of the Indian people."

[2] Lord Irwin's announcement provided for: "The setting up of a conference in which His Majesty's Government should meet representatives both of British India and of the States for the purpose of seeking the greatest possible measure of agreement for the final proposals which it would later be the duty of His Majesty's Government to submit to Parliament. . . . The Ministers of the Crown, moreover, have more than once publicly declared that it is the desire of the British Government that India should, in the fulness of time, take her place in the Empire in equal partnership with the Dominions. . . . I am authorised, on behalf of His Majesty's Government, to state clearly that in their judgment, it is implicit in the Declaration of 1917 that the natural issue of India's constitutional progress, as there contemplated. is the attainment of Dominion Status."

for a time cleared the air and gave a measure of hope to many
in India by the promise of Dominion Status. But the tide of
confidence ebbed again with the debates in Parliament, where
the opposition was assured that there was nothing new contemplated in the proposals and that no date was suggested in
the vague phrases which had been used by the Viceroy concerning their fulfilment in "the fulness of time."

How can we account for the fact that, after India's magnificent contribution toward winning the War, when Indian
leaders emerged from the conflict on the whole so loyal to
Britain and so ready to welcome any adequate offer of a real
advance in self-government, within a decade they had become
so hostile and embittered and had so completely lost confidence
in the Government? How can we explain the fact that the
apparently generous offer of Lord Irwin of a round table conference and of Dominion Status, both of which they had so
long demanded, should be flatly rejected and that the Indian
National Congress at Lahore on December 31, 1929, should
vote almost unanimously for complete independence? It is
most important to realize the causes of this defection if we
would understand the situation in India and other lands that
are now seeking full self-determination.

India's contribution to the War was remarkable. When
Indian patriots might have sought their own national ends
during the hours of the Empire's peril there was complete
unanimity among all Indian parties that political activity should
be suspended and that Britain and the Allies should be supported in the War. Men like Sir Surendranath Bannerji, Sir
Sivasamy Iyer and Mr. Gandhi actively engaged in recruiting,
as the last mentioned had twice before come to the aid of the
British Government in previous wars in South Africa. "The
part borne by India in the War and the sacrifices made by her
people for the common cause are represented by an addition
of over £153,000,000 to her debt, the sending overseas of
800,000 combatants and 400,000 non-combatants, and the
foodstuffs and other supplies at the cost of much privation
among the poorer classes." [1] Doubtless the peoples of each
country, reading only their own press, exaggerated their particular contribution, but India emerged from the War expecting
some reward for her sacrifices in the form of more democratic

[1] *Encyclopedia Britannica,* 1926, New Vol. II, p. 428.

self-government.   Instead it seemed to her that she was met only by an insult.

India's Disaffection

Several outstanding causes account for India's disaffection in the decade following the War: (1) The Rowlatt Act; (2) the Amritsar massacre and the indignities that followed; (3) a long series of repressions, arrests, trials and imprisonment of some twenty thousand Indian college graduates and students in 1921, and an even larger number in 1930; (4) deeper than all and underlying all, the fundamental racial antagonism produced in them by the seeming insolence of their "superior" Anglo-Saxon rulers.   Finally, this antagonism was fanned to a flame of racial bitterness and hatred at a moment of political crisis through *Mother India,* a book written by Katharine Mayo, an American.

It will require sympathetic understanding to appreciate the growing distrust and drifting apart of these two great peoples. Granted the sense of responsibility on behalf of a people whom they are convinced are so divided that they cannot successfully govern themselves, it is difficult to see how in most cases the British could have done otherwise than they did.   Though somewhat unimaginative and tardy, doing the right thing just a little too late, as so often happened in the case of Ireland, most Anglo-Saxons would have told them, as Roosevelt did somewhat impertinently concerning Egypt, that they must either "govern or get out."   So, they governed.

But equally it must be understood that the best Indian leaders have today the same love of liberty, the same determination to achieve and maintain it at any cost, quite irrespective of whether they are ready for it or not, as have the British themselves, or as the American Colonists had in 1776.   The average Anglo-Saxon who believes that he is called to take up the white man's burden of governing "lesser breeds without the law" is utterly incapable of understanding the present situation in India.   The people of India no more want Anglo-Saxon rule than would the citizens of Chicago or New York wish to be under a German or British régime even if it could be shown that these governments would prove to be more honest and efficient than the present misgovernment of these American cities.   Sympathizing, then, both with the difficulties of the

British and the aspirations of the Indians, let us note the principal causes that drove them apart.

1. *The Rowlatt Act.* If the Montagu-Chelmsford Reforms had been offered soon after the War, as we have said, they would have been enthusiastically received. Instead came the Rowlatt Act, "Bill No. 1, of 1919," passed within three months of the Armistice.[1] This gave the Government powers for internment without trial in seditious districts, including the suspension of Habeas Corpus in emergency, and rendered any Indian citizen liable to arrest and confinement without public trial or legal defense. And this "flagrant evidence of distrust" was felt to be the reward of loyal India for her part in winning the War! A now united people flamed in indignation and protest, yet this "Black Act" was insistently passed by the official majority with a practically unanimous India bitterly opposing it. National days of mourning were observed.[2] There were soon uprisings that led to "the tragedy of Amritsar." However administratively justifiable the bill may have been— and doubtless the Government knew of much more sedition than did the people—it was a cardinal blunder in statesmanship. That it was unnecessary was proved by the fact that it was finally repealed without having been once used. But the damage had already been done. Within five months the Act had resulted in the death of nine Europeans and four hundred Indians, and the Punjab, which had furnished almost half the Indian army, was on the verge of revolt.

2. *The Amritsar Massacre.* When Mr. Gandhi, who was slowly recovering from a long illness contracted during his war recruiting, heard of the passage of the Rowlatt Sedition Act, he was filled with indignation and called for a general *hartal,* or day of national mourning, when all business should be suspended. In Delhi and other cities violence occurred and several people were killed. Martial law was proclaimed in Amritsar where five Englishmen had been killed and some property destroyed. Although order had been restored before

---

[1] The Government had interned several hundred suspected revolutionaries at the close of the war. These were investigated by special process without public trial. Public protest against this led to the appointment of a special committee under Justice Rowlatt.

[2] Sir Michael O'Dwyer says: "I am confident that there would have been no outbreak but for the Rowlatt Bill." *India as I Knew It,* p. 266.

General Dyer reached the city, in the excitement of the moment, after having forbidden all meetings, the General opened
fire upon a large crowd of people assembled in an open square
in the center of the town.   The conservative Englishman, Sir
Valentine Chirol, thus describes what took place: "Nothing
can justify what was done at Amritsar where the deliberate
bloodshed at Jallianwala has marked out April 13, 1919, as a
black day in the annals of British India. . . . Without a word
of warning, he opened fire at about 100 yards' range upon a
dense crowd, collected mainly in the lower and more distant
part of the enclosure around a platform from which speeches
were being delivered.   The crowd was estimated by him at
6,000, by others at 10,000 and more, but practically unarmed,
and all quite defenseless.   The panic-stricken multitude broke
at once, but for ten consecutive minutes he kept up a merciless
fusillade—in all 1,650 rounds—on that seething mass of humanity, caught like rats in a trap, vainly rushing for the few
narrow exits or lying flat on the ground to escape the rain of
bullets, which he personally directed to the points where the
crowd was thickest.   The 'targets,' to use his own word, were
good, and when at the end of those ten minutes, having almost
exhausted his ammunition, he marched his men off by the way
they came, he had killed, according to the official figures only
wrung out of the Government months later, 379, and he left
about 1,200 wounded on the ground, for whom, again to use
his own word, he did not consider it his 'job' to take the
slightest thought. . . . On his own showing, he deliberately
made up his mind whilst marching his men to Jallianwala, and
would not have flinched from still greater slaughter if the
narrowness of the approaches had not compelled him regretfully to leave his machine-guns behind.   His purpose, he declared, was to 'strike terror into the whole of the Punjab.' "[1]

Once again the action of General Dyer was, from a military
point of view, administratively justifiable and probably put an
end to local rioting, but it struck about as much terror into
the Punjab as did the battles of Concord and Bunker Hill into
the American colonists.   The Amritsar Massacre was followed

[1] *India Old and New,* pp. 177, 178, Sir Valentine Chirol.   Together with
a great multitude of his fellow-countrymen, "Amritsar was the critical event
which changed Mahatma Gandhi from a whole-hearted supporter into a
pronounced opponent."

by humiliating punishments, public floggings and whippings, and monstrous "crawling orders," where "innocent men and women were made to crawl like worms on their bellies" down a certain road where a lady missionary of the "superior" race had been roughly handled by a crowd. After the tardy investigation by the Hunter Committee, General Dyer's action was condemned by the House of Commons but condoned by the House of Lords, and a fund of $130,000 was presented to him with a jewelled sword. The report of this approval of his action only deepened India's indignation. The Duke of Connaught, representing the King-Emperor in opening the new Parliament of India, said: "The shadow of Amritsar has lengthened over the fair face of India."

The bitter resentment against General Dyer and others can only be understood in the light of the vivid memory of the Mutiny of 1857 by both sides. The British describe that revolt as a military sedition; the Indian National Congress calls it the First War of Independence. We have always been told of the massacre and the well of Cawnpore, but Indians remember the well at Ujnalla where vengeance upon nearly 500 men was demanded for the lives of two Englishmen.[1] The well known English writer, E. J. Thompson, in *The Other Side of the Medal,* reminds us that "the two cruellest massacres of Europeans occurred long after a policy of indiscriminate vengeance had been put into operation."[2] "British troops burnt down villages along their route of many hundreds of miles, turning the country into a desert."[3] "The English killed their prisoners without trial and in a manner held by Indians to be the height of barbarity, sewing Mohammedans in pig skins, smearing them in pork fat before execution, burning their bodies, and forcing Hindus to defile themselves before blowing them from the mouth of a cannon."[4] There were wholesale destructions of regiments.

The Rowlatt Act, the Amritsar Massacre remembered in the light of Mutiny, and the Khalifat question which aroused the

---

[1] H. H. Greathead wrote: "The sacrifice of five hundred villainous lives for the murder of two English is a retribution that will be remembered." *Letters During the Siege of Delhi,* p. 15.

[2] *The Other Side of the Medal,* E. J. Thompson, p. 66.

[3] *Ibid,* p. 82.

[4] G. T. Garratt, *An Indian Commentary,* p. 112.

Mohammedans, all increasingly united leaders and people against the Government.[1]

3. *The repression, arrest, trial and imprisonment* of so many of the outstanding leaders of India was a third cause as well as a result of the growing unrest.   Men like Mr. Gandhi, the Ali Brothers, Motilal and Jawaharlal Nehru, and finally in 1921 some twenty thousand, chiefly intellectuals, college graduates and students, were sent to prison.   One must not too severely blame the Government for trying to maintain law and order; neither can one wonder at Indian leaders resenting what seemed to them such tyranny.   Motilal Nehru, the outstanding leader of the Swaraj party in the National Legislative Assembly at that time, described the British Government in India as "the greatest and most powerful terrorist organization in the country." [2]

Eighty thousand Sikhs had volunteered as soldiers in the World War and since the Mutiny had been noted for their loyalty to Britain, yet up to May, 1925, some fourteen thousand of the Akali Sikhs had been thrown into prison, and many were clubbed down or fired upon before the Jaito shrine under their vow of non-violent protest.[3]   There doubtless was again administrative and legal justification for the Government's action but it all helped to spread disaffection throughout North India.   Lord Reading made the unwise suggestion to have the Prince of Wales visit India at this pitifully inopportune moment.   The boycotts and hostility with which he was met in some cities, and the costly and elaborate police protection required for him, were evidence of the underlying unrest and resentment of the people at that time.

4. *Fundamental antagonism to their "superior" Anglo-Saxon rulers* is a more potent source of unrest and disaffection than all other causes combined.   Far more deadly than the shooting at Amritsar is the long accumulation of grievances against the governmental, cultural and social superiority of the ruling race.   The British civil servant is just, efficient and

---

[1] Thus the official Central Committee of distinguished Indians writes: "Within a year the whole political atmosphere underwent a complete change, and goodwill and friendliness gave place to suspicion, distrust and racial hatred which combined to produce a situation of serious unrest." *Report of the Indian Central Committee*, p. 10.

[2] Sir Reginald Craddock, *The Dilemma in India*, p. 221.

[3] Zimand, *Living India*, pp. 241-243.

reserved; but to the Indian he seems cold, aloof, unimaginative, unsympathetic. On the author's recent journey across India an Indian official in the railway compartment, referring to the Englishman who had just left, said: "They all hate us." Nothing could be more untrue, yet this was his impression after a lifetime in their company.

Despite the decree of the British Parliament in 1833 that "no native of our Indian Empire shall, by reason of his color, his descent, or his religion, be incapable of holding office," racial discrimination has been long continued in the administration of India. Indians resent being excluded from the best English clubs. The distinctions against them are often similar to those against Negroes in the South of the United States—except for lynching. Nothing in this chapter should be interpreted as implying that the British are worse than the Americans in the matter of race prejudice. On the whole, they are probably somewhat better. But this racial superiority and cleavage shows itself in almost all relations. There are many offensive monuments with memories of the Mutiny that are resented by Indians and which have to be at times guarded from mutilation, like those of General Outram in Calcutta, Neill in Madras and John Lawrence in Lahore.[1]

Typical of this unconscious racial arrogance, the Viceroy, Lord Lawrence, said: "We are here by our own moral superiority."[2] Lord Shaftsbury said bluntly: "I do not see the use of political hypocrisy; it does not deceive the natives of India; they know perfectly well that they are governed by a superior race."[3] Lord Roberts always counted Indians to be an inferior subject race: "It is this consciousness of the inherent superiority of the European which has won for us India."[4] In one of his provocative speeches Lord Curzon condescendingly in-

---

[1] Under the statue of the latter was the defiant inscription: "Will you have the pen or the sword?" After it had been mutilated several times the wording was changed to "I have served you both with the pen and the sword." This is typical of the change of attitude which is taking place widely in India.

[2] Sir Michael O'Dwyer, *India as I Knew It*, p. 407.

[3] *Indian Affairs*, 1889, p. 160.

[4] Sir George Arthur, *Life of Lord Kitchener*, Vol. II, p. 177. Roberts writes at the time of the Mutiny: "When a prisoner is brought in, I am the first to call out to have him hanged." "By the middle of February the rebels will be, please God, nearly exterminated." *Letters Written During the Indian Mutiny*, Dec. 28, 1857, and February 26, 1858.

formed India "that truth was rather a Western than an Oriental virtue, and that craftiness and diplomatic wiles have in the East always been held in much repute." [1]   Aldous Huxley thus describes the Englishman in India: "Three hundred and twenty million Indians surround him; he feels incomparably superior to them all, from the coolie to the Maharajah." [2]   Very many of the English feel keenly the ingratitude and disloyalty of the Indian.   One lady, in writing to the Calcutta *Statesman* urging all right-minded people to contribute to the fund in appreciation of General Dyer, says: "Have Indians forgotten how they were plundered and persecuted by self-seeking robbers and tyrants, in the evil days before the British Bulldog pinned them to the dust?   Those were dire days indeed." [3]   To sum up these quotations which could be multiplied indefinitely, we may quote from one of India's greatest missionaries: "It would be a complete mistake to suppose that the discontent in India is either limited to certain classes or that it is the product of agitation.   It is as widespread and as deep in the land as are its poverty and its hunger. . . . It is these two facts, the hunger of the common people and the hauteur of the foreign ruler, that have brought the administration of India to the present crisis." [4]   It is this assumed racial superiority which, like a suffocating atmosphere, encompasses the Indian and the Oriental in every dependent country of Asia.   He feels it in almost every contact of his life.

Such asserted superiority produces automatically an inferiority complex in the subject race.   Repeatedly educated Indians quote the words of Sir John Seeley: "If the feeling of a common nationality began to exist there only feebly . . . from that day almost our Empire would cease to exist. . . . Subjection for a long time to a foreign yoke is one of the most potent causes of national deterioration." [5]   All of this Mr.

---

[1] *Living India,* p. 52.   S. Zimand.

[2] *The Bookman,* Feb., 1926.   G. Lowes Dickinson writes: "Of all the Western nations the English are the least capable of appreciating the qualities of Indian civilization. . . . Between him and the Indian the gulf is impassable."   Essay on *The Civilization of India,* pp. 18-19.

[3] Quoted by Edward Thompson, *The Other Side of the Medal,* p. 15.

[4] Nicol MacNicol, *The Making of Modern India,* pp. 8-10.

[5] *The Expansion of England,* by Sir John Seeley. Over a century ago in 1824, Sir Thomas Munro wrote: "Let Britain be subjugated by a foreign Power tomorrow, let the people be excluded from all share in the govern-

Gandhi has in mind when he speaks of "the slave mentality" which has resulted in India; and when Mr. Gokhale says: "A kind of dwarfing or stunting of the Indian race is going on under the present system.   We must live all our life in an atmosphere of inferiority."   Coupled with this racial prejudice there has been the growing distrust on the part of Indians of the reality of British promises.   The Queen's Proclamation of 1858 clearly promised to make no distinction between the different classes of the subjects of the Crown, as between British and Indians, in appointment to all offices.   Liberal Englishmen in India point out that this and other promises have been violated openly and that both Viceroys and Secretaries of State repeatedly have made it quite clear that they did not intend to keep it.   Also some of the promises made to India during the War were forgotten as soon as it was over.   With these broken promises came also the weakening of the faith in the impartiality of the standards of the British judiciary.

In the summer of 1927, coming at just the psychological moment of a political crisis in India, Katharine Mayo's *Mother India,* a brilliantly written book dealing with child marriage and the physical evils of India, caused an amazing increase of racial bitterness and of aversion to the British Government which it sought to praise.   It was widely read in England and America and deeply resented in India as cruelly unjust.   Miss Mayo had gone to India with influential introductions from the India Office in London which had warned her, "Whatever you do, be careful not to generalize."   Miss Mayo's visit came just at a time when, nearing the close of the tentative trial of the decade of dyarchy, the whole question of India's future constitution was at stake.   The natural result of reading *Mother India* would be to conclude that such a degraded and degenerate people as she describes are not, and never could be, capable of self-government.   Whatever its purpose, this was exactly the result the book achieved.   It was given wide and free distribution and made use of by the reactionary diehards in Parliament and the British Tory press, and it became a powerful political document.   We must clearly distinguish

ment, from public honours, from every office of high trust and emolument, and let them in every situation be considered as unworthy of trust, and all their knowledge and all their literature, sacred and profane, would not save them from becoming in another generation or two, a low-minded, deceitful, and dishonest race."

between the issue as to the *factual* character of the book, with the consequent need and result of social reform, and the *political* aspects of the book with their consequence of racial hatred and estrangement. The first might have been wholly good, the second wholly bad. It is with the second political aspect that we are here concerned.

Now that the atmosphere has been cleared, if the writer may speak for himself, he would say that in his opinion, while most of the statements in the book are matters of fact, the total impression is false and misleading. If one should write a book confined exclusively to lynching, racial prejudice, graft, crime and bootlegging, and call it *America* it would be false, though every line of it might be a statement of fact.[1]

We see no adequate reason to question Miss Mayo's *bona fides*.[2] To our knowledge she has been unostentatiously contributing money for the aid of India's womanhood. We also gladly believe with the *Indian Social Reformer* that "her book has stimulated action which otherwise would not have come so soon. Indian opinion is almost morbidly sensitive to Western criticism." The book doubtless has done good and will yet do more. But undoubtedly it has also done great harm, embarrassing at times the British Government which it was apparently intended to praise. Throughout the book its violently anti-Indian and pro-British bias is manifest. In our opinion the book is misleading and unjust at several points:

a. *Its sweeping and devastating generalizations,* often based upon inadequate facts.

b. *"Its subtle calumny, breathed by a trusted friend* in such a clever way that it cannot be disproved."

c. *The attribution of all of India's woes to sex depravity.* Miss Mayo writes: "The whole pyramid of India's (the Hindus) woes . . . rests upon a rock-bottom physical base. That base is, simply, his manner of getting into the world, and

---

[1] Mr. Gandhi felt that the book was powerfully written as "the report of a drain inspector," giving a graphic description of the stench exuded by the open drains. *Young India,* Sept. 15, 1927.

[2] Miss Mayo's declared purpose should be remembered: "In shouldering this task myself, I am fully aware of the resentments I shall incur; of the accusations of muckraking; of injustice; of material-mindedness; of lack of sympathy; of falsehood perhaps; perhaps of prurience." *Mother India,* p. 26.

his sex life thenceforward."[1] We need not repeat here t
chamber of horrors that follows.

Whatever part Miss Mayo's book may have played, it v
in the bitterness created at this time that the Madras meet
of the Indian National Congress turned from Dominion Sta
that had for forty years been the goal of the Congress,
complete independence of the ruling race.[2]

Among the many replies to Miss Mayo's book, one instr
tive psychological reaction is found in *Uncle Sham,* written
an Indian, Mr. H. L. Gauba, wherein he seeks to hold up th
United States to the same process of attack and ridicule back
by statistics and quotations drawn from "authoritative Ame
can opinion." A brief quotation or two will at once indic
the character of the book and India's reaction to *Mother In*
The author says in his Foreword: "I write that the truth ab
American life may be made known as fearlessly and as
as Miss Mayo has made known what she only believed
the truth about India. It is perhaps also necessary to ex
that the facts set out are confined either to the writer's
observations in the United States or to authoritative Amer
opinion on the subjects treated." In his chapter on the *V*
he writes: "Uncle Sam leaves few virgins unravished. . .
will appear from the sequel, the American girl begins to t
of marriage and sex at the age of four or five, at twelve
is old enough to know the physiological details of anato
of her boy friends, by sixteen she has tasted of the delic
mysteries of life, by twenty-five she has had perhaps four
five encounters into the domains of matrimony, at thirty s
is sterile, infected, abnormal. This is the sum and substan
of the life of an average daughter of Uncle Sam. This su

---

[1] *Mother India,* p. 29. In October, 1927, the chief missionary organizati
of the country, *The National Christian Council,* issued a statement to th
people of India and the West: "The picture of India which emerges from
Miss Mayo's book is untrue as to facts and unjust to the people of Ind
The sweeping generalizations that are deduced from the incidents that ca
to the notice of the author, or, that are suggested by the manner in wh
these incidents are presented, are entirely untrue as a description of India
a whole."

[2] "There can be no doubt that Miss Mayo had as much to do with th
passing of the Independence Resolution as all other factors put togeth
It was cold iron that entered deep into the vitals and found lodgement
the heart itself." K. T. Paul, *India in 1928, The Student World,* A
1928. p. 113.

ry is borne out by the evidence set forth below." [1]   The
thor follows with descriptions of the American game of
rip poker" illustrated with copious quotations from Bernarr
cfadden, H. L. Mencken and Judge Lindsey's pictures of
erican high school youth.   He thus quotes H. L. Mencken:
ew York is the capital of Satan, and no woman there is a
ictly A. 1 virgin, and yet, on the contrary, in New York it
a punishable offence to discuss even the weaknesses of the
onstitution of the United States." [2]

We found *Uncle Sham* a best seller on the news-stands all
er India.   When the writer met Mr. Gauba in Lahore in
ovember, 1929, he asked him two questions, thinking that
haps his stay in America had been as brief as that of Miss
yo in India.   To the question of how long he had been in
United States, he replied: "I have never been in America." [3]
en asked if he thought *Uncle Sham* a true picture of Ameri-
life he said: "It is as true and as false as *Mother India*.
e only sought to show that anyone can write a book like
Mayo's on any country.   The first copy of *Uncle Sham*
came from the binders was sent by the author to Miss
o with the inscription: 'From one Drain Inspector to
er.'"

ch are the things that nations are reading about each other
time of strained international relations and racial antago-
.   As Dr. MacNicol writes of *Mother India:* "Such a book
his poisons the relations between peoples."

It is quite useless to say that before India is entitled to free-
om she must put her own house in order and accomplish the
cial reforms that are so desperately needed.   As Stanley
nes well says: "India will not face her past until she is sure
her present."   She will neither admit nor can she adequately
eel her own deep social need while she is humiliated and burning under the sense of wrong inflicted upon her by the for-
igner, to whom she is tempted to attribute all her woes.   She
els that she has been autocratically ruled from Whitehall
ven thousand miles away, and again her leaders quote Ram-

---

[1] *Uncle Sham,* by H. L. Gauba, Indian Edition, p. 65.
[2] *Americana,* Martin Hopkinson, London, p. 295.   *Uncle Sham,* p. 59.
[3] Yet he states in his Foreword that his facts "are confined either to the
ter's own observations in the United States* or to authoritative American
ion."   Thus his whole book is founded on a falsehood.

say MacDonald as saying: "India is governed by a bureaucracy which, though officers may come and officers may go, goes on forever." "Up to the present moment the Government has been an autocracy, a despotism." [1]

India demands substantial self-government today. This will be less costly than the foreign rule of "the most expensive government in the world." Mr. Gandhi, in his last letter to the Viceroy before his arrest, wrote: "Take your own salary. It is over 21,000 rupees per month ($7,770 a month or $93,000 a year) besides many other indirect additions. The British Prime Minister gets £5,000 per year, a little over 5,400 rupees per month at the present rate of exchange. You are getting over 700 rupees per day against India's average income of less than 2 annas (4 cents) per day. . . . You are getting much over five thousand times India's average income. The British Prime Minister is getting only ninety times Britain's average income. On bended knee I ask you to ponder over this phenomenon." [2]

Ramsay MacDonald wrote in 1910 after his visit to India: "Two generations ago we said we should welcome this awakening. We urged India to it; we prepared for it. Now that it has come we are afraid. We spy upon it; we deport its advocates; we plan to circumvent it. . . . It has been an attitude of friendship at first and of bitter opposition later." Admitting the great value of the Pax Britannica, he continues: "On the other side of the account, however, is the great loss to India that this peace has been bought at the price of her own initiative. That is the real objection to all attempts to govern a country by a benevolent despotism. The governed are crushed down. They become subjects who obey, not citizens who act. Their literature, their art, their spiritual expression go. . . . They cease to live. . . . This loss of initiative and of self-development is greater as regards India than almost any other country. . . . The source of most of our failures is a lack of sympathetic imagination."

When Mr. MacDonald asked the leaders of India, some twenty years ago, "What is your conception of the end that is being worked out by our Indian administration?" Mr. Gokhale replied: "Self-government within the British Empire"; while

---

[1] *The Awakening of India*, pp. 11, 146, by J. Ramsay MacDonald, 1910.
[2] *India and the Simon Report*, p. 180.

Arabindo Ghose said: "A free and independent India."   These
are exactly the two replies that are made today, the first by
the majority of the Indian members of the Round Table Conference, the second by the Indian Nationalists.   Mr. Mac-
Donald concludes his book with these prophetic words regarding India: "We cannot keep her back.   Her destiny is fixed
above our will, and we had better recognize it and bow to the
Inevitable." [1]

-----

[1] *The Awakening of India,* 1910, pp. 197, 218, 268, 311.

CHAPTER II

China of all the countries in the world today is undoubtedly the most chaotic and complicated, the hardest to analyze or to understand. Here is one-quarter of the human race in the midst of a vast transition, suddenly plunged from the ancient and medieval into the modern world, from an ancient static society into the volcanic upheaval of a new social order. In a word, China is in revolution. And a revolution that is not simple but highly complex; utterly different from the American, French or Russian revolutions, or from the non-violent revolution in India. China has independence but lacks unity and order.

Spread over several centuries the West passed through an intellectual Renaissance, a religious Reformation and a series of political, industrial and social revolutions which transformed medieval into modern Europe. But "unchanging China" is now being forced into a fivefold revolution that is at once intellectual, industrial, social, political and religious. Five simultaneous upheavals are disrupting China. There is an intellectual and cultural revival somewhat similar to that which broke the stagnation of the Middle Ages in Europe, with the dethronement of Confucius as the chief source of authority, and the creation of a new language and a new literature. The industrial revolution, with the erection of some two thousand modern factories and the modernizing and rebuilding of her cities, has introduced China to the machine age and flooded her cities with proletarian labor. The beginnings of a social revolution are marked by the disintegration of the old family as the central social unit and the rise of new social institutions. The political revolution culminated in the overthrow of the Emperor, the Son of Heaven, head of the last of the eighteen dynasties, and the founding of the modern Republic of China in 1911 under the impulse of the new spirit of nationalism. The continuing revolution must now realize the three principles of nationality, democracy and social justice within the framework of a nominal Republic.

Finally, a moral and religious revolution is forcing itself upon distracted China. The old humanism of Confucianism, Taoism and Buddhism, which made their priceless contributions in the past in creating and stabilizing ancient China, can offer no hope of reconstructing a modern nation out of chaos. Some new system or force from without must unify and energize the country if it is to become an effective entity. Communism and Christianity are in actual fact two competing systems offering to reconstruct China, the one by revolution and a confessedly ruthless dictatorship, the other by the seemingly slower evolutionary processes of education and the patiently acquired disciplines of democracy. Neither of these systems is playing the part of an academic or theological or mystical escape from the actual problems of the modern world. They are two antithetic and contrasted systems, either of which will affect the whole political, social and spiritual life of the people. In the midst of changing moral standards China is facing the challenging issues of religion or atheism, the Christian and the anti-Christian movements, irreligious secularism or a moral and spiritual reformation.

Two short decades ago we saw in China a conservative people wearing the now antiquated queue. Under the Dowager Empress they had organized the Boxer Uprising to expel the hated foreigner from their ancient Middle Kingdom, the Celestial Empire, the center of the universe which was supposed to be surrounded by a completely barbarian world. For a century they had sought to keep out the "foreign devil" and maintain their proud and changeless isolation. Now all seems chaos and seething change. Twenty years ago these people were said to have no patriotism. Foreign influence had become so arrogant that signs were erected in some of the parks in the port cities reading, "Dogs and Chinese not allowed." Today a burning nationalism would abolish the remainder of the seventeen unequal treaties long held over a prostrate China, and would deprive the foreigner of his special privileges and immunities, especially in his "concessions." This fivefold transition or continuing revolution in China is not yet over; it has only just begun. And it must continue in the midst of civil war, economic depression, unemployment, famine and flood and every known form of human suffering. All its agonies, so terrible for the time being for the hungry masses, are but the birth pangs of a new civilization. China is not yet a united nation but a vast civilization in process of transition.

The Revolution is both caused and accompanied by *two conflicts;* that of two civilizations, oriental and occidental, and that between the new nationalism and foreign imperialism. As in the case of Japan and India, the impact of the West, with its commerce, industry, politics, education, literature, religion and social structure, proved a vast and disturbing counter-irritant to the peaceful East. Oriental humanism was confronted by industrialism, organization and scientific efficiency. The old social order was not adjusted to meet this demanding impact. The golden mean of China's philosophy of harmony and human happiness, with its self-complacency and conservatism, were forever shattered both for its revolutionary youth and for its seething masses. In a single generation the compass has swung a hundred and eighty degrees from changeless, petrified Confucianism to disruptive and destructive Communism.

As we have said, the second conflict is that between the new and volcanic Chinese nationalism and foreign imperialism. For a century it has seemed to China that this advancing imperialism has invaded and forced upon her its trade, its factories, its opium; it has gained foothold in encroaching concessions and courts, in the growing control of customs, tariffs and revenues; it has taken large sections of territory, parceled out spheres of influence and protected all foreign seizures and Chinese servitudes by gunboats, naval bases and garrisons. Even foreign education, culture and religion have seemed so associated with these evils that they have appeared as a part of this ever-victorious imperialism. Culminating in the shooting of Chinese workers and students in 1925, the new nationalism flamed with indignation and struck back, not blindly as in the Boxer Uprising, but with modern weapons and methods. The days of a now retreating imperialism are numbered. It has been the habit of many foreigners to lay all the blame for existing conditions upon the Chinese, and of many of the latter to place all the blame upon foreign treaties and nationals. But in a new spirit both of understanding and co-operation, each must realize, admit and rectify their own faults if China's problems are to be solved. While the nations of the West have caused and contributed to China's awakening, they have also hindered, handicapped and plundered her. They have been both a blessing and a curse. A shameless imperialism can no longer justify or maintain itself even before this prostrate nation.

One thing more must be realized if we really are to understand the inwardness of the situation in China. We must view the present transition in the light of the long perspective of China's past and of China's permanent character. When the newly-arrived foreigner gets pessimistic about the country "sinking into chaos" the Chinese only smiles. He is not hopeless or even excited. He sees not chaos but confusion. The latent memory of the long past is in him. He knows his country has weathered and survived a score or more of worse storms and crises. He knows there is an ingrained, inbred, persistent nucleus of culture and character that will in time overcome every military conqueror, modify and adapt every foreign system, whether the Mongol or the Manchu in the past or Communism or Christianity in the future. Just as Soviet Russia today is Czarism plus Marxism, but is and always will be truly Russian, so in the future there may arise a Chinese Communism or a Chinese Christianity, but it will surely and certainly be Chinese. China will bend but she will never break. She may be profoundly modified but will never be completely transformed. There is too much of survival value to be lost in her finished and stubborn culture of the past.

The Chinese have been a self-governing people for thousands

of years. During the last millenium the Mongols for two generations and the Manchus for some two and a half centuries imposed their dynastic rule upon the Chinese, but where are those peoples today? Being more backward and barbarous, they were first conquered and enriched by a superior Chinese culture, then cast aside and left behind by it.

China's early civilization surpassed that of primitive or medieval Europe. Her cultured people were dressed in silks more than a thousand years before Christ, when northern Europe was still clad in skins and centuries later in coarse wool and linen. China had invented and was using paper of high grade by 105 A. D. This discovery was carried through central Asia to Persia, Egypt and Spain, and finally reached Europe in the eleventh century, nearly a thousand years after its invention in China. The early discovery and use of the mariner's compass, of gunpowder, of furniture, wallpaper, landscape gardening and many other evidences of a high degree of culture and civilization placed her far in advance of Europe. She discovered the art of printing and the use of movable type nearly four centuries before Gutenberg. She was dining on fine porcelain when Europe was still using wooden trenchers. She had attained to high ethical standards and to notable achievements in law and order, so that twice the area of Europe was under a unified government when the western continent was distracted by internal strife and lawless disorder.

Even today, the moment soldiers or armed forces are withdrawn, no people become so quickly and completely law-abiding, unless it be the British. In the pre-industrial age no nation in the world had attained to a higher and more consistently coordinated and continuous state of culture. China had the largest single government cultivating order, courtesy and comfort. She was publishing the largest number of books of any country. In the time of Marco Polo in the thirteenth century China's civilization and culture as a whole were counted in advance of Europe. By the reports of the Jesuit missionaries down to a century and a half ago this preeminence of China persisted. And there is a nucleus and core of Chinese culture that will still persist beyond all changes and will absorb and modify all systems which challenge or confront her. In the confident outlook of such a perspective we shall view the present confusion or seeming chaos of this greatest transition through which China has ever passed.

The Revolution is being accomplished or accompanied by *two processes,* vast and simultaneous—*decomposition and reconstruction*—the rapid, destructive breaking down of the old order and the slow, constructive building up of the new. These two processes always accompany every thorough-going revolution, as in France and Russia. It is the destructive phase that seems more evident, disturbing and discouraging in China at the moment. But the Chinese have survived many periods of revolution, feudal strife and chaos in their long history. Their unbroken continuity and power of survival have been phenomenal. Even in the feudal age of Confucius "the world had fallen into decay"; and as late as the Taiping Rebellion, from 1850 to 1864, nearly half the provinces were devastated and some twenty million lives were lost. True friends of China must not, therefore, be disheartened or surprised at this phase of decomposition and destruction of the old civilization, with its institutions and sanctions, before the new has been formed and while there is as yet nothing to take its place. A shallow optimism and false sentimentalism which refuse to face the grim facts will not solve the crucial problems of China, but rather a fearless and sympathetic realism which is not afraid to probe to the bottom the evils of the present because of its unshaken faith in the future of China and her great people. In this faith let us note the principal evils that are prevalent in the present régime and then the constructive values that are being built into the creation of the new China.

Chaos in China

The dominant evils in China today seem to be militarism and civil war, lawlessness and disorder, corruption, the curse of opium, poverty and destitution resulting from these evils, and the consequent menace of Communism.

Militarism and civil war are devastating and disintegrating movements still continuing two decades after the founding of the Republic. This inheritance was bequeathed by Yuan Shi Kai, whose generals and their successors have been fighting among themselves ever since his death in the struggle for power. Each becomes a feudal warlord who creates, maintains and owns his army. To sustain himself he often insists that he must live upon the people, and that he must seize and control some railway. Thereupon traffic is suspended, the rolling stock is stolen or ruined, and the roadbed falls into decay. To finance himself he induces or forces the farmers to plant the cursed opium as a temporary "necessary evil" and a flood of moral corruption follows in the wake of this pernicious poison. His army becomes an economic pocket for the unemployed. Often unpaid, the soldiers appropriate their arms and turn free-booters. Soldiers become bandits and bandits become soldiers. The whole system easily degenerates into lawless violence.

Some of the generals are, or were originally, able and earnest though uneducated men. But the fighting is done sometimes with lead and sometimes with "silver bullets." Armies are bought and sold with money or by propaganda. Generals must be bribed, often periodically. Sincerity of purpose becomes more questionable when in any given war many of the generals have in the past fought against others now on their own side and beside generals now on the opposing side. Constant turnings, betrayals and breaking of promises do not gain the confidence either of the leaders or of the masses of people who alike suffer from the incessant warfare. In some provinces press-gangs carry off laborers from their homes, while women and girls suffer unmentionable wrongs at the hands of the soldiers. Over two million soldiers have thus been withdrawn from active production to live upon or often prey upon the country. To support them merchants and others must be taxed and retaxed. A single major war costs over ten million dollars gold. Actually nine-tenths and officially eighty-five percent of even the published portion of the budget, apart from interest on debts, is poured into military expenditure, while every constructive project languishes for want of funds.

With these infrequently paid armies quartered upon them, the helpless people must endure confiscation, and constantly duplicated taxes, often demanded for several years in advance and extorted by threats of violence and looting. Mr. Abend cites the illustration of the city of Changteh in 1929 taxed successively by five successive generals. The first two levied tribute on threat of loot. The next two combined to capture the city and according to Chinese reports they "looted every home and shop," carrying away to the mountains a million dollars in cash, tons of merchandise, some eighty women and girls, and thirty wealthy men whom they held for ransom.[1]

During the preceding year, 1928, the gifted Minister of Finance, Mr. T. V. Soong, stated to the National Economic Conference that China was at that time forced to support eighty-four armies, eighteen independent divisions, and twenty-one brigades, totalling more than two million men. Even though underpaid, the cash outlay had been $360,000,000 out of the national income of only $450,000,000, after loan obligations were paid. Thus the government, without any provision for education or civil expenses, faced a deficit of $60,000,000. There were eight civil wars and rebellions during the next year, 1929.

In the fight to maintain the existence of the National government, the President, Chiang Kai-shek, supported forty-six German military advisors on his personal payroll, including General Ludendorf's able assistant, Colonel Max Bauer. It must always be remembered that much of the burden of and blame for this foreign trained militarism is of foreign origin. Militarism in time develops into the negation of all government and of all rule. If "war is hell" it becomes in China chronic hell—hell for business, hell for government, hell for the starving people. It drives a desperate population ever nearer to that condition of poverty and despair which makes the country ripe for Communism.

Yet the demobilization of China's armies has become an almost insoluble problem. When the generals meet and agree

---

[1] Hallett Abend, *Tortured China*, pp. 76, 147, 154.

to disarm the conferences only break up with increased suspicion. Each general who regards himself as China's savior wants the others to disarm first. China can neither pay her armies nor disband them. General Ho Ying-ching estimated that to maintain the armies would cost $800,000,000 a year, at a time when China's national revenue was only some $432,000,000. The balance must be wrung from the impoverished people. Yet it is even more fatal to disband the troops. If dismissed unpaid they turn bandit as the only means of supporting themselves and the mere rumor of disbandment sends whole detachments over to join the ranks of the Communists in the field. It is difficult to see how the troops can be quickly dispersed unless some leader is strong enough to unify China, pay the soldiers enough to enter civil life, or secure a foreign loan to finance the building of public works, roads or railways to employ the disbanded soldiers. In the meantime China remains in chaos and is bled white by civil war and incessant militarism.

Lawlessness and disorder are the inevitable result of the present military situation. As we have seen, unpaid or disbanded soldiers turn bandit. Soldiers and bandits often loot cities during war time and villages in peace time. One typical farmer, recently robbed of everything for the third time, said that there was nothing left between him and starvation but to turn bandit himself. There has been no such robbery and lawlessness in China since the Taiping Rebellion. Another sign of lawlessness is the practice of kidnapping and holding for ransom. While we were in China rich men were being seized and held for ransom even in Shanghai. Both Chinese and foreigners are now in danger in a number of districts. We have seen prominent Chinese marked for kidnapping who dared not venture out in public alone. Lawlessness leads almost to anarchy in some districts and among certain classes. Students at times become infected with the spirit of radicalism and license, and there is little discipline or restraint in some of the colleges.

In the sense in which it is understood in the West, there has never been a strong central government in China. Rather the country was ruled by the family and the guild, under a disjointed individualism, held together by the momentum of tradition and precedent, under a loosely autonomous local democracy. The national government was a mere symbolical superstructure, far removed from the people. Taxes were farmed out and their collection often abused. Against frequent misgovernment the Chinese maintained their basic right of revolution. Yet it has been said paradoxically that though the Chinese are the most rebellious they are the least revolutionary of all peoples.

The failure of the central or provincial governments to maintain law and order has witnessed the widespread growth of banditry even approaching very close to Nanking and many provincial capitals, and at times entering the port cities. Nanking has not yet been able to maintain effective authority over more than four or five of the twenty-one provinces. It has been well said that banditry in China does not spring from lawlessness but that it is a barometer of economic conditions. Men rob in order to live. In fact, China's chaos today is basically economic.

In the province of Honan alone, which contains about one-fifth of the soldiers of China, it is estimated that there are some 400,000 bandits. The city of Iyang in that province changed hands between various bandit gangs some seventy times in 1930.

Bribery and corruption constitute the third evil from which China is suffering today in a wide-spread system that is called "squeeze." Fortunately it is a *system* and as such it may be corrected. It is not a necessary trait of Chinese character for in their business dealings the old Chinese guild merchants won a deserved reputation for honesty throughout the East; their word was as good as their bond. But in the period of decay of the Manchu dynasty, offices were shamelessly bought and sold. In the lawlessness of civil war the system has become much more wide-spread in both business and government circles, and with disastrous results. A single illustration will suffice. A generation ago the steamship lines of Japan and China were both in their infancy. Today the steamships of

Japan successfully girdle the globe, but a blight has fallen upon the Chinese lines. When one ship known to the writer was repaired recently, the captain demanded his ten percent in squeeze, the chief engineer ten percent and the first officer five percent. It cost twice as much to repair this ship in China as it would have in Japan. When it is running, the coal and all supplies are purchased with squeeze. Directors of the company, who are models of piety in loyalty to their family and clan, have no conscience in looting the profits of the company. Last year this ship with one other lost a hundred thousand dollars. Unfortunately this system spreads like the blight of a disease or a pestilence through the commercial and official life of China. In some quarters there has been marked improvement, but in the North especially things are growing worse. Many returned students from abroad are striving to be honest, but there is little hope of moral, economic or political recovery until an awakened national conscience and public opinion demand the correction of this system which is at present sapping the life of China, morally and economically.

The sweeping generalization was once made that the Chinese are honest and the Japanese dishonest, but so widespread is the growing system of squeeze that today the reverse would appear to be true. Traveling salesmen who cover both countries are reporting that prevailingly the Japanese are honest and are steadily becoming more so, while the pernicious system of squeeze is making the Chinese constantly more dishonest.

Many of the higher officials are true patriots who are not corrupted. But the system is discouraging and disastrous for many of the students returning from their courses of study in America or other lands. They are often unable to secure positions without the payment of bribes, and cannot rise or stand in favor with other officials if they refuse to countenance the system.

Nepotism, or favoritism for relatives, has been a direct outgrowth of the family system in China. Filial piety and the five relations of Confucianism involved as one's first duty loyalty to one's family, to ancestors however remote, and to dependents however humble. It was a virtue to favor a rela-

tive rather than to appoint the most honest or efficient man for
a post in a corporation or in the government.   Thus the great
statesman, Li Hung Chang, might with almost a clear Confucian conscience betray or sell out his country's interests if
only he amassed a fortune for his family.   Family loyalty was
absolute, national loyalty was dim, distant or unformed.   A
reformer in such a situation would find the system almost
solidly against him.   A whole network of relatives, super-
numeraries, grafters and incompetents would be thrown on the
defensive against a man who did not fit into the system.   Many
private companies, formed to build railways or conduct other
enterprises, have failed scandalously after squandering millions
under leaders who were often models of filial piety but guilty
of political or commercial corruption.   The *mores* of the Confucian five relations simply does not fit or function adequately
in the modern world.

It may help Americans to a more patient understanding of
China to recall the notorious corruption of city governments
in their own country at present, and even more the corruption
at the time of their own Revolution, if one goes back of the
halo of revolutionary romance to the reality of history.[1]

The Curse of Opium

The curse of opium in China has followed in the train of
civil war and lawlessness.   Both in its devastating moral and
social effects and in the highly lucrative nature of the trade,
opium may be compared to slavery and liquor as a major social
evil.   But especially it has proved the curse and ruin of China.

---

[1] Washington, after a visit to the Continental Congress in 1777, wrote:
"If I were to be called upon to draw a picture of the times and of men,
from what I have seen, heard, and in part know, I should in one word say
that idleness, dissipation and extravagance seems to have laid fast hold on
most of them.   That speculation—peculation—and an insatiable thirst for
riches seems to have got the better of every other consideration and almost
of every order of men.   That party disputes and personal quarrels are the
great business of the day whilst the momentous concerns of an empire—a
great and accumulated debt—ruined finances—a depreciated currency—and
want of credit (which in their consequences is the want of everything)
are but secondary considerations, and postponed from day to day, from
week to week, as if our affairs wear the most promising aspect."

With many of her other evils it was the foreigner who first introduced the drug.[1]   The friction created by the contraband traffic which China struggled to exclude was one of the causes which led to the so-called "Opium War" between China and Great Britain.   To China the invading white barbarian seemed to represent opium and plunder.   He appeared to be a veritable "foreign devil."   The Chinese Commissioner finally seized and destroyed twenty thousand chests of the drug.   A British fleet blockaded Canton in 1840 and after two years of defeat China signed the Treaty of Nanking in 1842.   Five of her ports were forcibly opened for trade and she was compelled to pay an indemnity of twenty-one million dollars, including six millions for the cost of the opium destroyed.

The curse of opium spread until her old army was rendered almost useless through opium smoking during the Taiping Rebellion, from 1850 to 1864.   From 1906 to 1913 by heroic efforts China almost abolished the raising of opium, and in 1913 the Government of India, having generously responded to her efforts at reform, finally ceased all export of the drug to China.   But in the political chaos which followed the Revolution of 1911, the generals forced the farmers into the raising of opium to produce sufficient revenues to carry on their wars. The use of the drug not only impoverishes its addicts, but the widespread growth of the poppy decreases the food production, contributes to famine conditions and to moral degradation by making slaves and sots out of excessive users.

Among others, four foreign nations have been particularly guilty in the matter of the opium traffic with China—Great Britain, Portugal, France and Japan.   It would require a volume to describe the British opium trade with China, both before and after the "Opium War."   In 1906 liberals in the House of Commons condemned the traffic, but the lucrative evil still persists.   If we study the official figures showing the

[1] The poppy plant was introduced by the Arabs in the eighth century.   In the sixteenth century it was produced for medicinal use in India and China. In 1620 tobacco was brought to China from the Philippines; later it was smoked with opium and finally opium was smoked alone.   The British East India Company and private smugglers carried on a lucrative trade in the drug with China and after 1810 the Americans also.

proportion of net opium revenue to the total budget revenue in the various countries and colonies concerned, the very large share derived from opium will be apparent in the following table, especially in the British colonies. These figures indicate the proportions of revenue but not the thousands of Chinese opium addicts who suffer in all these colonies.

Percentage of Opium Revenue to Total Budget Revenue.[1]

	1926	1927	1928
Straits Settlements	30.5	34.0	32.3
Federated Malay States	14.6	13.6	12.3
Brunei		20.7	21.6
British North Borneo	22.7	21.2	19.2
Hong Kong		11.6	11.0
Netherlands Indies	5.4	4.8	4.9
French Indo-China with			
Kwang-Chow-Wan	10.0	10.0	8.0
Formosa	3.42	3.5	2.7
Siam	18.2	16.7	16.5
Macao		32.6	27.1

The marauding Portuguese began to infest the coasts of China in the sixteenth century and in 1557 settled in Macao near Canton. Their cruelty, kidnapping and licentiousness became proverbial. For a long time they maintained themselves chiefly by three sources of revenue in Macao, opium, gambling and licensed prostitution. The proceeds of their gambling hells were at one time divided between the Church and the State. A thorn in China's side, they could pour opium into the country from this port. The Chinese would long ago have swept this pest hole into the sea in moral indignation had it not been protected by unequal treaties and foreign gunboats. In recent years under invaluable pressure from public opinion exerted through the League of Nations, the Portuguese have been trying to put their house in order.

The French have a bad record in the manufacture of drugs in France and in the opium trade in China. The large French

---

[1] These figures can be verified at the League of Nations in Geneva or in the government reports of the various countries.

settlement in Shanghai is a lucrative center for the traffic which pours this poison into China. The French have been receiving $150,000 Mexican a month for the illicit opium monopoly in their concession. In February, 1926, a thorough investigation was made of the French concession and the names and addresses of some forty large dealers in opium were obtained, in addition to the location of their opium dens which were providing the Chinese with six thousand pipes for smoking. A protest concerning these opium centers was sent to the French Consul in Shanghai and to the French Minister in Peking. After giving due notice to the opium dealers, an "investigation" was conducted and the whole traffic was whitewashed and denied. For three years the French have defeated every effort to clean up their settlement.

Apparently nearly all the French officials in China are implicated. The writer saw the signed report of the French official, René Baurens, specifying in detail the shameful part of the French Syndicate of Opium Protection in the traffic. Baurens complained that he had not been getting his fair share of the graft with the other officials. Because of his complaint he was dismissed and later transferred to Indo-China. There is no doubt about the open disgrace of this French traffic in opium. The writer went out in broad daylight and was able without difficulty to see the French opium dens, and through Chinese agents himself purchased opium which was being sold in quantity. Anyone can find it except the French officials who connive at the traffic. ·

The French and Chinese in the opium ring approached the foreign International Settlement and offered them $250,000 Mexican a month for the privilege of the opium monopoly there. To their great credit the offer was refused. It was almost the one body with a good record that we found in China.

The French pour their opium into mid-China. The Japanese are flooding Manchuria and North China with the drug and its more deadly derivatives. The writer by personal inspection in Manchuria found the Japanese in their concessions carrying on this deadly trade. They protect their own subjects and the

Koreans from using the drug but exploit the Chinese merci-lessly. We saw a whole series of Japanese "Foreign Goods Shops" selling morphine and heroin to Chinese customers and providing sheds where they are given injections or powders and can sleep off the effects of the drugs. Within one square of the Japanese station, in their own concession where the Chinese cannot prevent it, at number 2 Lan Shu Tung, we saw some fifty Chinese smoking the drug in the Japanese dens, and purchased opium without difficulty through the Chinese guide. Just before we arrived in Mukden 148 large boxes of heroin shipped from Hamburg, Germany, to a well-known Japanese dealer, were seized and destroyed by the Manchurian Govern-ment, and shortly after 239 boxes were seized in Harbin. These drugs are being poured into Manchuria and North China at the present time, where the Japanese are flagrantly violating Article 17 of the Hague Opium Convention. It is earnestly to be hoped that for the honor of this great nation this stain may be removed in the near future. The same may be said of the British tropical colonies, where, although always protecting their own nationals, many of the Chinese coolies and laborers are encouraged to form the deadly habit of opium smoking.

Although foreign nations must take their full share of blame in connection both with the past and present situation, the writer is compelled to say regretfully that *the Chinese offi-cials are today far more guilty in connection with the opium traffic in their country than all other nations combined.* The Commissioner of Finance of the province of Hupeh with head-quarters at Hankow, in his official returns for income for the single month of September, 1929, showed that two-thirds of the tax collections of the province came from opium. Out of the total revenues of some $3,000,000, opium yielded nearly $2,000,000, wine and tobacco, $50,000, the salt tax $50,000, and the stamp tax $60,000. In Hankow twenty-four opium dealers offered $130,000 a month for a monopoly of the trade.[1] Two of the most lucrative provinces alone have been furnish-

[1] Abend, *Tortured China,* pp. 98, 99.

ing $10,000,000 a month to the National Government from opium.

There is an opium ring in Shanghai headed by the "Three Musketeers," who are members of the Black and Red secret order. These men are as well-known in China as Al Capone is in Chicago. They seek to control not only the opium monopoly, but the gambling, some of the kidnapping, crime and, when necessary, murder and assassination in Shanghai.

The Chinese Government refused to allow the League of Nations' Commission of Inquiry into Opium Smoking in the Far East, which had been welcomed in all the other countries concerned, to investigate the facts regarding opium in China. Indeed they could not face such an investigation today without disgrace. Within a few hours' travel of Nanking are wide plains carpeted with the white velvet of poppies. They are the curse of Szechwan and other provinces. The Opium Suppression Association of Nanking, under General Chang Chin-Kiang, has made earnest efforts to stamp out this monstrous evil, but their work will remain ineffective until those higher up are willing to pay the price of ridding China of the most terrible poisons known to man. If the Nanking Government takes over the opium monopoly as proposed, the temptation will be almost irresistible to exploit their suffering people for profit. Thus opium remains one of China's major problems.

Poverty, unemployment and desperate economic need have naturally followed the evils just mentioned of civil war, lawlessness, corruption and the demoralization of opium, especially when the natural calamities of famine and flood are added. Business is hampered and crippled with exorbitant or illegal taxes. Railways, that were once a gold mine of revenue, are diverted or ruined. Wages are desperately low and the cost of living has increased. Unemployment is widespread. Recent graduates from middle schools or colleges cannot find work. Students are often discouraged or depressed, or fall a prey to pessimism, cynicism or despair. Many turn to promised radical panaceas for a solution. In northern Honan and Shansi we found people living on leaves and roots; from Shantung they were migrating to Manchuria. In the famine districts of the northwest many were dying.   In 1929 some two millions starved to death and two millions more were estimated as "practically certain" to die before the next harvest.   The Red Cross Commission estimated that "thirty million Chinese are continually attempting to sustain life on less than the minimum required for subsistence."   Although India is poorer, it is undoubtedly true that this one-quarter of the human race in China is suffering more acutely in its economic life today than any other portion of the entire world.

The basic poverty of China is difficult to realize.   The average farm of some five acres must support an average family of 5.7 members.   The annual family income is only about $147 a year, or $2.30 per capita a month.[1]   The United States has 265,000 miles of railway, China some 7,000; the former has 300,000 miles of surfaced motor roads, China less than 1,000; the former has a million miles of graded dirt roads, while China has only some 10,000.   Where there is a harvest in one province and famine in the next, there is no economic transportation for the grain to the point of need, nor can surplus grain from abroad be economically transported to famine areas.

Investigation of historical records indicates an average of about one famine a year in China during the Christian era, or 1828 famines between 108 B. C. and 1911 A. D.   During the drought years of 1877-1879 there were from nine to thirteen million deaths.   In imperial days there were granaries and warehouses for the needy but these have been destroyed since the Revolution.   Drought and flood are both natural causes of famine.   The effects of both are catastrophic in the present political situation.   Either too much or too little rain spells misery for multitudes.

Space forbids a further review of the evils from which China is suffering. China's philosopher and fearless reformer, Dr. Hu Shih, counts "poverty, disease, ignorance and corrup-

[1] Professor J. L. Buck, Nanking University, *Annals of the American Academy of Political Science,* 1930, p. 109.   The average density of population in East Central China on cultivated land is 839 per square mile, compared to 48 in the United States, 77 in Denmark and 1238 in Japan.

tion, the four cardinal enemies of the nation." Illiteracy is undoubtedly one of China's great handicaps. There have been far fewer in the educational institutions of China than in India. When they claim about six million pupils it is but half the number of those in India. The educational system inevitably suffers from the present national disorder. Disease also takes a terrible toll in China from bubonic plague, cholera, typhoid, dysentery, smallpox and tuberculosis. Though no reliable statistics are available, the death rate is undoubtedly over thirty per thousand. Ancestor worship makes for large families. The average woman in China is said to bear nine children. Infant mortality is, of course, very high.

The Menace of Communism

Communism arises as a counsel of despair when the foregoing evils of militarism, lawlessness, corruption, opium and poverty combine to furnish the fruitful soil for its growth. It must be remembered that Russia borders upon China for thousands of miles and after the failure of their immediate program in the West, Russia turned to the East, concentrating her efforts upon China as her first hope.

On our last two tours around the world we found China the one country seriously and immediately threatened with Communism. We say this in spite of many factors in the situation that are adverse to this system. The Chinese of the older generation, after centuries of training in the doctrine of the "mean," have an inherent aversion to radical theories and organization, and their whole family system would naturally present a barrier to Communism. But no Confucian golden mean dominates the minds of China's students or labor today, and the family system is becoming impaired. China has no great fortunes or vast wealth to share. Her few fortunes are quickly subdivided or dissipated in one or two generations. As Dr. Sun well said: "The real problem of China is the problem of poverty, not the problem of unequal distribution." You can communize wealth but not poverty. China's small landholdings are a barrier against the division of property. There are no vast estates to divide. The Land Committee of the

Kuomintang Party reported in 1927 that only 15 per cent of China's soil is cultivated. Of the four-fifths of the population which is rural, approximately 150 millions own land themselves, 136 millions are tenants, 30 millions are agricultural laborers and 20 millions have no regular means of livelihood. Thus 65 per cent are landless, only 12 per cent of the rural population own enough land on which to live in contentment, and three-quarters of China's rural population have no interest in the present system of land distribution.[1] Here is more than a sufficient dispossessed population for a desperate and destructive revolution. Wages, hours and conditions of work are the worst in the world in China. There is a vast proletariat to appeal to.

Communists in China told the writer frankly that they look for the continuance of civil war, divisions in the Kuomintang Party and the psychology of despair occasioned by unemployment, privation and hunger as the best hope of their cause. Even in 1930 they claimed 150,000 men in the Red armies then fighting openly in eight provinces, and five million peasant sympathizers. They already have seized control of scattered districts in four southern and several western provinces under Communists or local Reds. They confess that their cause has been hindered by the undisciplined cruelty and barbarities of their short-lived rule in Canton and Hunan, but look upon China as a happy hunting ground during the period of social decomposition while civil war continues and the above evils are rampant. As Communism is presented to landless peasants, unemployed or underpaid labor or cynical and desponding students, it seems to offer the simple promise of a panacea for all wrongs, apparently based on a high idealism, with its promise of social justice by immediate communal sharing and cooperation. Meanwhile Russia is pointed to as the triumph of the system. If China sinks lower, Communism will offer itself as their last hope in despair.

Many factors have favored the spread of Communism in China. Dr. Sun had asked for the help of a Lafayette to aid

---

[1] *Foundations of Modern China,* Tang Leang Li, p. 251.

his country in her Revolution. He turned first hopefully to America. In 1923 he had demanded part of the customs revenue at Canton to support his government. British, French and Italian gunboats appeared on the scene as a threat, with a still larger fleet from the United States. He finally turned in despair to Russia, the only country that would give him aid, as Lafayette had to the American colonists. Russia abrogated her unjust and unequal treaties with China and sent successively three able men to represent her there: Joffe, Karakhan and Borodin.

On May 30, 1925, during a strike of Chinese workers in a Japanese cotton mill, less than three months after the death of Sun Yat Sen, came the "Shanghai Massacre" when the foreign-officered police unwisely fired into the ranks of the students and workers. Twelve were killed and a larger number wounded. Less than a month later the foreigners fired into a procession of students and workers at Canton and forty-four were killed. The news of these two affairs, which was flashed all over China, had an effect similar to the "Amritsar Massacre" of General Dyer in India. Strikes and demonstrations were held all over the land. A partial boycott on British trade lasted for more than a year.

During the same period, seemingly offering the hand of friendship, the Russians were founding the Communist University for the Toilers of the Orient in Moscow, and a little later the Sun Yat Sen University there to train several hundred picked Chinese students.

Borodin, aided by thirty Russian military experts in Canton, began to train the partisan army that was soon to conquer China and to strengthen the Kuomintang Party. By injecting a revolutionary spirit, strict party discipline, and organizing the workmen and peasants, he was loosing forces of disorder that later got out of hand, threatened Chinese society, left numbers of workers unemployed and produced indescribable confusion.

After Chiang Kai-shek had turned against the Communists with a campaign of extermination and repression in Nanking, there followed the collapse of the Chinese Soviet Republic in

Hankow and Borodin was sent back to Moscow. But the movement had left a lasting and powerful influence in China.

When the writer was in the foreign office of a neighboring power in 1930, he was shown a map of China on which twenty-two areas were marked in red, which were even then in control either of Communists, or local reds, or bandits who found the red banner of Communism a convenient cloak or excuse for pillage and destruction, but which neither the central nor any provincial government could control. In central and southern China more than 30 million people in scattered areas have been living under the domination of so-called "Communist bands." The Nationalist troops are often undermined by propaganda and will not fight seriously against the armed peasants and Communist armies.

While in China the writer met a leading Communist who on the occasion of his last visit had been a prominent Chinese pastor. This man, after reviewing the strength of the various elements and forces making for their cause, said: "Communism alone can save China; Christianity cannot do it. You will be working in the colleges of this city this week. But before you begin we have captured half the student body in the city. We are working day and night among the students and in the ranks of labor. In the end we shall capture China by a dictatorship. Then we shall unite the largest country in the world and the most populous, which will include the bulk of eastern Asia with a population of 560 millions. Nothing but our united dictatorship can save China from sinking in its present chaos."

The Reconstruction of China

As we have already seen, there is a constructive as well as a destructive process observable in China today. Although the country has not now and never has had a strong central government, despite delays, discouragements and humiliations in the erection of the outward political framework, all the while the new China has constantly been in the process of building from within.

The beginnings of this new movement may be traced for more than a century back to the introduction of Western culture. Robert Morrison, the first Protestant missionary, had landed in Canton in 1807. However benevolent in intent, he carried with him all the implications of China's fivefold revolution. As Emerson said: "Wherever a man comes there comes revolution." Dr. Yung Wing, the product of a mission school and the first Chinese to graduate from an American college, had brought the initial group of 120 Chinese boys for education in the United States. They were recalled to China in 1881. Since then there has been a continuous stream of Chinese students in America. They number at present about 1500, a larger number than in any other country except Japan. Five of the most influential members of the present cabinet graduated from Yale, Harvard, Columbia, California and Oberlin.

The relation of these two large republics that confront one another across the Pacific is likely to remain close and fruitful. The two countries have many similarities in area, climate and conditions. The two peoples have many psychological affinities. Both are democratic and preeminently practical, commercial peoples. They have a similar sense of humor, and even common faults and dangers in their materialism. If the United States will continue to play the role of one of China's best friends—if *best* friend" would seem too presumptuous or exclusive in view of our lack of sympathy and sagacity in recent years, as in our failure to meet Sun Yat Sen's appeal for aid—America may make a unique contribution to the remarkable development that will take place in China in the coming decades. Julean Arnold, Commercial Attaché in China of the United States Department of Commerce, estimates that China will require in the near future 100,000 miles of railways at a cost of five billion dollars, together with other mechanical and commercial developments in like proportion. It will make a great difference whether the United States is a far-sighted and real friend of China during her period of reconstruction, or merely a commercial Shylock.

The material, economic and industrial awakening of China is evident even in the midst of political chaos. Of the modern cities, Canton is only a type and a fore-runner. During seven years of stress and storm, in the midst of civil strife and revolution, the dark, unsanitary, over-crowded native city has been transformed into a modern city with many fine buildings. In all directions wide, modern paved streets have been opened up, and these are only typical of the new highways of thought now breaking through the people's minds. Hundreds of motor cars and buses fill the streets and carry passengers out into the country. The city is electrically lighted and has a new automatic telephone service and a radio broadcasting station. Efficient traffic officers and a new police system make for good government. The old temples that stood often for conservatism and superstition have been demolished or discarded along with much of the old order that was both good and bad. Millions of dollars have been spent on the new city. We met the Mayor of Canton and his large and efficient staff, all students returned from America, Britain, Germany and Japan, who are welcoming and utilizing modern ideas in a city that for nearly a century strove to keep out the hated foreigner and all his ways. And Canton, Shanghai, Tientsin and Hankow are typical of the new cities that are being built or renovated all over China. Once the land of isolation and the walled city, China is becoming the land of modern communications. The very city walls, picturesque as they are, are often being torn down and opened up for modern boulevards, as was done with the walls of Paris.

As in the case of Japan, China sought first the outward and material rather than the inner spirit of the new era, but she will be driven to a complete revolutionary transformation of all her life. An industrial revolution, bringing both ultimate material well-being and immediate menace to victimized classes, has entered China as a disturbing factor. The old system of peasant agriculture with small holdings and cottage handicrafts has been menaced by the introduction of machinery to replace hand labor and industry organized for mass production. Within two decades some 2000 modern factories have been established in the industrial belt affecting fifty cities.[1]

With the pouring of a new proletariat into the cities, fifty million people along the coast and the railways are feeling the influence of the industrial revolution. The old guilds which united all classes are giving place to modern Chambers of Commerce for the employers and Labor Unions uniting the workers. The two parties of an industrial class war are being formed. A rapidly rising cost of living, with high prices and higher rents, has outstripped the slower rise in wages, bringing a wave of social and industrial unrest, which radical organizers and intellectuals have been quick to exploit.

Wages in China are the lowest in the world and hours and conditions of labor correspond to the worst conditions found during the industrial revolution in England in the eighteenth century. A report of the Chinese Ministry of Agriculture and Commerce showed that the maximum daily wages of the workers in 29 principal industries ranged from 20 to 50 cents, gold, while the minimum average was but 4½ cents a day. For 220,000 women employed in these industries maximum wages ranged from 2½ to 42 cents a day, and minimum wages from 1 to 17 cents.[2] The squalor and misery of the early days of English industrialism are being reproduced in China. The new Ministry of Industry, Commerce and Labor is endeavoring to provide better working conditions. The Arbitration Act of April, 1928, the Labor Union Law of 1929, and the Factory Law of 1929 demand better wages, hours and conditions, but there are terrific obstacles to enforcement. The lawless war lords, some foreign employers who hide behind extra-territoriality, the difficulty of Chinese employers competing successfully with these foreign employers, and the restless and radical tendencies of Chinese labor are among the obstacles encountered.

---

[1] In 1888 the first Chinese cotton mill was erected in Shanghai. There are more than 120 cotton mills today with 3,700,000 spindles and an investment of $150,000,000 gold. There are some 500 electric companies and power plants.

[2] A. P. Finch in *Current History*, June, 1927, Report of 1923. *The New World of Labor*, p. 17.

In the last two decades China's trade has increased 600 per cent to approximately one and a half billion dollars. Her exports of fifty years ago were practically limited to silk and tea. Today they are tenfold greater and comprise over seventy items. Half a century ago China imported cotton, piece goods and opium. Today her imports have multiplied over tenfold and many items each aggregate more than half a million dollars in value. With the establishment of law and order China's trade will increase enormously. Every ten cents added earning capacity of labor provides forty million dollars increased purchasing power.

Although China's natural resources were over-estimated by early travelers like Marco Polo, and later Baron von Richthofen, they are nevertheless considerable. China's coal reserves are many times larger than those of any other Asiatic country and possibly larger than the whole of Europe. She produces ninety per cent of the world's antimony and sixty-three per cent of its tungsten. Her cotton production is second only to that of the United States. The early home of silk, her production like that of Japan in recent years can be improved and greatly increased. Her labor supply, although not at present economic, is potentially the largest and among the hardiest of the world. Millions of human beings are still being used as pack animals at unit costs more than ten times greater than American freight rates. According to the Government Bureau of Economic Information, China has 295,000,000 gainfully employed, or more than seven times the working force in the United States.

China has need to industrialize. The "farmers of forty centuries" on an area of crops half as large as the United States cannot sustain nearly four times the latter's population. There has been a rapid growth of a new labor movement guided by members of the Kuomintang, by students, radicals and laborers themselves. A development of class consciousness and class conflict has been a recent phenomenon largely produced by the Communists. The Chinese in general, and labor in particular, are probably more capable of developing the strike and the boycott as weapons than any other people.

The first boycott in the present century was in 1905 against the immigration rulings of the American Government. The first anti-Japanese boycott began in 1908. The boycott against the twenty-one demands in 1915 disrupted Japan's trade for years and forced her to change her policy. The heavy loss in Japanese trade was followed by the establishment of new factories in China. The Chinese boycotts against the British because of racial discrimination, the exclusion of Chinese taxpayers from representation in municipal councils, and acts of violence against Chinese labor and students led to a serious crippling of British trade.

The Seamen's Strike in Hongkong in 1922 called out 50,000 men and paralyzed the industrial life of that city for three months. The total loss of trade to Hongkong in fifteen months was over $300,000,000 gold. Soon afterward sixty labor organizations were formed in Shanghai alone and fifty strikes occurred. In this one field at least the Chinese are learning the power of solidarity so effectively utilized by the Japanese. Largely by the power of the strike and boycott China has recovered Shantung, won tariff autonomy, obtained the surrender of two British concessions and Weihaiwei, and has made headway toward the abolition of extra-territoriality. She has discovered a defensive weapon less costly than war and far more effective. This bears some similarity to India's use of non-violent non-cooperation under Gandhi.

The intellectual Renaissance of China is quite different from the earlier movement in western Europe. The latter was a rebirth of an ancient way of life from Greece and Rome and a rediscovery of forgotten human values. The movement in China discards the obsolete portion of their ancient learning based on authority and ancestor worship. It seeks to adopt the scientific spirit of the West and to re-evaluate their own ancient culture. Sixty years ago there was but one news-sheet in all China, and that was the oldest in the world. Today there are hundreds of daily newspapers and twelve hundred registered periodicals in circulation.

Dr. Hu Shih traces the beginning of the awakening to a controversy among Chinese students studying in America. The first declarations of the movement published in China in 1917 created a revolution in Chinese literature which marked the first stage of the Chinese Renaissance. The intellectual leaders of China turned from a thought life, dominated by the authority of the past, to the scientific attitude of mind. This involved first the creation of a new language as an adequate vehicle of expression. As dead as Latin, the classical Chinese had been petrified by the examination system for two millenia, stultified and unintelligible to the common people. Dr. Hu Shih drew up the eight principles that were to be the basis of the new and living language whereby men were to write as simply as they spoke. By 1920 the Ministry of Education had adopted the new method of writing and a flood of new periodic literature came into being in full self-expression in the new style. This literature reflects much of the best thought of two hemispheres from articles on the new psychology, equality for women and birth control, to the re-evaluation of the best products of the Chinese mind for centuries. It is a movement of criticism, of doubt, of protest, and of reform which was deeply needed to penetrate the solemn "face" with which China had long protected her worst evils.

The Student Movement began in 1919 as a protest against the decision of the Versailles Peace Conference and, like the political movement of Chinese students in the second, tenth and seventeenth centuries, became a powerful factor in China's reform. The organization of students in their own party, the Kuomintang, was stimulated and solidified by Russian influence, for the Chinese have hitherto shown a fundamental lack of organization.

While Dr. Hu Shih led the intellectual revolt, James Yen, a graduate of Yale, organized the invaluable Mass Education Movement. It had begun by his trying to teach the 200,000 Chinese coolies in the labor battalions in France to learn the thousand commonest characters. This movement developed a new technique in learning and in the production of new literature. Children or adults can be taught to read by this method in a few weeks. If at least 80 per cent of the Chinese people are illiterate, that would mean three hundred and twenty millions, including seventy million children of school age. This includes two hundred million adolescents and adults who have passed the school age and are permanently illiterate, unless they can be reached by this system. The Mass Education Movement makes its first drive for the hundred million illiterate youths who are responsive and eager to learn. A four months' course, of an hour each week night, or a total of 96 hours, at a cost of one dollar for the term, gives the rudiments of education to these eager students. The second period of the movement includes intensive training in citizenship. The book work is followed by training in sanitation, modern farming and the creation of model districts.

The whole campaign is community-wide, it is voluntary, and it is made locally self-supporting. Over 3,000,000 books have been sold which are used by an even larger number of people. Graduates receive the proud diploma of "Literate Citizen." This movement has great possibilities for the future in this land.

The Political Revolution is the most clearly marked phase of the reconstruction of China. The man who led and embodied the revolutionary movement was Sun Yat Sen. He was born in 1866 near Canton, the son of a Christian peasant father. At the age of thirteen he went to study in Honolulu where, for five years, he imbibed American ideas of democracy. Among the first graduates of modern medicine in Hongkong, he dropped his practice after China's defeat in the Sino-Japanese war in 1894, and became a revolutionary in an attempt to overthrow a monarchy which had lasted for two millenia. He spent years in exile in Japan, America and Europe, organizing the Chinese all over the world. Following the Revolution in 1911 he was chosen as China's first President. This office he surrendered to Yuan Shi Kai after three months to secure the unification of the North and South. After Yuan had diverted and prostituted the revolution to the ends of his personal ambition, Dr. Sun led a second revolution in 1925.

By the swift coup of 1911 a parliamentary republic had been established in name, but it was in reality only a thinly disguised military dictatorship. Chinese village life has always been democratic and will eventually furnish the basis for the future democracy of China, but national life has always been autocratic. The revolution of 1911 was a bourgeois revolution, a change of leadership from the corrupt Manchus to a handful of intellectual leaders. The second revolution of 1925 was the beginning of a national movement that was to include not only students and merchants but the dumb and dangerous masses of workers and peasants.

In 1924 Dr. Sun reorganized the Kuomintang Party, which was in many respects patterned after the Communist Party in Russia.[1] It proposed a program of national reconstruction to be realized in three stages: 1. the period of military tutelage, 2. of educative training of the people; and 3. of constitutional government, or true democracy. After two decades of civil war China is still largely in the state of military tutelage bordering on dictatorship and the people have not yet been educated in preparation for democracy.

With all his many faults Sun Yat Sen was a true patriot, a fearless revolutionist, and a high-minded idealist who bequeathed to his people the heritage of a new symbol of national unity, which China had lacked, a political party, the Kuomintang or National People's Party, and a program for national reconstruction embodied in his three principles. He furnished a sufficient basis for the swift apotheosis which exalted him as the almost infallible Father of his Country. His will, dic-

---

[1] The Kuomintang provides for a frankly one-party government on the principle of "democratic centralism." The supreme authority is the Party Congress which elects the Central Executive Committee of 36 members and 21 deputies. Between congresses the Central Executive is the supreme party authority, which in turn elects a Political Bureau. The Kuomintang is based on the principle of party dictatorship and the individual is supposed to be the unquestioning instrument of the party. The party now suffers from internal dissension and the forcible domination of factions. Its membership in 1929 was 422,022 of whom 172,796 were officers and soldiers. Later soldiers numbered 23 per cent, workmen 29, liberal professions 25.7, students 10.5, merchants 4.3, and peasants 7.5 per cent. This party claims dictatorial power during the "period of tutelage."

tated just before his death on March 12, 1925, is recited weekly in government schools and on all state occasions.[1]

Dr. Sun bequeathed to his people as ideals his Three Principles of nationalism, democracy and justice, or "the people's livelihood." [2] These play the same part as slogans or watchwords as did the "liberty, equality and fraternity" of the French Revolution. They were a Chinese adaptation of Lincoln's government "of the people, by the people, for the people." The principle of nationalism or patriotism is to supplement proverbial Chinese loyalty to family and clan. Democracy, or the people's sovereignty, is to take the place of former autocracy and of the loose individualism of China which leaves her helpless as a rope or "sheet of sand." The people's livelihood, or decent living conditions for the masses, is imperative as the economic foundation for the whole reconstruction of society.

Dr. Sun says: "The principle of livelihood is socialism, it is

[1] "For forty years I have devoted myself to the cause of the people's revolution with but one end in view, the elevation of China to a position of freedom and equality among the nations. My experiences during these forty years have firmly convinced me that to attain this goal we must bring about a thorough awakening of our own people and ally ourselves in a common struggle with those peoples of the world who treat us on the basis of equality.

"The work of the Revolution is not yet done. Let all our comrades follow my *Plans for National Reconstruction, Fundamentals of National Reconstruction, Three Principles of the People,* and the *Manifesto* issued by the First National Convention of our Party, and strive on earnestly for their consummation. Above all, our recent declarations in favor of the convocation of a National Convention and the abolition of unequal treaties should be carried into effect with the least possible delay. This is my heartfelt charge to you.

"(Signed) Sun Wen.
"March 11, 1925."

[2] Lectures of Dr. Sun, on the *San Min Chu I,* published by the China Committee, Institute of Pacific Relations, Shanghai, 1927. In place of scientific birth control he urges an increased population that China may cope with her more rapidly multiplying enemies! A virile nationalism must meet the menace of foreign imperialism. Foreign trade is pictured as a loss to China. Students are warned of the danger of "squeeze" or graft; and are reminded that character must be the basis of all national reconstruction.

communism, it is utopianism." [1]   This is to be realized by
equalization of land ownership, the regulation of capital, and
the socialization of the unearned increment of land values, all
to be attained by evolutionary and constitutional methods.
Obviously China's first difficult task is to restore security and
political unification.   However long this process may be
delayed, we must believe that the principles of nationalism,
democracy and justice will yet be realized in her national life.

The social transformation of China is not so obvious but is
even more far-reaching than the political.   Old China centered, not in the individual as in the West, but in the family
as the heart of Chinese society, where all attachments and
relationships were riveted.   The patriarchal system developed
large clans so that some villages are inhabited by a single clan
and the majority by only two or three.   The family controlled
its members and shared in collective responsibility for each
individual.   Ancestor worship and strict filial piety crystallized
Chinese society into fixed forms.

An ancient guild, in some cases over a thousand years old,
ruled each trade, fixed prices, determined relations, acted as
legislature and judiciary, and exercised the functions of a
state.   Patriotism was non-existent, as dim and distant as the
abstract conception of "humanity" to a socially unawakened
provincial.   The system developed a locally free people of
scholars, gentlemen and peasants, but was utterly lacking in
unity or efficient national organization.   Even the present Nanking Government, which is the best that China has known for
generations, has never controlled more than four or five
provinces.

The old patriarchal, solidified, joint family of China is being
gradually shattered.   Youth is initiating the "individual home
movement," where young couples decline to live with their
parents.   Woman, in place of a secluded domestic in humble

---

[1] *San Min Chu I*, p. 364. Dr. Sun says: "We should even claim Communism as a good friend . . . Why do members of the Kuomintang
oppose the Communist Party?" p. 428. Yet, "class war is not a cause of
social progress, it is a disease," p. 391. It must always be remembered that
Dr. Sun never flirted with Communism nor tried to utilize Soviet Russia
as a tool until he believed that the United States had failed him.

subjection, is demanding and is being given a new status in public life, in education, business and government. Two out of the fifteen members of the early Central Administrative Council, the highest organ of the National Government, were women. There is now freer social intercourse between the sexes. There is a growing conception of the value and rights of the individual and also of the importance of cooperation, team-play and national unity. These lessons and ideals, however, will take decades rather than years for attainment and will try the patience of China, and much more that of the impatient West. But a vast movement of social change has begun which will utterly transform this ancient Middle Kingdom.

A moral and religious reformation is the fifth and final form of reconstruction which will probably take place in China. That reformation will doubtless ultimately take the form, not of the revival or development of any of the ancient religions, but either of a Christian civilization akin to the West, or of a Marxian, materialistic Communism in organic relation to Soviet Russia. Either alternative would involve a thoroughgoing reformation. The Chinese, when uneducated, are very superstitious but seldom mystical or deeply religious. They are preeminently a practical, pragmatic, and moral people. They have potentially a deep moral conscience, but are usually undeveloped in an appreciation of spiritual values. It is very difficult for them to believe in or appreciate the unseen.

The average Chinese in the past inherited the influence of three religions in one—Confucianism, Taoism and Buddhism. From Confucianism he received his feudal ethical code, his filial piety, ancestor worship, propriety, conservatism, toleration and pragmatism.[1] From Taoism as formulated by Lao-tse he derived his stoicism, impassiveness, democracy, patience and calm; but also a later growth of degenerate superstitions. From northern Buddhism he inherited most of what little religious life he had, however spiritually undeveloped or however superstitious he may have been.

---

[1] "To give one's self earnestly to the duties due to men and, while respecting spiritual beings, to keep aloof from them—that may be called wisdom." This indicates the proverbial Chinese attitude to things seen and unseen.

Christian missions were one form of the influence of the Occident upon the Orient. Christianity was introduced by Nestorians from the seventh to the ninth century. It was reintroduced by Catholics and Nestorians from the thirteenth to the fourteenth century, but again died or was crushed out. It was introduced for the third time by Roman Catholics in the sixteenth century, and that community now numbers some two millions, having had at one time about three thousand missionaries. The first Protestant missionary landed in 1807. In 1926 the Protestant missionary body numbered about eight thousand and the number of baptized Protestant Christians about half a million.

The anti-Christian movement developed in 1926 and 1927 as one manifestation of intense anti-foreign nationalism and also as the result of Communist propaganda. Foreign missions and their converts were accused of complicity with foreign imperialism, exploiting capitalism and unscientific superstition.

Protestant missions have widely promoted education by a system of schools, colleges and universities, including some of the best institutions in China. They have introduced modern medicine, hospitals, medical schools, and public health programs. They have taken an active part in famine relief, in fighting opium, and in social reform. Sun Yat Sen, Feng Yu Hsiang and President Chiang Kai-shek were all deeply influenced by Christianity and at one time or another were avowed Protestant Christians. At various times about half the cabinet have been Christian men, including H. H. Kung, Minister of Commerce; C. T. Wang, Minister of Foreign Affairs; and Wang Chung Hui, former head of the Ministry of Justice. The two last were sons of Chinese pastors, while the first was the president of a Missionary College. The influence of Christian men has been out of all proportion to their numbers in China. Dr. Edward Hume, late president of Yale-in-China, makes this conservative statement of missionary work in that land:

"A few outstanding things can be recorded that do not require the measuring-rod of figures. First of these is modern education. From the first the Jesuits were teachers and men of science. . . . The Roman Catholic missions today have important higher educational institutions in a number of cities throughout China. . . . Protestant higher institutions number twenty-four and their total enrolment in schools of all grades is just short of 300,000.

"With education of every grade, as introduced by the missions, came the spirit of investigation. Their influence was what paved the way for the abolishing of the old order of government examinations, and sent thousands of eager youth to America and Europe, as well as to Japan, to secure for themselves what education could give. It was these schools that laid the foundation of such movements as the abolition of foot-binding. Today, no school in China will permit any girl to be enrolled who has bound feet. So, too, from the schools came the movement for personal hygiene, for the planting of trees, for the pursuit of science.

"Another vivid example of what missions have done is to be found in the hospitals and dispensaries everywhere. Three hundred and eighty-one men and 118 women doctors are today bringing the benefits of modern medicine to China, ably aided by 320 nurses. No form of missionary endeavor has done more to make the foreign worker beloved than medicine. Side by side with the hospitals and dispensaries, and working through them, are the schools for the training of Chinese students in modern medicine and modern nursing. It was these schools, founded by missionary doctors and nurses, which led the way for the program of Government education in these fields. These teachers prepared the first medical textbooks, set the standards high and started the stream of medical and nursing graduates, already of considerable dimensions. The genuinely scientific quality of the teaching imparted in the newer schools of today is attested by the teachers in our American schools and hospitals, who find them capable of the truest scientific attitude in the laboratory and the most human relationships with their patients.

"Add to these the orphanages and homes for widows, the leper asylums and institutions for the blind and deaf, and the visible accomplishments of missions form an impressive list. More than all these, however, has been the product in human life. Watch the stream of graduates from the mission schools and colleges and you find among them many of the illustrious names on the roll of the diplomatic service, in the government ministries, presidents and deans of colleges, heads of modern hospitals, bankers, jurists, teachers, clergymen, publicists, men and women that China cannot dispense with. Again, the missionary has been one of the most effective students and interpreters of the life of China to the world outside." [1]

[1] *New York Times,* April 24, 1927; *China Yesterday and Today,* pp. 165–167.

The Leaders of China

India stands or falls with Gandhi, and Turkey with Mustafa Kemal. Japan is led by a group of leaders who cooperate, and China by a number of individualists who find it very difficult to do so. In Nanking we met the President, five of the Cabinet Ministers, four out of the five heads of the departments of Government, and a score of the principal officials.

President Chiang Kai-shek and his wife, who is a graduate of Wellesley, invited us to dinner. It was a simple meal, as simple indeed as the President's whole life. He is a strong, silent, well-poised man, the least communicative we met in the whole of Asia. He is a vigorous leader, a good fighter and a shrewd politician. Born in 1887, he early became military secretary of Dr. Sun in Canton. Forced to flee from that city with Sun, he received some military training in Japan and later in Moscow where he was sent to study Russian methods. Later he was placed in charge of the Whampoa Military Academy in Canton, where, with General Galens and other Russian experts, he trained the future officers of the celebrated Northern Punitive Expedition of 1926. In less than a year they captured half the provinces of China, and within two years had brought the whole of China under the Nationalist colors, although not under the control of Nanking.

He subdued China, broke with the Communist régime at Hankow and tried to unify the country on the basis of Dr. Sun's three principles and his advance from the military stage to that of political tutelage. The government has remained, however, a military dictatorship driven to rely more and more on force. For some reason, perhaps beyond his control, he has failed to unite the Kuomintang party but has seen it sadly split and divided. He has been hitherto powerless to win decisive and final victories over the Communists, even on the field of battle, and unable to meet the enthusiasm and idealism of their propaganda, which is similar to that of his own earlier army when the Northern Punitive Expedition began. He has failed to win the confidence and support of the left wing of the Party, of Canton in the South and of the military leaders in the North like Feng and Wen. Whatever its faults and shortcomings, he has given China the best government she has had for generations.

With the President have been most of the members of the strong Soong family, sometimes ironically called the "Soong dynasty." The sturdy old Methodist mother is a strong character and a devout Christian. The eldest daughter married Dr. Sun Yat Sen, the late President, and as his former fellow-worker and widow holds aloof from the present government, with her left wing revolutionary sympathies. The youngest daughter is the able wife of President Chiang Kai-shek. The second daughter married Mr. H. H. Kung, the Minister of Industry, Commerce and Labor, a lineal descendant of Confucius of the seventy-sixth generation, and former president of a Christian college. The eldest son is T. V. Soong, the most brilliant Minister of Finance that China has ever had. A graduate of Harvard in economics, with banking experience in New York, he has striven heroically to balance the budget and restore China's damaged credit.

C. T. Wang, the son of an Episcopal clergyman, former National Secretary of the Y.M.C.A. and a graduate of Yale with honors, is the brilliant and fearless Minister of Foreign Affairs of the Nanking Government. He was a young revolutionist in 1911, and later, as a representative at the Paris Peace Conference, refused to sign the Treaty of Versailles because of the loss of China's rights in Shantung. He negotiated with Japan for the return of the Shantung railway to China, and with Russia for the recognition of the Soviet Republic and the management of the Chinese Eastern Railway, as well as being the aggressive diplomat who has endeavored to abolish extra-territoriality and the unequal treaties of the foreign nations. His success in spite of China's weak international position has been remarkable.

It is noteworthy that a good proportion of the Cabinet, and a majority of the heads of departments in the Nanking Government are Protestants, and that most of the subordinate officials were trained either in Protestant institutions in China or are returned students from America. There is no reason to doubt the genuineness of the conversion of President Chiang Kai-shek to Christianity. He had something to lose and little to gain by such a step and it was probably due to the genuine Christian influence of the group mentioned above, including the members of his family.

Unique in this group, or rather outside it, is Marshal Feng, often described as "the so-called Christian general." In 1922 the writer spent four days with General Feng and his far-famed "Christian Army." He is a man of impressive presence, every inch a soldier. Like Chinese Gordon, he is a stern disciplinarian, but a passionate lover of men. He was born in 1880, and as a poor peasant boy and untutored coolie he was driven into the Chinese army to get his bread. When stationed as a common soldier at Paotingfu he was so bitterly prejudiced against Christianity that he took delight in firing with his rifle through each letter of the sign in front of the Presbyterian Mission Chapel. In his ignorance he honestly believed that the missionary doctors in the hospitals were secretly stealing the eyes and internal organs of little Chinese children to make a mysterious liquid with which to send their telegrams. The death of the martyrs at Paotingfu in the Boxer Uprising touched the heart of Feng. In 1912, Feng, now a young major, attended Dr. John R. Mott's meetings in Peking, and was converted to Christianity. No sooner had he become a Christian than he began to work earnestly among his fellow-officers and soldiers and in time conceived the project of building up a Christian army.

When the writer met the Marshal about ten thousand of his troops had become Christians. Somewhat like Cromwell's Ironsides, his men might neither smoke, drink, nor gamble, yet he held their deathless devotion, sleeping on the ground with them on the field of battle and sharing their frugal life in time of peace. When we were with him, as Governor of Honan Province he rose at four, and after his devotions studied Chinese and English. For an hour he worked with his own hands daily in the iron foundry and his officers were compelled to learn a trade. He gave us his motor car while he walked or rode a bicycle. Daily we met nearly a thousand of his Christian officers at 7:30 A.M. after their drill, each with his notebook and New Testament.

Bitterly resentful of the encroachments of foreign imperialism, the Marshal finally gave up the fundamentalist character of his early ascetic religious practices. He has several times turned toward Moscow for help but he openly repudiated Communist excesses and cruelty and told Borodin to leave China. Alternating between his Oriental and Occidental loyalty to persons and principles, he has often seemed to change sides and has gained a reputation of treachery among his enemies.

Guided by a few fundamental convictions, he is a village Cromwell with a peasant mind that at times plunges on impulse, whether right or wrong. Up to his lights he will strive for China's unification, and the realization of the three principles of nationalism, democracy and social justice, especially the last. As a man of peace he would strongly prefer the educational, evolutionary strategy of a Christian civilization, but it would be quite within the range of possibility for him or for China, piecemeal or as a whole, to plunge into Communism as a last desperate resort. For when there is a loss of faith in national leaders Communism makes a palpable and imperative appeal to anarchic China in chaos.

China's Alternatives

If it is out of the question for China to set the clock back and revert to her classic isolated past, if neither Confucianism, Taoism nor Buddhism has the power to reconstruct China in her present chaos, as we have suggested, her future development will probably be in one of two directions. It may be in the rich diversity of a modern development of Christian civilization, which should keep the balance between freedom and order, between liberty and social justice, between the individual and society in a constructive, evolutionary development. The other alternative is for China to choose the system of Marxian materialism with a Communist dictatorship and all that emanates from it. During the present decade and at this very moment China is standing at the parting of the ways. In their initial divergence they seem close together, but in their final goal these two paths lie the poles apart.

It is assumed in Russian propaganda and by inexperienced youth, labor and peasants in China that the system of Soviet Russia can be offered as a swift and certain panacea in the midst of chaos. A sudden *coup d'état,* a few days or weeks of fighting, a division of the landed estates and large fortunes, the workers take over the factories, the hated foreign imperialists are driven out, the missionary schools and hospitals are closed, all share, all cooperate and all live happily ever afterward. It all looks so simple and promising. It seems to glow with the promise of a high idealism. It is founded on the age-long right and even duty of the Chinese of revolution, and its palpable materialism is so congenial to their pragmatic temper. It comes ever closer with the apparent failure of other systems and methods. It shifts nearly all the blame upon the imperialist and capitalist, upon the hated foreigner and the envied man of wealth.

But the imagination of the realist reels before the concrete picture of this system realized in flesh and blood. China is not Russia. She has not the oppression of four centuries of Czarism to goad her to moral indignation. She has no great wealth, no vast Czarist and nobles' estates and government lands to divide. She lacks the developed oil, coal, manganese, timber, grain and many of the rich resources and favorable conditions of the U. S. S. R. She cannot even feed herself. She has a densely over-crowded population that can perish by millions in a real and ruthless revolution. But more than all this there is an unrealized element of tragedy in the situation. The writer desires to speak here with perfect sympathy. He has a natural love for the Chinese people. To him they are the most kindly, courteous, polite, gentle, peaceable, home-loving people in the world.

But once you get them above the boiling point, once their blood pressure rises to the degree of volcanic explosion, if we may mix our figures of speech, no people on earth is capable of greater cruelty or more complete callousness to slaughter and loss of life than the Chinese. We make this statement with regret but we base it not upon theory but upon experience. The actual practice where Communists have come into full control, or where the opposition has recaptured areas from them, has been so often one of extermination or ruthless slaughter in fear or self-defense, that we can picture what this dictatorship would mean if extended district by district over the whole of China. Stalin, with all the rich resources of the U. S. S. R., can just manage to feed Russia, but neither he nor any dictator on earth, Chinese or Russian, could feed starving China through the chaos of a Communist revolution and the decades of delayed reconstruction that would tragically follow. Compared to it the suffering of the whole Russian revolution would be child's play.

Walter Bagehot had some wise words on the strength and weakness of a revolutionary dictatorship: "The representative despot must be chosen by fighting. . . . The head of the government must be a man of the most consummate ability. He cannot keep his place, he can hardly keep his life, unless he is. He is sure to be active, because he knows that his power, and perhaps his head, may be lost, if he be negligent. The whole frame of his State is strained to keep down revolution. The most difficult of all political problems is to be solved—the people are to be at once thoroughly restrained and thoroughly pleased. . . . But I need not prove in England that the revolutionary selection of rulers obtains administrative efficiency at a price altogether transcending its value; that it shocks credit by its catastrophes; that for intervals it does not protect property or life; that it maintains an undergrowth of fear through all prosperity; that it may take years to find the true capable despot; that the interregna of the incapable are full of all evil; that the fit despot may die as soon as found; that the good administration and all else hang by the thread of his life." [1]

It must be clearly recognized that China in this situation presents the challenge of the East to the West and to the world. We all have a concern in China. Nationals of all nations with their life and property are at stake on a great scale. Since the

---

[1] Quoted by Professor A. N. Holcombe in *The Spirit of the Chinese Revolution,* pp. 98–99.

isolation of "hermit nations" and "middle kingdoms" in water-tight compartments is a thing of the past, every awakened human being who has risen above the level of mere animal existence must be concerned with a quarter of the human race. For good or ill, East and West have already met in China, and never the twain can be separated again. Trade and commerce, prosperity and peace, understanding and cooperation, a gigantic China in reconstruction with enormously increased purchasing power and production will affect us on the one hand. On the other, famine and flood, war and revolution, poverty and pesti-lence, Communism and hatred, the destruction of life and property, with endless international complications and dangers, will force upon us the challenge of the East as a sinister men-ace. To use a somewhat vulgar phrase, we cannot let China "stew in her own juice." A quarter of the world cannot be isolated.

Whether we like it or not, our commerce, our missionary schools and hospitals, our official and unofficial representatives are there already. Out of some 12,000 Americans living in China, somewhat more than half are missionaries and members of their families. American missions represent a capital invest-ment of some $80,000,000, with an annual cost of several millions, while American business represents an investment of $70,000,000 with vast possibilities of trade when China enters upon her period of reconstruction with the colossal building of roads, railways and factories that must follow.

There is a total of about 320,000 foreigners resident in China.[1] Twelve thousand of these are Americans, as compared with 61,739 Chinese in the United States.

In our relation to China there are three possible courses of action open to us. The first is that of foreign intervention, whether military or political, by the concerted action of the powers. The second would imply the other extreme of with-drawal as completely as possible, leaving China to her fate

---

[1] These include 198,206 Japanese, 85,766 Russians, 14,701 British, 12,000 Americans, 3,657, Portuguese, 2,733 Germans, 2,715 Frenchmen. There are 3,500 American residents in Shanghai alone representing some 250 American firms.

without either interference or aid. The third would suggest unofficial, non-military and non-political cooperation of all the true friends of China for her complete reconstruction and rehabilitation. We favor the last alternative.

The first alternative of intervention and interference has been tried repeatedly without success and often with disastrous failure. We may remind ourselves of the menace to the prosperity of the Far East and to the peace of the world by the selfish scrambles of the powers for concessions, spheres of influence, and the intended partition of China. The international relief expedition after the Boxer Uprising of 1900 was disgraced by looting and wanton destruction of life and property, as were subsequent punitive operations with their harvest of bitterness and hatred. The powers were able neither to rehabilitate China nor to keep peace among themselves.

The proposed financial consortiums of 1913 and 1920 were failures. The first backed the wrong man, Yuan Shih Kai, and the second failed through disharmony and distrust. The arms embargo of 1919, where Great Britain, the United States, France, Japan and other powers agreed not to export munitions to China, broke down through the jealous exclusion of Russia and Germany, and through the nationals of the signatory powers themselves breaking the agreement. The Nine-Power Treaty arising out of the Washington Conference of 1921–1922 failed again because of the exclusion of Russia and Germany, because of the aversion of China to foreign tutelage and because of the inability of the powers to cooperate or present a united front.[1]

At present Mr. Hallett Abend, both in his articles in *The New York Times* and in his book *Tortured China,* is typical of a group which advocates "benevolent intervention." If China resisted, "there would be war of course. But it would be a short war and not costly in either lives or money. Seizure of the ports would be a simple matter, and this would be quietly followed by foreign military control of the railways. Foreign

---

[1] A. N. Holcombe, *Can the Nations Cooperate in the Rehabilitation of China, Annals of American Academy,* 1930, p. 347.

gunboats strung up the Yangtze River would cut the country in half. . . . The costs of such an intervention should and could easily be borne by China."[1] Of course! They could be borne as easily as was the cost of the conquest of India by India herself. Imperialism, however benevolent, should always be made practical and self-supporting! But, in the light of the record of more than a century, however benevolent the intentions, in the end China is usually exploited and the imperialist powers always disagree in their conflicting interests. It has been well said that any power can take China that wants it, and any power, or concert of powers, can keep it which can provide 400,000,000 able-bodied policemen to maintain law and order by an odious foreign imperialism.

Intervention would almost inevitably have the same effect that it did in Soviet Russia. It would hasten China's unity in the face of a common foreign foe. A foreign army could easily and quickly seize military objectives and impose its brief rule by force. But it would rouse the deep and growing resentment of China's millions and call into operation their most formidable weapon of the strike and boycott. Most important of all, it would throw China into the arms of Soviet Russia which, in the guise of the savior of China for the Chinese, could more easily shape and reorganize that vast republic upon Communist lines. By no accident, or impulse, or combination of circumstances, and upon no provocation whatever of the loss of life and property, should the United States or Britain be betrayed into the fatal policy of intervention. Only those working consciously for a Communist China should advocate such a course.

The second alternative to intervention or interference would be withdrawal. But that would be even more disastrous. As we have said, we can never again isolate nearly an eighth of the world's land area nor a quarter of its population. We cannot afford idly to witness the growing danger to life and property in China, nor let it sink under a ruthless dictatorship of Communism.

---

[1] *Tortured China,* Hallett Abend, p. 302.

The third alternative remains, of practical cooperation with China to aid her in her period of reconstruction. It is fortunate that the powers were never in a better mood to cooperate nor in a more favorable situation genuinely to assist China than in this hour of her supreme need. A number of them have had painful lessons in the results of intervention in China, Russia and elsewhere. Japan is still suffering from the effects of her twenty-one demands made upon China during the war. Communists would like nothing better than foreign intervention, which many believe they tried to provoke in the Nanking incident.

What then can foreigners and foreign nations which are true friends of China do under present conditions? We believe that among others three things are possible:

1. In full faith in China's proverbial power of recovery from just such situations, let all foreign nations genuinely and heartily cooperate for the maintenance of the complete sovereignty and integrity of all China and of the open door for trade. Let them render every reasonable assistance that is asked to enable China to regain her footing and reestablish law and order under her own government.

2. Let everything possible be done to strengthen rather than withdraw or retreat from the great and varied practical work of missions, especially under a growingly indigenous leadership. We say this in spite of the impatience of much of the modern temper with the whole idea of missions and even of religion itself. There are always in every land some over-zealous fundamentalists concerned merely with theological or ecclesiastical proselytizing. But such is not the character of the missionary movement as a whole, which is likely to play a powerful part in the reconstruction of China, unless the country goes Communist.

3. Let us, in full cooperation with Chinese Leadership, be ready to aid in concrete plans for the economic reconstruction of China. The West already has made a notable contribution to the Orient in education and in modern medicine. There remains one field today where China imperatively needs help. That is in the reconstruction of her economic life. In former

times waterways and public granaries were maintained, often with adequate budgets and reserves. Recent years of internal disturbance have witnessed the destruction of some ancient institutions, the neglect of public utilities, the disappearance of accumulated reserves, and have left China helpless in the face of natural calamities. Every few years now comes a drought, a flood or a pest of locusts, which could be successfully met by an organized community under a strong government, as America met the tragedy of the Mississippi flood. But in China such conditions easily develop into a famine for the afflicted population. This is becoming a recurring and increasing phenomenon. China may become chronically the "land of famine."

We have passed through districts where scarcely a blade of grass remained in sight. Yet many of these areas could be irrigated, as they have been in India, to make them free from all future famine. *What is supremely needed today is not so much famine relief as famine prevention; not emotional appeals, but a statesmanlike program of economic reconstruction; not pauperizing charity, but cooperation with the Chinese people to enable them once more to stand on their own feet.*

There are at present two prevailing causes of famine: economic disorganization and failure to gain control of the forces of nature, which now result in natural calamity. There is alternately too much or too little rainfall. The former breaks the river dykes and brings a devastating flood; the latter, in years of drought or scanty rainfall, with the absence of reservoirs and irrigation canals, causes famine. The total lack of a system of highways is a contributing factor to famine, and leaves the people of one locality starving for want of food which may be available in another. Automobile manufacturers of America could get their money back many times over if a portion of the cost of a few model roads were advanced. Irrigation projects could pay for themselves in full with interest and keep a revolving fund available for the rehabilitation of successive areas.

A staff of experienced engineers, both Chinese and foreign, is already available. During the last decade in experience gained under the China International Famine Relief Commission, in addition to its immediate relief work, 590 miles of dykes have been constructed, with fifty miles of irrigation ditches, 270 miles of drainage ditches, over 5,000 wells dug and 2,150 miles of good roads built. This work, which has relieved or benefited millions, cost approximately only $4,000,-000. The money received from foreign sources was considerably less than half of the cost of these projects as a whole. One loan of less than $50,000 reclaimed 30,000 acres of land from flood, which are now annually producing crops worth over $2,000,000. Another loan of $45,000 has permanently irrigated 14,000 acres and will yield more than 100 per cent of the cost in its yearly crops. Another loan of $250,000 is making possible the irrigating of 300,000 acres along the Yellow River. This will not only be recovered, but will pay for itself many times over. Partial surveys have been made of a score of new projects for which the people are appealing for aid and in which they are ready to cooperate by assuming their full share of financial outlay and complete repayment. But there are now no funds available to undertake these projects.

An initial sum of several million dollars available for *a famine prevention fund* would enable China to accomplish certain definite results:

1. It would keep alive a certain number of people. This is the least that it would do; for it is not enough merely to prolong existence for the poor under present conditions in China.

2. Followed by the work of the mass education movement, under the able leadership of Mr. James Yen, the whole standard of life in a given area may eventually be raised by education for citizenship training. Hundreds of rural cooperative societies have already been organized and are now successfully functioning in many districts under the China International Famine Relief Commission. This work should be extended.

3. The value of human life and its higher possibilities may be demonstrated among a people where the hard struggle for

bare existence has often left them callous to human suffering and privation.

4. Constructive projects can be undertaken and productive loans and investments made under the responsibility of the local gentry and officials and with their full cooperation. During the period of the repayment of the loans for irrigation projects, dyke and road building and reclamation work, a modern system of management and accounting would train the leaders in local self-government and organization, which is important for the future stability of a strong China.

5. When the next natural catastrophe of drought, flood or famine appears it would not be necessary to wait for months for an inexperienced commission to come from the West, but there would be already on the ground experienced engineers immediately to survey and report upon conditions, buy grain while it is cheapest, and provide, not eleventh hour famine relief in charity, but constructive projects of work for future famine prevention, enlarging their operations as required by the magnitude of the task in hand.

This whole plan is far removed from debilitating charity. It would be carried out under Chinese leadership and responsibility, but with a modern system of accounting, in full cooperation with foreign expert engineering skill provided at the request of China. Four-fifths of the money invested would be paid back with interest into a revolving fund. It would enable the Chinese in certain stable areas to undertake permanent productive projects. It would help China in successive areas to regain her footing, which unaided, she cannot do.

If human life is worth anything, anywhere, it is of value in China today. As soon as America emerges from her own financial crisis and industrial depression, the time will have come to help China to save herself. Can we turn our backs upon the greatest need in the entire world today and leave one-quarter of the human race to sink into chaos and misery without lifting a hand to help them?

CHAPTER III

Upon visiting Japan again after an absence of seven years the outstanding impression one receives is the poverty of the country and of the people themselves together with their titanic accomplishments. Without the ancient heritage of India in religion and philosophy, or the relatively rich natural resources of China, Japan is the one nation of the Orient always able to compete with the West on their own ground at almost every point. The first to absorb Western civilization, in the face of terrific handicaps Japan has lifted herself to the third place of power on sea and land in the world today. As the last outpost of the Orient, the leader of Asia in material accomplishments, and as the first and most complete point of Asiatic contact with the Western world, Japan may yet lead the way to a needed synthesis between the two strategies of life, between the scientific control of the West and the inward spiritual detachment of the East.

The opening of the country by Commodore Perry's fleet in 1854, the Restoration of power by the regent Shogun to the Emperor in 1868, and the adoption of the Constitution in 1889, little more than forty years ago, marked the birth of modern Japan. Two incidents on our recent visit served to illustrate the phenomenal progress of Japan since these events. These were connected with Viscount Shibusawa, the aged financier, and Prince Tokugawa, descendant of the Shogun.

The former, the grand old man of Japan at the age of ninety, sometimes called the J. P. Morgan of his country, has witnessed the almost entire transformation of his people during his lifetime. He told us that he was a boy of thirteen when Commodore Perry's fleet of American gunboats first arrived in 1853, and returned the following year when Japan opened her long-closed doors to the modern era. At that time he believed that the world was a solid cube and on its flat top there were only four countries in existence—Japan, Korea, China and India. After Perry's arrival he had to enlarge his flat world and to add two more lands, America and a country called Europe. At that time he was in favor of resisting the American fleet, but the shot fired from the Japanese battery on the shore splashed harmlessly in the water about half way to its destination. Fortunately, the counsel of old and wiser heads prevailed, and Japan was opened from that time gradually but completely to the influence of the Western world. What changes this one man has witnessed during his own lifetime! He has seen Japan transformed in almost every aspect of its life as it sought to assimilate the whole complex of Western civilization, entering in a few decades into a political revolution, an intellectual renaissance, a religious reformation, and an industrial and social reorganization almost unparalleled in history. His memories of Townsend Harris, America's first statesmanlike representative, of General Grant's visit to Japan, of Theodore Roosevelt and of Japan's participation in the conflicts with China and Russia and in the World War, marked several of the milestones of his country's remarkable advance. He has seen Japan surrender in a day her ancient feudalism for imperial solidarity, abandon isolation for final cosmopolitan membership in the League of Nations, and gradually yield her traditional autocracy to growing democracy. At the age of twenty-eight he served the last Shogun in the old feudal days, when trade, commerce and finance were looked down upon as only a shade above the occupations of the outcaste. He was among the first to enter these despised professions and became Japan's leading banker, for forty-three years president of the First Bank of Japan, now one of the "Big Five." He held office as president, director or adviser of some sixty corporations and was identified with scores of philanthropic and social welfare organizations.

Prince Tokugawa, President of the House of Peers, lineal descendant of the regents or great Shoguns who ruled Japan for two and a half centuries and banished Christianity in bloodshed from the land as a proscribed religion, was a boy of five at the Restoration of the Emperor Meiji in 1868, when the Shogun and all the two hundred and sixty-two feudal lords surrendered their fiefs, and the boy Emperor took the great Charter Oath. He witnessed the progress of Japan during the entire forty-five years of the Meiji era. He was his country's Representative Delegate at the Washington Disarmament Conference to restrict the modern fleet of Japan together with those of the Western powers. He is Governor of the League of Nations Association of Japan. It was suggestive to meet him and hear him preside at a Pan-American luncheon where just beyond him as he rose to speak we could see his ancient ancestral castle surrounded by its great moat, now the residence of the Emperor. Rising in the center of Tokyo it is typical of the spirit of strong and sturdy feudal Japan which still persists at the heart of the modern nation. Prince Tokugawa's constant effort for closer international friendship and his repeated testimony as to the value of Christianity to Japan strikingly show how far his country has traveled in a single generation from isolation, feudalism and the complete prohibition of Christianity as a dangerous foreign religion.

Japan's Resources

Let us examine Japan's material limitations and the relative poverty of her resources and then her achievements and progress during the modern era. The area of Japan proper is 148,756 square miles, less than that of the state of California, and in material resources it is much poorer, having less than half the arable land of that single state. Japan is formed by a chain of volcanic islands of sand and lava, beautiful in scenery, but lacking in most essential raw materials. Of all the land in Japan only 15.8 per cent can be cultivated, which is less than any other great nation. This may be contrasted with England's 77 per cent, Germany's 64 per cent and the United States' 46 per cent.[1] The size of the average farm in Japan is only two and a half acres, and 91 per cent of the farmers have less than five acres of land apiece.[2]

About 46 per cent of the farm land is worked by poor tenants who own no land. The average monthly income of the peasant proprietors is only $56.26 and of the tenants $39.58. The average farmer has a deficit of $17.41 a month in agriculture and 29 per cent of the farmers are forced to seek some supplementary income.[3] The tenant ends the year in debt. His annual per capita cost of living is only $80.16, which is less than one-fifth of that of the average American farmer. The whole population of Japan has only one-quarter of an acre in crops per person; China has nearly twice that amount, and the United States twelve times that area in crops and thirty-six times the amount in pasture land per person. Nowhere in the world has agriculture been so intensive and so efficient in the utilization of land. Each farm looks like a garden; not an inch seems wasted.

About half the land of Japan is occupied by forests. Though artistically beautiful these are not of high commercial value and their total area is only about 8 per cent of those of the United States or of Canada.[4] Japan is forced to import timber from America. In the number of head of stock per 10,000 of the population, British India has 15,627, the United States 10,202, and Japan only 304.[5]

A comparison of relative wealth and income of various countries reveals the fact that Japan's total wealth of $51,-171,000,000 is about one-eighth that of the United States and her per capita income of $109 is less than one-sixth that of

---

[1] Agricultural figures are quoted chiefly from the reliable authority of Dr. S. Nasu in *Land Utilization in Japan,* see p. 173.

[2] *Ibid,* p. 30. Average area of arable land under peasant management is 2.69 acres. The farm population of 26,943,000, or 5,561,608 families, is 52.19 per cent of the total number of households. *Ibid,* pp. 178, 179.

[3] *Land Utilization in Japan,* pp. 197-200.

[4] *Ibid,* p. 68.

[5] *Ibid,* p. 193.

the latter.[1]   The annual income of the United States of approximately ninety billion dollars in normal times is almost twice the total wealth of Japan.

In raw materials Japan is fundamentally lacking in the three essentials of modern industry—coal, iron and oil.   Her most vital weakness is her poverty in iron ore.   Her imports total over $50,000,000 in iron and steel yearly.   Her total reserves are little more than the output of the United States in a single year.   She produces little or no coking coal for her steel industry.

Of oil, she produces less than half of her industrial requirements and has to import 150 million dollars worth a year of mineral products and 300 million of cotton.[2]   In the last thirty-five years she has had an adverse trade balance in all but six years, four of which were during the World War. During the last sixty years Japan has been forced to borrow abroad $1,250,000,000, less than half of which has been repaid.   Her two chief exports are both threatened: her luxury product of silk shipped to America is menaced by artificial rayon, and her export of cheap cotton goods to Asia by the mills of China and India and by the political unrest of these countries which cripples trade.   The outlook for her industrial future is somewhat serious.   She has had about a million unemployed during 1931 and has been suffering from business depression ever since the World War.   Not more than a fifth of her university graduates can secure positions within a year after graduation and most of these are inadequately paid.   A flood of cheap labor pouring in from Korea has proved to be a further embarrassment.

Sir Frederick Maurice shows the practical impossibility of Japan going to war with the United States because of lack of resources and raw materials in the following comparison:[3]

---

[1] *Ibid*, p. 26.

[2] *Ibid*, p. 72.   *Economic Annual*, 1929, p. 134.

[3] *The Forum*, March, 1926, p. 815; the figures are taken from the *Statesman's Year Book*.   The United States produces about 60 per cent of the world's copper, 65 per cent of the oil, and 40 per cent of the world's coal.

	United States	Japan
Pig Iron	40,361,000 tons	78,000 tons
Steel	45,000,000 tons	nil
Copper	950,000,000 pounds	100,000,000 pounds
Coal, bituminous	422,000,000 tons	27,000,000 tons
Petroleum	23,500,000,000 gallons	60,000,000 gallons

Japan faces a most serious population problem. At the time of the 1925 census there were 59,736,822 in Japan proper and 83,456,929 in the Empire, but if we add the average yearly increase of over 902,781, we have a population for Japan proper in 1931 of 65,153,508 and for the Empire of over 90,000,000. In density of population Japan ranks next to Belgium, Holland and England, but if arable land only is considered, Japan has the densest population in the world, four times as great as British India and twelve times that of the United States.[1] This density is ever increasing. There is no adequate outlet for this overflow as the Western world is largely closed against Japanese immigrants and there are only 676,000 Japanese residing abroad, after decades of effort to settle Manchuria and other regions. The Japanese are a home loving rather than a pioneering people.

The population of Japan remained practically stationary at about 30,000,000 for three centuries before the Meiji Restoration in 1868. Her birth rate has now increased to 33.6 per thousand. Her death rate has decreased through industrialism, sanitation and preventive medicine to 19.8, leaving a large annual increase in population of 13.8 per thousand.[2] Japan's population is now doubling every forty years. At the time of Margaret Sanger's visit to Japan the authorities were suspicious of the birth control movement and her books were prohibited. But today we find editors, intellectuals and social workers in favor of this latest reform, and 68 birth control clinics are now operating in Tokyo alone. The move-

---

[1] For every 250 acres, the United States has a population of 79, British India 260, and Japan 950.

[2] *Financial and Economic Annual Department of Finance*, p. 3; Japan *Year Book*, 1930, p. 36.

ment is as yet reaching only a fraction of the population, and religion, social custom and political expediency are still on the side of a larger population.   As there is no hope of emigration lessening the pressure of population on the means of subsistence, the growing consumption of foreign foodstuffs, the increasing pressure of economic want and social discontent may force the government to be one of the first after Russia to adopt a completely modern attitude toward scientific birth control.   This seems the only alternative to economic and social catastrophe.

Japan's imports of rice have steadily increased for the last thirty years and now represent 12 per cent of the home production. [1]   With 55.78 per cent of the population urban, and over half a million a year pouring into the cities, the slums and factory districts are becoming increasingly congested. The Social Department of Tokyo reports 62 sections of the city where the destitute are living.   These are usually low lying and unsanitary.   Many of the houses consist of only "three mats" in rooms of six by nine feet.

We visited the slums of Tokyo and Kobe.   In the former 34 per cent of the people are living and often working in one small room which affords each family of five less than eight square feet of space, or about that occupied by a double bed.   The other 66 per cent in the slums have an average of less than ten square feet per family.   The inhabitants are underfed and overcrowded until they have to sleep side by side, men, women and children crowded together.   From such families eighty per cent of the prostitutes have been forced into their present lives by poverty, the impoverished parents frequently renting out the girl for a period of years.

In her industrial evolution Japan has been ground between the upper and nether millstones of competition and poverty. She is forced to compete with the massed wealth and efficient industrial organization of the Occident, and the cheap labor and larger supplies of raw materials in China and other Oriental countries.   Fourteen rich families control the bulk

---

[1] *Land Utilization*, pp. 174, 175.

of the wealth and industries of the country, especially the three great companies of the Mitsui, Mitsubishi and Sumitomo families, while the masses of the people are poor. There is evidence of the terrific strain to which the whole population has been subjected by the pressure of modern industrialism and of the increasing population upon the inadequate food supply. Japan, already overpopulated, in a few years will be approaching dangerously near the saturation point in population and the breaking point in economic and social strain.

In the end an industrial country must depend upon raw materials, labor, mechanical skill, power, capital and markets. In none of these is Japan's position satisfactory. Her labor, which is her chief industrial asset, though apparently plentiful in an over-crowded population, is not really cheap. Labor has been agricultural and is attached to the land. Workers are driven into the cities most unwillingly and only by necessity. Of girl recruits secured for the factories, 84 per cent return to the farms as soon as they have worked out the advance made to their parents. These girls are kept in the factory dormitories and not allowed to leave the grounds without permission. Close supervision hinders the growth of trade unionism but also the contentment of the workers, so that there is a large annual turnover, ranging from 40 to 60 per cent in textile mills. A spirit of autocratic paternalism and of feudalism still lingers in Japanese industry.

The unit cost of labor is low but its collective cost is high as efficiency is sacrificed to low wages. The average daily wage is only $.85, $1.17 for men, $.48 for women. A girl entering a cotton mill begins at 30 cents a day, while 39 cents is the average wage for cotton spinning. Female workers in the United States average from $2.09 to $4.00 for a ten hour day, that is, from five to eight times the Japanese wage.[1] Of the entire labor force in industry 51.4 per cent are women and 12.46 are under sixteen years of age, 208,674 of them being girls.[2]

Japanese factories are over-crowded with workers and the

---

[1] *Japan's Economic Position,* J. E. Orchard, pp. 339–352.
[2] *Japan Year Book,* 1930, p. 184.

output per worker is small. Low wages and long hours add to their inefficiency. Seventy-five per cent work more than 10 hours and 31 per cent from 11 to 12 hours a day, with from two to four rest days a month. An American spinner tends from 2 to 6 times as many spindles on the same yarn as the Japanese. The American worker has three times the output and often four times the wage of the Japanese. Wage costs per pound of yarn are somewhat less in America than in Japan. Japanese labor also lacks mechanical ability and experience. They have not the Yankee knack for machinery. There is a scarcity of capital and the interest rate is high. There has been wide dissatisfaction with Japanese goods, especially during the over-shrewdness shown during wartime, but trade associations have been successfully raising the level of integrity and improving the standard of quality of output.

In the matter of power Japan is one of the least of the coal consumers. Her annual per capita consumption of coal is but half a ton, compared with that in the United States and Great Britain of 4.4 tons. She has large water power resources, but in developed power Japan stands fourth and in per capita power only eighth in her total national production, or about equal to Spain. Of all the countries in Asia Japan is making the most strenuous efforts to develop her industries.

Thus a review of material conditions in Japan, leaves with us the final impression of the severe limitation of her natural resources and of the general poverty of her people. Her achievements and accomplishments in spite of these handicaps are all the more remarkable.

Japan's Achievements

Anglo-Saxons look back to the Magna Carta oath in 1215 more than seven centuries ago. Less than seventy years ago the young Emperor Meiji, at sixteen years of age, on April 6, 1868, in the presence of the court nobles and leading feudal lords who had surrendered to him their power, took the famous coronation Charter oath which has been the cornerstone of the great changes of the new Japan, to the effect that: "All governmental affairs shall be decided by public discussion; both rulers and ruled shall unite for the advancement of the national interests; all evil customs of former times shall be abolished; knowledge shall be sought for all over the world."

The old feudal Japan centered in an Imperial House descended from the Sun Goddess. The present Emperor Hirohito is the one hundred and twenty-fourth in an unbroken line of rulers of one house for more than two thousand years. The old spirit still survives among the unawakened portion of the masses, who devoutly believe that the reigning sovereign is decended from heavenly ancestors. The same is true of the conservatives, as when Dr. Masujima writes: "The Japanese Sovereign is superhuman because he is absolutely virtuous and above all human temptation, and he would not condescend, as history has shown, to do otherwise than good to his people." But the rising tide of a new democracy is shown in the growth of the movement of organized labor, the organization of peasant unions, universal manhood suffrage which now gives the vote to the working masses, and the proposal for the early enfranchisement of women. Driven by the force of economic need, by ever more liberal ideas in education, by modern industrialism and the reform movement, democracy is steadily advancing in Japan.

Almost in a day Japan turned from isolation to a place of growing importance in the cosmopolitan world, from medieval feudalism to modern centralized and representative government. Casting aside the armor and the spears, the bows and arrows with which the young Shibusawa and his friends fought, she set out to learn the best modern military science of the West, quickly springing into the place of the third power in the world on sea and land.

On a former visit the writer found not only "socialism" but even the word "social" in all its connotations under suspicion. Today with wiser tolerance the government is allowing wide reading and discussion of all social theories. They have, however, a very powerful and efficient police system, always conservative and sometimes reactionary and unwise. It is doubtful, however, whether the full liberty of public discussion that is proverbial in Hyde Park, London, would be immediately safe and successful among a population so likely to be swayed by the mob mind as are the workers of Japan.

The growth of the new liberalism is in evidence in the foreign policy of Baron Shidehara, thus far a true liberal, and in the new attitude and relation to China. The costly boycotts that followed the Twenty-one Demands upon China, while the Allies were occupied in the World War, and the rising demand of her own liberals have led Japan into more enlightened and cooperative foreign relations. In one group of fourteen liberals that we met in Japan all favored the ultimate independence of Korea, if its integrity and the protection of Japan against Russia could be guaranteed.

In nearly all departments of life Japan's advance during the last sixty years has been phenomenal. Since 1868 her combined exports and imports rose from $19,230,500 to over two billion dollars, an increase of one hundredfold in sixty years.[1] Her cotton spindles increased thirteenfold in the last thirty-five years, to six and a half million.[2] She is the third largest consumer of cotton, next to the United States and Great Britain. The value of her raw silk exports rose from 41 million dollars in 1902 to 372 millions in 1928, a ninefold increase.[3] Japan now produces 60 per cent of the raw silk on the world's markets, ranking first among the nations. The material is supplied entirely by farmers.

The annual value of her manufactured products increased from 685 million dollars before the war in 1913, to three and a half billions in 1927. Bank deposits advanced during the same period from one to nearly six billion dollars.[4] The revenue of the government increased from 29 million dollars in 1872 to one billion dollars in 1928.[5] Japan's war wealth increased from 16 to 43 billion dollars between 1913 and 1921. Despite the post-war depression her wealth today is estimated at 51 billions. This would be double that of Italy's 25 bil-

---

[1] *Financial and Economic Annual,* 1929, p. 126.
[2] *Year Book,* 1930, p. 381. This is 4 per cent of the world's total, one-fifth of that of the United States.
[3] *Land Utilization,* Nasu, pp. 8, 9.
[4] *Economic and Industrial Development of Japan,* by J. Inouye, p. 2.
[5] *Economic Annual,* p. 29.

lions and nearly as great as France's 60 billions, in spite of the greater resources and longer period of modern development of these nations.[1] Japan's per capita wealth increased from $250 in 1904 to $865 in 1924.[2]

In industry in the last thirty-five years she increased the number of her factory workers from 25,000 to 1,898,872 in 53,680 factories.[3] This is still a relatively small number of workers compared to the 26,943,000 of the farm population. Despite Japan's lack of resources, and the aversion to industry of both its military and peasant classes, it is the government that has been chiefly responsible for the introduction of new industries. It has built railways, established and managed textile mills, iron and steel works, banks, shipyards and shipping lines. It has provided capital, granted subsidies and protected manufactures, but after the Chinese War in 1894 it gradually handed over industry to private hands. Industry was stimulated by each of Japan's wars, with China in 1894, with Russia in 1904, and by the World War in 1914.

Japan's advance in almost every field has been steady and consistent. After the death of the great Emperor Meiji in 1912, and during the short reign of the more feeble Emperor Taisho Tenno, Japan's manufactures were sold in every country in the world. She had lent money to Russia, France and Britain. She had enforced her will at the Versailles Conference, and Japanese scientists had become famous in research. She had become the third maritime power in the world both in warships and commercial tonnage, and the growth of her navy was only curbed by the Washington Conference. This was a surprising advance for this isolated, medieval people that had looked with wonder upon the tiny "black ships" of Commodore Perry's little fleet in 1854. At the time of the London Conference they possessed warships of the first line with a tonnage of some 600,000 with 80,000 officers and men. The first

[1] *World Almanac*, 1930, p. 295.
[2] *Land Utilization*, Nasu, p. 26.
[3] *Year Book*, 1930, p. 379; *Economic Annual*, p. 91.

small Japanese-built steamer was launched in 1898, yet in twenty-two years her merchant fleet of three million tons ranked third among the world powers.[1]

According to Sir Frederick Maurice, Japan emerged from the World War with the third navy and the second army in the world. Her people, however, are peace loving and all her financial experts know that war with America, even if there were no fighting, would cause the collapse of her two principal industries of silk and cotton and expose her to the peril of social revolution from the army of her unemployed.

Japan's first railway was opened in 1872. The mileage had increased from one to nearly twelve thousand by 1930 and her railways are now carrying one billion passengers annually. Lacking in many other resources, Japan has developed her fisheries into perhaps the most scientific and lucrative in the world, with an annual catch valued at 175 million dollars, which has increased threefold in the last sixteen years.[2] Her development of the culture pearl, where the oysters are artificially caused to produce real pearls, is an example of her scientific ingenuity.

The Labor Movement

The Japanese labor movement has been one result of industrialization. With the rising cost of living pressure for better labor conditions has come from the trade unions, and also from the influence of international opinion from countries with higher standards. Japan, like India, is very sensitive to world opinion. Under its pressure midnight work for women and children was abolished and the legal age for child labor was raised.

The present labor movement began in 1912 with the organization of the Friendly Society which became the parent of the present General Federation of Japanese Labor. Trade Union membership in June, 1929, numbered 321,125, which is only about 6.7 per cent of the industrial population. Among

---

[1] *Economic Annual,* 1929, p. 208.
[2] *Year Book,* 1930, p. 363.

obstacles to effective organization are the paternalism of Japanese industry and the active opposition of the government manifested through the police department.   Next to Soviet Russia, Japan places greater reliance upon her strict police department and her spy system than any other country.   Police attend all labor meetings, and, disguised as students, enter the classes of liberal professors.   In 1928 approximately a thousand workers and intellectuals were arrested as Communists.   Some of these were kept in prison for two years without trial.

The labor movement of Japan is weakened by three divisions and the farmer movement by as many more.   Four proletarian parties participated in the general election of 1928. Only eight members were returned to parliament out of 466 in 1928, and, owing to their divisions, only five in 1930.   The proletarian vote in the last election totaled 502,313.   It will be only a matter of time until they learn the value of solidarity which has been so effective in the life of Japan.

As a result of this growing unrest on the part of labor, there were three or four hundred strikes a year, even in the hard times following the War.   The Japanese laborer, though usually patient and hard working, when aroused is volcanic in temperament like the molten lava underlying his mountainous islands.   This was manifested in the sudden and fierce rice riots of 1918 when some 300,000 took part in violent demonstrations against the high cost of living.

During one visit to Japan we first met the employers in the paternal organization for the "Conciliation of Capital and Labor" and then went down into the slums to meet a dozen labor leaders.   One of the employers had just stated that there was no serious unrest among the workers and that they would be quite content if left alone.   The labor leaders laughed this statement to scorn.   One of the labor leaders was trying to support a family of eight on a little more than a dollar a day. He had been forced to give one child away because of the pressure of poverty.

Another then told us his story.   He had worked long hours for twenty-five cents a day, but finding it impossible to support himself and his family on this amount, he started to work

overtime to increase his income.   Although working long after
the regular hours he could only make fifty cents a day.   He
found it difficult to support his family even by adding two or
more hours to the regular shift of fourteen hours a day.   At
times on a change of shift, he had to work for thirty or more
hours at a stretch.   For two weeks straight he worked twenty
hours a day with only four hours for sleep.

After fourteen years of such work, his health was broken
through lack of rest and proper nourishment.   He said: "My
body was broken, my mind dulled, and my whole character
was disintegrating.   I had no time for my family, no interest
in production or in anything else.   I lost my skill.   I had sunk
with the masses of my fellow-workers into poverty and had become like a part of the machinery.   Then the trade union
movement came and I seized upon it with hope, for it gave us
a chance to fight for higher wages, shorter hours and one rest
day a week.   But this is only our first step.   Frankly, we are
out to completely abolish industrial slavery and the capitalist
wage system.   They may not recognize our unions or ac-
knowledge that we have any rights, but we shall yet become
strong enough to enforce our will."

Another of the leaders said: "To be frank with you, we are
all radicals and out to abolish the present system, because the
government, the capitalistic courts, and the big business men
are all united against us.   We have arrived late upon the scene
in the labor world, but we have started with advanced ideas
and principles.   Today we are persecuted, hounded, and betrayed, but in the end we will win.   If a few of us meet together to discuss the calling of a strike, or even the forming
of a labor union, the police can punish us on suspicion without
trial.   Several hundred men in the labor unions have been
thus persecuted.   The police, the severe laws, 'special orders'
and all the forces of militarism and capitalism are used to crush
our labor movement.   The employers dismiss our leaders
whose names are placed on the blacklists of the government and
of the business men.

"Another injustice which we have to deal with is the labor
spy system.   Spies are scattered among the workers to learn

their plans. They seek to stir up dissenion, undermine the workers and leaders, and break up their unions like the Fascisti in Italy. The government and capitalists have used ruffians and gamblers, who are members of the so-called 'Nationalistic Society' which is used to fight labor. These ruffians make raids on the labor meetings, using violence and sometimes seriously injuring those who are taking part. Many have been wounded and several killed by these tools of capital and the government. The police shadow our leaders and frequently raid our headquarters. But we are not discouraged. We will win justice in the end; we are out for no halfway measures; no 'welfare' or paternal schemes will satisfy us; we want nothing less than social justice."

Japanese Education

In education Japan's progress has been remarkable and consistent. She has largely achieved the purpose of the Imperial Oath of 1868: "Henceforth education shall be so diffused that there shall not be a village with an ignorant family, nor a family with an ignorant member." This was the determination and this has been the achievement of that little group of Samurai warriors who stood behind the boy Emperor. The real educational system, which was begun only in 1872, has achieved a high standard of literacy in spite of the difficulty of the complicated written language. With an enrollment of 11,792,690, which is slightly larger than that of India with its vastly greater population, the government claims that 99.47 per cent of the boys and 99.38 per cent of the girls are in school. The statistical system differs from that of the West, however, and there are many illegitimate children and others who are not counted. The conscription examination reveals that less than one per cent are illiterate. Japan's .94 per cent of illiteracy compares favorbly with 7.7 in the United States, 92. in India and 8.2 in France.[1]

In Japan in 1878 only 43.2 per cent of the children had been in school, while in 1925 there were 99.4 per cent.[2] Facilities are

[1] *World Almanac,* 1930, p. 788. *Japan Year Book,* 1930, p. 166.
[2] *Land Utilization,* p. 35.

offered every child for a six year period of compulsory education paid chiefly by a tax on the local community. Heretofore the opportunity above this grade has been severely limited. Education in Japan is highly systematized, centralized and standardized. Most of the students wear uniforms of a semi-military type, though compulsory military training among them is highly unpopular and militarism is being increasingly discredited. The aim of the educational system in Japan has not been to develop exceptional ability, so much as to standardize the nation with a supply of well-trained instruments of national policy. This, of course, tends to stamp out originality, but inculcates loyalty.

The students are hard-working and take themselves seriously. They have considerable political influence and take part in organizing labor and the peasants. Higher students' have to absorb two systems of culture and at least two languages, including the memorizing of several thousand characters of their own language, and many hours a week of English. In consequence a student cannot graduate from the university before he is twenty-five or twenty-six. The system is democratic in so far as every social class attends the same primary schools, while in higher institutions the ruling power is not with the individual will of the teacher but the public opinion of his class and the students acting as a corporate body, as is the case in China and Russia. American students are tame and obedient in comparison to democratic student control in these three countries. The Japanese system develops mass production and social action, rather than a high degree of individual initiative or moral courage either on the part of students or faculty.

Heretofore the Japanese system of education has been on the whole scientific, technical and materialistic. "Moral education" has been based on the Imperial Rescript on Education supplemented by textbooks for developing moral character and virtue. Although formal, the whole system has tended to train the students in the loyalty, obedience and solidarity which made Japan what it is and which the authorities most desire to maintain.

The authorities have become alarmed at what they nervously call "dangerous thoughts" on the part of the students.   In 1926, students of the leading colleges were arrested for "dangerous thoughts" and kept under arrest for more than nine months without trial.   It is characteristic of bureaucracy in this as in other lands, that they should appropriate, even in the financial depression, a million dollars to check this tendency by chairs of History of Buddhism, Oriental Philosophy, and Oriental Ethics in the universities, and to increase the number of supervisors and inspectors of students.   They have also partly removed the ban on teaching religion as they begin to see that a purely scientific and materialistic education furnishes an excellent preparation for Marx, Lenin and atheistic Communism.   The two hundred bookshops in one student neighborhood in Tokyo are more thronged than bookstores in any other country, with the writings of Marx and Lenin more in demand than any others.   From fifty to sixty books a year on Russia are now published in the United States, but the number of such books published in Japan is greater than in any country in the world outside of Russia itself.

The state Shinto religion is taught and practiced in the schools beginning with the Sun-Goddess myth story, and inculcates reverence for ancestors, worship of the ruler and intense patriotic nationalism.   The Government will also probably call both upon Buddhism and Christianity to help them stem the rising tide of unrest and revolt.   They may not see that what is needed is not increased inspectors and formal teachers of "safe" thought, but social justice for the unemployed and for underpaid labor and peasants.

It is to be hoped that they may see this in time and they will do so if history repeats itself in Japan.   Time and again a movement that started among the young intellectuals as radical and "dangerous" thought, when tempered by experience, has become a more widespread progressive liberalism. In ever-widening circles it permeates public opinion and is taken up by an ever more liberal press.   In time, before it is too late, government responds, at least by compromise, and takes an advanced step.   While other peoples swing to the more sudden and violent extremes of reaction and revolution, slowly but surely, in solidarity, in unbroken continuity with her great past, Japan always advances. The surviving *genro* or elder statesman, Inouye, once a dangerous young Socialist radical and now a mild liberal, is typical of this tendency in Japan.

So it will probably be with the present "dangerous thought" movement. Saturated with the Marxian demand for social justice, when tempered by experience, these very students in official and commercial life will become more advanced liberals demanding and effecting many of the changes needed in the present unjust economic order. When these ideas have permeated the press and public opinion the government will doubtless respond in action. Thus the present phase of "dangerous thought" may prove one of the most hopeful movements in Japan.

This steady advance of Japan is well illustrated in the case of the suffrage movement. The Emperor as the Son of Heaven and the Shogun as military dictator were once autocratic rulers. This power was shared with the 262 feudal lords. After the Restoration in 1868 a small group of young samurai were the real rulers of Japan. In 1890 there were 500,000 eligible voters; in 1927 there were approximately 3,000,000; on February 20, 1928, there were 13,000,000 who had attained the right of universal manhood suffrage. [1] A bill granting the municipal vote to women passed the Lower House in 1930. The feminist movement has reached astonishing proportions and has won for woman suffrage the avowed approval of all three major political parties. They will probably be given the vote within another decade.

At no point is Japan's advance more marked than in the steady march of democracy, of growing liberty and of freedom of the press. The influence of naval and military men in governmental affairs is diminishing. The vigorous protests of the naval authorities against the ratification of the London Naval Agreement were unavailing. This was a victory for

---

[1] *Japan Year Book*, 1930, p. 70.

civil representative government as against the old form of dual authority. Japanese education and industrialism have been two principal factors in the growth of liberalism. The influence of the press has steadily grown. There are nearly 1200 daily newspapers and 2800 weekly and monthly periodicals. The daily circulation of the principal papers is larger than any in New York or Chicago. The new Trial by Jury Act went into effect in 1930. There is wide religious tolerance. The proposed Religious Organizations Bill recognizes Christianity, Buddhism and Shintoism on a basis of full equality. In few countries of the world has there been a finer spirit of cooperation in social service between leaders of various faiths as witnessed by their joint annual conferences. Another sign of progress is found in the growing strength of reform movements. The anti-prostitution movement has recently seen licensed quarters abolished in four additional provinces. A temperance campaign to raise the juvenile drink age limit to twenty-five years has won wide support.

In the light of all the evidence an impartial observer could hardly deny the poverty of Japan's resources on the one hand, nor on the other, her marvelous accomplishments in spite of them.

National Characteristics

As a people the Japanese have never suffered defeat at the hands of man, nor have they been broken by any natural calamity. The Japanese live in one of the two great earthquake regions of the world. During the last half century Italy has had 27,672 earthquakes, and Japan 26,562. [1] There are still 54 active volcanoes in Japan. The delicate seismograph instrument shows a slight tremor almost with the frequency of the human pulse. The great earthquake of September 1, 1923, which was followed by a tidal wave and fire, destroyed three-quarters of Tokyo, the third largest city of the world, and all of Yokohama, the chief port of Japan. Her losses were greater than in her war with Russia, which included 99,331 killed, 46,-476 missing and 103,733 wounded. The property loss due

---

[1] *Year Book,* 1930, p. 19.

to the great catastrophe reached two and a half billion dollars. Not only were the ruined cities rapidly rebuilt, but they were remodeled with wide streets and costly earthquake-proof buildings. This titanic task with its countless civic improvements was completed within seven years, in spite of severe financial depression. The true greatness of the Japanese people was shown in their quiet fortitude and their undiscourageable spirit in overcoming apparently insurmountable obstacles. They are like the pearl oyster which they have studied and by a delicate operation have caused to produce pure pearls. Every pearl represents a pain. Japan's pearl of great price of character will be produced, and is even now being formed, out of great suffering. A people with traditions of Plymouth Rock and Valley Forge should be able to understand, appreciate and admire the collective accomplishments of this indomitable people.

The people of Japan are more remarkable than their material accomplishments. Indeed these can only be understood in the light of their character. Of all their characteristics probably loyalty is the most important and the basis of all the others. This seems to be inculcated until it is ingrained in almost every home, every school, every class of society. Individually the Chinese outwork and under-live the Japanese in Manchuria, the Koreans, the Filipinos, and often the Americans in California, but they have as yet little solidarity, unity or capacity for cooperation, hence the contrast in the present situation in China and Japan today. Dr. Nitobe is penetrating but a little too severe in his criticism of his own people when he says: "Our achievements are due not to towering figures who lead us, but to an impersonal collective entity—a sort of corporation consisting of mediocrities. . . . The rise of Japan is due to a strong and well maneuvered national unity on the one hand, and on the other a quick adjustment to the material superiority of Western civilization."[1]

Allied with their loyalty and social solidarity is their capacity for organization. They have a remarkable gift for learning

---

[1] *Japanese Traits and Foreign Influences,* Inazo Nitobe, p. 27.

from all sources and for utilizing the best of what they learn. They seldom blindly adopt, but nearly always adapt the innovation to their own needs, often improving upon it. If it be argued that their civilization is borrowed, then it must be admitted that so is that of practically every other modern nation. Their energy and painstaking toil account for much of their success. For the most part they have still preserved the fine simplicity of their life. Their love of beauty is proverbial and characteristic, and far in advance of Americans and most Europeans. Living closer to nature than does the West they often make of life an art. Their innate politeness is far in advance of the cruder and younger Republic of the West across the Pacific. There are, of course, differences of manner and etiquette that may easily lead to misunderstandings between Orient and Occident. The annoyance or impatience of the Westerner is a misdemeanor in the eyes of a Japanese. To show anger is to him evidence of gross ill-breeding. A blundering, blunt or crude frankness which wounds the feelings is not easily forgiven. Their indirect method of expression avoids, if possible, the unpleasant and controversial.[1] With the people of China, Korea and India they have a vast capacity for conciliation and compromise. They seldom push issues through to logical but unpleasant conclusions. Even in deep suffering they present to the world either a stoic or smiling countenance. Their long isolation makes each Japanese, even more than an Englishman, an island in himself. He does not and usually cannot break his intense reserve. Associated with all this is an extreme sensitiveness, both as individuals and as a race. No other country is so sensitive to public opinion.

The Japanese are often accused of dishonesty. A commercial civilization like that of China readily develops the conviction that honesty is the best policy, while a feudal, military régime like that of old Japan develops the characteristics of courage and cunning. Business was at first despised as beneath the dignity of the samurai warrior. Moreover, the early years of European intercourse were often marked by shameless ex-

[1] See an excellent analysis of Japanese character by G. C. Allen in *Modern Japan and Its Problems*, Chapter I.

ploitation on the part of foreign merchants and the Japanese were forced to compete with them at a disadvantage. The old smoking room myth of employing Chinese tellers in Japanese banks because of their honesty was, of course, never true, but it will die only a slow and lingering death. There are still scandals of bribery and corruption both in Japan and the United States, neither of which has as yet achieved the moral level at this point of the older countries of Britain, Germany and Scandinavia. But Japan is steadily advancing in her standards of honesty. Scandals are usually attacked and exposed and public opinion is ever demanding higher levels of conduct.

Japan has the vices of her virtues and to understand her past is to sympathize with her present. The magnificent feudal castle and moat of the ancient Shogun, now the residence of the Emperor stands as a constant reminder that the heart of this great city and of all Japan is still largely feudal and oriental, despite occidental surface innovations and institutions. The old Japan lived on after the Restoration of 1868, in things both good and bad. The custom of old Japan of the prohibition of the publication of the news of any important event has furnished a precedent for the control of news, especially from Korea or Formosa. Old Japan was always under tutelage to its feudal masters. Under the Shogun the people's lives were minutely regulated. The same tendency was perpetuated by the police regulations of the new order and it was most natural to continue these in Korea where they were galling and offensive. The adoption both of general education and conscription further facilitated the inculcation of obedient loyalty. But loyalty untempered by other virtues may become a danger and a means of evil as well as of good.

A Typical Leader

We have spoken of Japan's limited resources and of her titanic achievements, but no mere compilation of statistics nor abstract statement of national characteristics will enable us to grasp and understand the actual situation in present day Japan. It would help us to clothe a skeleton of facts with flesh and blood if we could have a biography of some Japanese leader such as Viscount Shibusawa or Prince Tokugawa, who could embody for us both the life of the old and of the new Japan in contrast. It may be even better if we take a man from among the common people, Kagawa, the Gandhi of Japan. Indeed he reminds us of Gandhi in many ways, a frail and emaciated figure with scarcely a sound organ in his body, yet like Gandhi an indefatigable worker, a benefactor of the poor, a friend of little children, a guide and organizer of labor, a leader of the despairing farmers, the arousing conscience of a self-satisfied church, the St. Francis of the slums of Japan.

Kagawa was born in Kobe in 1888. His father was a Japanese official who died when Kagawa was six years old. He was adopted by a rich uncle in whose luxurious home the boy had everything he could desire. His uncle was an ardent follower of Shinto, the primitive cult of Japan, a combination of nature worship and hero worship, nationalized into a patriotic cult to uphold the state. It makes no appeal to reason or emotion and has no moral code. Ethically and theologically weak, its chief emphasis is upon the past. Confucianism, borrowed from China as a system of ethics based upon the five human relationships, confines itself to the present life. Popular Buddhism introduced from India in 552 A. D., with its religious worship, its sensuous Nirvana, its pantheon of gods and superstitions, places its emphasis upon the future life. Kagawa, like most Japanese, had received his patriotism from Shinto, his ethical standards from Confucianism, his religious hopes and fears from Buddhism.

But he was not satisfied. His whole soul cried out for moral purity. His own father had died of dissipation. His elder brother had had seven concubines. His family for three generations had been maintained only by concubines. And he himself, the son of a concubine, was sent to school from a concubine's home, with a feeling of shame upon him. Deeply dissatisfied, he was seeking some way of moral escape, some adequate dynamic of character. While attending a government school he joined a voluntary Bible class to study Christianity, conducted by an American missionary, Dr. H. W. Myers. Gradually the story of Jesus the Carpenter of Nazareth, who poured out his life for the poor, gripped the heart of this young idealist. When he finally informed his uncle of his intention to become a Christian he was driven from his home as a penniless outcast. Dr. Myers took Kagawa into his own home and treated him as a son.

During his course of study, while preparing himself for his life work, he contracted tuberculosis. Seeking recovery, he went to live with a poor fisherman in his hut upon the seashore. Coughing and feeling his pulse, when all efforts at recovery seemed to fail, he finally resolved upon a desperate venture. If he had only a short time to live he would have his fling before he died, and live at the full. His way of having his fling was not a course of dissipation such as his relatives had known, but to place his life in the midst of the greatest human need and misery that he could find in the slums of Shinkawa in Kobe. When we asked him why he chose the slums when he had tuberculosis, he said: "I thought that I had only a few years to live and I wanted to do all I could in that short time for the people who needed me most."

This slum of Kobe is one of the worst in the world, inhabited by some twenty thousand outcasts, paupers, criminals, beggars, prostitutes and defectives, who live like homeless dogs in human kennels of filth and vermin and disease. During the thirteen and a half years that Kagawa lived there the slum was thrice stricken with plague, five times with cholera, twice with dysentery, thrice with smallpox, and every year without exception with typhus. At the time of the smallpox epidemic in 1917 his was the only house that escaped, death entering every other home in the neighborhood. Infant mortality in these slums was four times the rate elsewhere in Japan.

Dr. Myers says of Kagawa's work in the slums: "We felt that in giving him permission to go there we were signing his death warrant, but he would take no refusal. He lived on $1.50 a month and the rest of the money given for his support and all else that came into his hands went to help the poor and suffering about him. He gave away all his clothes except what he had on his back, and to provide for somebody who was hungry he often went without a meal. Strange to say, this heroic treatment cured his disease.   He was preaching day and night during these years, visiting and nursing the sick, studying and writing, and doing the work of six ordinary men."

Here he lived in a little room six feet square, without a bed, without a stove, without a table or a chair.   After some years in the slums he went to America to study, spending from 1914 to 1916 at Princeton.   Upon his return to Japan many lucrative positions were offered him, but he refused them all and returned to his little room in the slums.   Sharing his mat with a beggar he contracted chronic trachoma, from which he has suffered ever since.

Kagawa is a Christian Socialist.   One of his first tasks was to organize labor to improve their wretched conditions.   He found women working from twelve to seventeen hours a day, at a daily wage of from twenty to fifty cents.   With nine-tenths of the laborers receiving less than a living wage, and with 92 per cent of the families of Japan trying to exist on less than $250.00 a year, he set to work to improve these appalling conditions of poverty.   He did not ask for charity. He demanded social justice.   He led the striking workers in Kobe in 1921.   Some 35,000 workmen of the shipbuilding yards marched in a procession of protest several miles long. The employers closed the works and enlisted military force, but it required the exertions of two battalions of soldiers and four thousand police for the suppression of the strike, when for the first time in Japanese history blood was shed in this connection.   The strike failed, but the sympathy of Japan was with the strikers.   Kagawa was sent to prison with a hundred and twenty others for disturbing the peace.   For years government detectives and spies dogged his steps.   Five times he was arrested for his fearless vindication of the rights of labor and for his articles printed in the newspapers attacking the government for their neglect of the poor.

After aiding the industrial workers, Kagawa next took up the organization of the poor farmers and tenants in agrarian districts.   Farmers' unions were started, cooperative societies, patterned after those in Denmark, were organized and a paper was published for the guidance and help of farmers. With the awakening of the women of Japan Kagawa introduced a third newspaper called *The New Womanhood*. After studying the labor movement at first hand in Great Britain, Germany, Holland and countries abroad, meeting Ramsay MacDonald and others leaders, Kawaga organized the first Labor Party of Japan and became a member of its executive committee.

Immediately after the great earthquake he organized an expedition and opened a relief settlement in the midst of the devastated area. Here with the aid of eighty picked students from the universities, he worked for months in the midst of the refugees.

In 1930 Kagawa was called by the Mayor of Tokyo to a government position as the head of the Social Bureau of the municipality at a yearly salary of $9,000. Although desperately in need of money, he refused the salary in order to retain his freedom, undertaking the duties of the office as a voluntary worker. Here he introduced a program of municipal socialism, looking after a hundred and forty institutions and a staff of eight hundred employed workers. He endeavored to put the social work of the city of Tokyo on a cooperative basis. His Unemployment Insurance Bill was adopted by the Municipal Assembly and went into effect in February, 1930. The Mayor adopted his social budget for that year in toto, and added $25,000 for eleven additional settlements. When the city made him a personal donation of a thousand yen, he immediately donated it to the "Save the Baby Society." The whole Municipal Assembly gathered for a three hour lecture on his social program. Following his experience in Kobe and Osaka, Tokyo is now his laboratory, but all Japan is his field.

When he was earning some $15,000 a year in royalties on his writings, he devoted every cent to downtrodden humanity. From the money received from his books and other sources he has already given more than $100,000 to aid in his social settlements, the impoverished labor movement, and for his Japanese fellow-workers in Japan, Korea and Formosa. The earthquake, however, destroyed all his books and plates and ended most of his royalties.

In the three cities of Kobe, Osaka and Tokyo he is now supporting and conducting five labor dormitories, three kindergartens, three fresh air summer camps, three cooperatives, credit union pawn shops, and medical clinics where the poor are furnished free medical aid, scientific contraceptive information and needed treatment for birth control.

Kawaga started the Peasants' Union with a contribution of $5,000. He is principal of Osaka Labor School, which he inaugurated with an initial gift of $2,500. He is president of the Cotton Mill Workers' Union of Osaka and is a former president of many other unions. He acts as advisor to the Federation of Labor, the Peasants' Federation of Labor, the Society for the Abolition of Licensed Prostitution and other social organizations. His Kobe Settlement Clinic has given free treatments to over 273,000 in the last few years and the Osaka Clinic gives some 5,000 treatments a year.

In addition to the Consumers' Cooperative and Credit Union he has organized five Student Cooperatives in Tokyo in the five universities to teach the cooperative movement to students in order to enlist their leadership in later life among peasants and workers.

Kawaga is a prolific writer, a novelist, a poet. In all he has written more than fifty books and pamphlets and more than a million copies of his works have been sold. His *Beyond the Death Line* has exceeded 200,000 copies sold, his *New Life* 250,000, *The Shooter at the Sun* 100,000, *From Star to Star* 100,000, *Emancipation* 45,000, etc.

In the library of one of the larger cities of Japan the librarian told the writer that nearly one-fifth of all the books in use at that time were by this popular young author. As a novelist he frequently attacks some social evil by some book written with a purpose like that of *Uncle Tom's Cabin*. Not limited to his own writings, he has translated and published in Japanese a score of volumes by Josephus, Eusebius, John Ruskin, George Eliot, Albert Schweitzer, Lange's History of Materialism, Bowne's Metaphysics, the writings and life of John Wesley, David Livingstone, and many modern writers. As a versatile artist he sometimes illustrates his own books by clever pen sketches and drawings. In his lectures, during which he holds his audiences spellbound for as many hours as he has strength to speak, he frequently illustrates his talks with his rapid brush on large sheets of white paper which he tosses over the back of his blackboard as they are used in the course of his address.

Kawaga would appeal to Americans as more romantic if, like Mr. Gandhi he were a Hindu, or a Buddhist, or if he were anything else than a Christian of the flaming type of the first century. But he is first and foremost a religious man. From this he draws the motivation for his whole life. He organized his first church in the slums of Kobe. Here he had to meet his impoverished congregation at six in the morning before they started their day of toil. His religion is at once personal and social. He believes that we must Christianize society and socialize Christianity. He is a pacifist with a hatred of war. He is a practical mystic. Like Gandhi he unites inward spiritual adjustment with tireless outward social activity.

It was his conviction that the churches of Japan were afflicted, as in some other countries, with the dry rot of intellectualism and sophistication, that they were lacking in social vision and passion. Moreover, the Christian community was too small a force to make its opinions effective. Not because he was impressed by mere numbers or statistics, but for the sake of a vital and dynamic social and spiritual movement, he said: "We must strive to get a million Christians in Japan. Then, and not till then, can we hope to have Christian principles and solutions applied to our political, social and religious life." Accordingly he launched the "million movement" which was later incorporated in the Kingdom of God Movement, which has now been taken up officially by the churches of Japan.

When we last saw Kagawa he was out on tour in connection with this movement, speaking four, five and six times a day. His manner is quiet, yet he moves his audience, apparently without any effort on his part, from laughter to tears. He fills to overflowing halls, theatres and churches and at times the railways run special trains that people may come from a dis-

tance to hear him speak.   When Communism is appealing to
inexperienced students as a panacea or shortcut, he is one of
the few men in Japan who has sufficiently mastered the economic principles of Communism, Socialism and Capitalism to
be able to fill the largest halls with students, answer their social
questions and meet them on their own ground.

Like Gandhi of India, Kawaga seems to have some hidden
source of energy.   He does the work of half a dozen men, yet
the chairman of his committee told the writer that he had
hardly a sound organ in his body.   His heart is affected; his
lungs bear the scars of tuberculosis; he has trouble with his
nose and throat and kidneys.   From trachoma one eye is totally
blind and the other is so weak that he has to read with a powerful magnifying glass.   After one of his night meetings recently
he had the return of a slight hemorrhage.   His physician told
the chairman of his committee to cancel all his meetings for a
month.   At the end of the month the doctor counselled further
rest.   The chairman said: "What did Kawaga do but say he
would begin meetings the next Sunday and that if we would not
organize them he would make his own arrangements.   During
that month of 'rest' he had written, or rather dictated because
of his eyes, three books or pamphlets.   Yet he insisted on
'going to work' again at once as he had been idle long enough."

Such is the life of this Christian Gandhi of Japan.   Liberal,
daring, hopeful, he is coming to grips with the challenging
social problems of his day.   In him we find embodied the hope
of a new Japan.

Japan and America

Japan's vital interests are closely bound up with the two
countries that lie to the East and West, China and the United
States.   With the latter her relations have been particularly
close.   In contrast to the ruthless opening of China to foreign
exploitation, Commodore Perry, with great patience, negotiated a treaty of "peace and amity" with Japan on March 31,
1854.   At no time did he even threaten to use force.   His fleet
was laden not only with guns, but with gifts from the Western
world, indicating its commercial and scientific advancement.

The United States was fortunate in its appointment of Townsend Harris, a merchant of New York, as its first consul-general. His wisdom, tact and patience slowly opened up Japan to friendly foreign intercourse with all the nations and won the enduring gratitude of the Japanese. By his wise foresight in the first treaty with America he helped Japan permanently to escape from the curse of opium.

Japan's rapid advance during the succeeding decades was in striking contrast to the exploitation and plunder of China by foreign nations. Calling in more than three thousand foreigners as experts and teachers, for thirty years Japan labored with titanic energy to modernize and reform her entire national life. Feudalism in Europe had been abolished only after warfare and bloodshed. In Japan the enlightened feudal chiefs surrendered their power to the emperor without a blow, embodied in one of the most amazing documents in history. Without violence also Japan gained freedom from extraterritoriality and was admitted to the family of nations in 1894, a relationship which America had advocated for many years. From America she adopted the principles of her public school system and men like Dr. Murray and Dr. Verbeck helped to organize the national system of education and the Imperial University. [1] Within four decades Japan became the only literate nation in the Orient. From America especially she received the humane and liberal influences of the foreign missionary, her impulse in trade and manufacture, her plan of prison reform, the example of a new home life, a new status for women, a new frankness and friendship in diplomacy. The United States in 1863 generously returned to her the indemnity from the Shimonoseki incident. For fifty years there had been no quarrel between the two nations.

Complications arose later over the question of Oriental residents in the United States and opposition to the Japanese in California on the part of organized labor began to develop in 1905. At the time of the San Francisco earthquake in 1906

---

[1] From Great Britain Japan derived most of her political and financial reforms, from France her first military system, which was later formed upon the German model, and from Germany her medical science.

Japan contributed more than half the total amount for relief sent by all the rest of the foreign countries. In order to smooth out local friction and provide "a maximum of efficiency with a minimum of friction" President Roosevelt entered into the "gentleman's agreement" in 1907 under which Japan, upon her honor, gave passports to the United States only to her officials, merchants, travelers and students, but not to laborers. This agreement she meticulously fulfilled. In spite of the efforts of the President and of the Secretary of State, Mr. Hughes, the exclusion act was passed in 1924 whereby "no alien ineligible to citizenship" might enter the United States. If the Japanese had been placed upon a quota basis like the European nations, with two per cent of the foreign born of each nationality residing in the country in 1890 to be admitted, it would have involved the admission of only 154 Japanese a year into the United States. This infinitesimal number could have been assimilated without difficulty by any one large city in the country. But in the most tactless and harsh way, with a maximum of friction and a minimum of efficiency, our leaders in Congress insisted on this invidious discrimination against Orientals in contrast to Europeans.

The exclusion of the Japanese in a manner so gratuitously offensive, in their view practically branded them as inferiors, by legislation passed insistently in the face of every plea and protest, by the nation that had been accounted Japan's best friend. It came as a terrible shock to this proud people. Seemingly a direct insult, it was like a blow in the face, or a deep and lasting wound to their national pride and honor. It was timed exactly seventy years after Japan had opened her doors and had made the most strenuous efforts ever made by any nation in history to organize her life on Western lines. Japan has always recognized not only the right but the duty of every country to protect itself against indiscriminate immigration. She is not greatly concerned whether 154 Japanese or none emigrate to America, but she is concerned as a matter of principle over her national honor. It was never in the mind of the Japanese a question of commercial gain, or a convenient outlet for their surplus population, but of essential equality.

Were all peoples ultimately "free and equal," according to our Declaration of Independence, or were some people like the Japanese, to be excluded as outcasts, permanently inferior? The blow of exclusion fell upon Japan just after the devastation of the great earthquake, and for many of her leaders it was a similar shock, far deeper and more lasting in its effects.

Can we imagine Great Britain or France going out of their way to pass discriminatory and invidious legislation, admitting all tourists save those from the United States and Mexico, or can we conceive the effect which such an exclusion would have upon our people? But even this utterly fails to convey to our thick-skinned and insensitive race the literally heart-broken feeling of the very best Japanese leaders. This has grown no less in the seven years since the exclusion act and it will not lessen in the future. "Discrimination begets discrimination, and it is not at all inconceivable that the time may come when the United States will be as eager to escape discrimination in China and Japan as the latter countries have endeavored to escape it in the United States."[1] But we should not wait until we are compelled to right this wrong. If we cannot have a "gentleman's agreement," we can at least have legislation that will avoid gratuitous insult. The best people both in America and Japan will continue to regret this legislative blunder and will never be satisfied until it is rectified for the sake of American national honor as well as that of Japan.

---

[1] Payson Treat in *The Far East*, p. 517.

CHAPTER IV

KOREA'S ASPIRATIONS

As we left Korea one scene stood out as typical. It was the annual garden party given by the Governor General, Viscount Saito, on the occasion of the Emperor's birthday. We were in the palace grounds of the old King of Korea with its beautiful buildings of classic Chinese architecture and could look back upon three thousand years of ancient Korean history. Before us was the fine modern building of the Government-General offices, built of solid granite and furnished with the most beautiful marbles and metals from Korean quarries and mines, typical of the brilliant development of the latent resources of the country under Japanese rule.

From the ancient palace we could look back in retrospect upon the history of this "land of the morning calm," with the glory of its classic past as the former teacher and guide of Japan in Confucian and Buddhist culture, but also with the humiliation of being a generation ago "without doubt the worst governed state in Asia." [1] But we could also look forward in prospect with mingled feelings, and wonder whether all this advance in material efficiency is to be for the benefit of an extending and conquering Japanese imperialism at the expense of a growingly impoverished Korean tenantry, dispossessed of lands they had once owned, or whether it is to be for the benefit of an increasingly free, prosperous and loyal Korean people. In a word, is Korea to become an embittered "Ireland," with its peninsula "pointing like a dagger into Japan's very heart," only waiting the hour when she may hope to strike her enemy; or is she to become a contented and loyal part of the Empire, and a grateful ally. That question can be answered only by

---

[1] Payson Treat, *The Far East*, p. 386.

Japan's future policy, not in words but in deeds. For by her deeds she will win either the grateful loyalty or the implacable enmity of this people. She will rule either by wise liberals or by blind militarists who will drive Korea into revolution.

Ancient Korea and modern Japan met at this garden party given by the Governor General. The former could look back upon three thousand years of classic culture enriched by her powerful neighbor, ancient China. But her long history had culminated in the corrupt government of the last King and Queen. A man could be sued for the bad debts of his profligate relatives or robbed by a swarm of grafting officials; hence enterprise had almost ceased. Some public offices were sold to the highest bidder. Many of the officials and members of the landed aristocracy had become a predatory class. The common people, often fleeced by their corrupt officials, found it safest to remain poor and live in hovels. There was no incentive to habits of thrift or industry and but little protection of life and property. Such a condition might have continued indefinitely in some distant island or isolated country. But in this buffer state between the three turbulent and unequal powers of Japan, Russia and China, all concerned in the vacillating palace intrigues of the King and Queen, it was impossible. It seemed almost manifest destiny that the country should be taken over by Japan, the most powerful of the three nations at that time, and the only one that could take seriously the reforming and modernizing of Korea.

Modern Japan was also in evidence at the garden party, from the Governor-General proposing "banzai" to the Emperor, to the ubiquitous military officers in uniform and civil officials in formal dress. It was only fifty-six years after Commodore Perry's fleet from the United States had knocked at the unwilling doors of ancient Nippon, that an awakened, modernized Japan had knocked yet more loudly at the portals of this hermit nation. Both Japan and Korea resented, though they could not effectively resist, their modernization. In this process impregnable Japan could retain her independence, but Korea could not. As master in her own house, Japan eagerly called in foreign instructors and modernized her entire material life. She

increased from $1,000,000 at the beginning of the Japanese protectorate, to $149,000,000 at the present time, expended on the almost unparalleled program of reforestation, the development of railways, ports, irrigation, subsidies to farmers, village associations, etc.

During the two decades of Japanese rule the trade of Korea increased from $29,848,000 to over $400,000,000 or more than thirteenfold. During the first decade the increase in trade was greater than in the Philippines or any region in the whole Far East. While imports increased about tenfold, exports multiplied more than twenty times during the two decades. The budget increased from $24,370,500 to over $97,000,000; while the entire production of the peninsula rose from $200,000,000 to over $1,000,000,000, or a fivefold increase. The products of agriculture increased more than three and a half times; forestry, mining and fishery products increased from three to nine times, while the output of manufacturing rose from $7,-500,000 to $172,000,000, or twenty-threefold.

Thirty years ago, under their own autocratic and corrupt administration, there were no railways, few roads and no modern industries. Today there are some two thousand miles of railway in operation and almost as much more approved or in process of construction. Seoul is now on the longest railway in the world, from Tokyo to Paris. With the railways have come better highways and good hotels in the big cities. One of the most remarkable achievements has been in forestry. The ancient forests of Korea had been ruthlessly cut down for firewood and the bare hills had left the people a prey to both flood and drought. During the last two decades, the Japanese claim that by government and private undertaking more than three million acres have been planted with over three billion trees. The whole landscape is gradually changing and the rainfall will in time be increased.

The fisheries of Japan itself are probably the most scientific and successful in the world and the value of the catches in Korea has increased more than twelvefold under efficient Japanese management. The Japanese have aided the Korean farmer in scientific sericulture as a cottage industry. During the last twenty years a better strain of silkworms has been substituted, the number of the households feeding silk worms has increased nearly tenfold, so that now more than one-sixth of the homes engage in this subsidiary industry, while the volume of cocoons gathered has increased more than twenty-threefold.

Of the total population only 2.2 per cent, or 424,740, are Japanese. They furnish only one-fourth of one per cent of the agriculturists, but about 25 per cent of those who depend upon public service for a livelihood. The foreign trade has increased twelve times as fast as the Japanese population, and some of the increased resources have accrued to the Korean people, especially in the cities. Bank deposits in Korea have increased about fivefold during the two decades. Of the savings-account depositors of the Chosen Industrial Bank 51.7 per cent were Koreans, though they held but 20 per cent of the funds, with an average for every depositor of $21.26, as against $90.37 for each Japanese. There is evidence from a number of sources that the wealth of Korea is slowly but steadily increasing, although the city has been receiving more than the country and the Japanese more than the Koreans.

If we turn from the city to the country, during the first fifteen years of the Japanese occupation the area under cultivation has increased 35 per cent and agricultural production 53 per cent. The testimony of the most impartial observers shows that "the herculean efforts of the Japanese" continue to aid the farmer. American cotton has been introduced, as well as diversified farming and stockraising, wide areas have been irrigated for improving the culture of rice, and the export of rice has been increased sixfold in two decades. Yet, according to the invaluable report of Dr. Brunner, "increasing debt, increasing tenancy and the undeniable restlessness of the population are not signs of a healthy and normal condition." While the average Korean has more money and probably greater purchasing power than he had twenty years ago, the increase has not kept pace with his desires or standards of living. Owner-cultivators are decreasing at the rate of eleven per cent, and tenants are increasing at the rate of twenty per cent a decade, while the reverse process has been taking place in Denmark. Government statistics show that while the population is steadily increasing, the size of the individual holdings in land is decreasing. The average tenant farmer has now only three acres, half of which is paddy-field for rice. Even this is more than the two and a half acres of the average farm in Japan. While the legal division of the crop between the landlord and tenant is fifty-fifty, in the south the renter's actual *net* share often leaves him but one-fifth of the crop. The average income of the farmer ranges from $100 to $170 a year, while his total taxes take from 8 to 10 per cent of this small income.

A survey in the south revealed that only 30 per cent of the owner-cultivators made a profit, while 95.9 per cent of the part-tenants and 96.9 per cent of the full tenants closed the year with a deficit. In the north two out of five families were found to be in debt and in the south about four out of five. These were paying an average of 36 per cent interest. In all regions many of the owner-cultivators have been compelled to mortgage their lands. Many are discouraged and some are having their mortgages foreclosed. With only 20 per cent of the land arable, and the farm population in the south rising to 900 persons per square mile, the carrying capacity of the soil is grossly overloaded, so that Koreans have moved in large numbers to Japan, Manchuria and Siberia where many have now settled. Generations of misgovernment under his old régime, where the farmer was preyed upon by the tax collectors and parasitic relatives, have left the Korean often indolent and lacking in enterprise. The Japanese in the country raise much more than the Koreans and the Chinese also outwork them. In this transitional period between feudalism and industrialism, the Korean farmer is suffering today as are the peasants in Japan itself.

Many Koreans will be unable to adjust themselves to the new era and will perish in the struggle for existence. Some are endeavoring to drown their troubles in drink. Many among the young are looking for some panacea, often turning, as the last hope of despair, to Communism, which is entering both from Siberia in the north, and in the south through students and laborers returning from Japan. Indeed Communism is making its widest appeal today in the three countries of the

Far East where peasants and labor are suffering most, Japan, Korea and China, especially in the last named.

Taking into account all existing conditions, the Japanese administration of Korea seems to have been materially efficient in the highest degree, although the Koreans have not had an equal share in the measure of prosperity with the Japanese. On the moral and spiritual side the effect of the Japanese occupation has not been so good. This is confessed by leading Japanese. Both drink and prostitution are licensed under the Government and both have increased greatly. The Government income from liquor has been large. With increased prostitution venereal disease has also grown. In an early treaty of 1876 the Japanese wisely inserted a provision which prohibited the importation of opium into Korea, thus passing on the boon which they themselves had enjoyed by the foresight of the American, Townsend Harris, at the time of the opening up of Japan.

The Korean Indictment

After observing the undeniable and gratifying material advance of Chosen under Japanese rule, let us hear the Korean statement of their case. We shall quote no one man, but rather give a composite statement of the practically unanimous opinion of the ninety-nine per cent of educated Koreans who passionately desire their independence. Perhaps one per cent who are receiving the material benefits of office or profit under Japanese rule prefer the far more efficient foreign control, while many of the farmers are so poor and hardpressed in the struggle for bare existence that they are indifferent to political issues. As already stated, the Koreans make a threefold indictment against Japanese rule.

1. The Japanese policy of assimilation or absorption of the Korean people. The Japanese had modernized their own people in 1868 by militaristic methods and imagined that they could Japanize the Koreans almost as easily. One Japanese thus states their purpose: "I can see only one end. This will take several generations, but it must come. The Korean people will be absorbed in the Japanese. They will talk our

language, live our life, and be an integral part of us. There are only two ways of colonial administration. One is to rule over a people as aliens. This you English have done in India, and therefore, your Indian Empire cannot endure. India must pass out of your rule. The second way is to absorb the people. This is what we shall do. We will teach them our language, establish our institutions and make them one with us."

The semi-official organ, *The Seoul Press,* in stating the policy of the Saito régime, says: "We will not waver in our determination to Japanize the Korean people." The Japanese language is made the medium of instruction in the schools instead of Korean. It takes more time than any other subject. The Koreans feel that their personality is violated, that their history, their culture, their most sacred traditions, all that makes them Koreans will in time be eliminated. This they deeply resent. They no more wish to become Japanese than the Japanese would wish to become Koreans. The Japanese informed the writer that they are now writing the Koreans' history for them by a combined committee of Japanese and Koreans and will then teach it in their schools. The Koreans have not forgotten the invasion of the Japanese regent Hideyoshi in 1592, who devastated the country with great loss of life and destruction of property. At the Governor-General's garden party, the Koreans pointed out the inscription attributing the destruction of the palace, not to Japan's fierce campaign, but to the Korean mob. So far, at least, the policy of assimilation seems to have been futile. The most bitter enemies of the present regime seem to be the Korean students in the government schools and those who study in Japan.

2. A dictatorship and autocratic rule by an alien power is the second indictment of the Koreans. They claim that the Japanese make their laws, appoint the officials and naturally keep most of the lucrative and important offices for themselves. The early rule by the Japanese seems to have been particularly harsh and militaristic. They tried to impose on the Koreans the experience of Japan all at once. Dr. Brunner tells us that in the first ten years there were over sixty major changes of policy put into effect, only to be revised after a year or two.

Even now the police inspector has very wide powers: "He issues permits for public gatherings, and attends them to censor the speeches and stop the meeting if he thinks the sentiments given utterance to are not in accord with what he imagines to be public policy; if he feels it to be necessary, he may arrest the speaker and detain him for examination." Although Viscount Saito and many of the higher officials are men of sympathy and understanding, all too many of the minor officials are unimaginative, unsympathetic and harsh, subjecting the Koreans to a thousand pin-pricks. These under-officials are the only ones with whom the common people come in contact. The Korean is seldom allowed to criticize the Government. If he does so it may be treated as a seditious utterance. Little liberty is allowed the press. The three papers owned by Koreans have all in turn been suppressed and several editors have served terms in prison. At the time of writing the Korean daily *Dong-a Ilpo* has been forced to suspend publication. In the *Seoul Press* of April 18, 1930, the Director of the Police Bureau warned the press representatives of the transgressions of this paper in printing articles by George Bernard Shaw, an article by the Korean patriot Dr. Yun on the success of Czecho-Slovakia, and continues: "In its issue of the 16th inst. the daily published an article by Mr. Villard, chief editor of *The Nation*, on the success of the liberation of Negro slaves, evidently with intent to give instigatory hints to the Korean race. . . . The authorities therefore summoned its representative responsible and gave a strict warning against such behaviour. In spite of this it repeated the practice, in connection with the suppression of its issue of the 16th inst., and this could only be regarded as flying openly in the face of the authorities. Such being the case, the authorities have been obliged to order the suspension of its publication. From the beginning of January last to the end of March, the paper was suppressed as often as 39 times, or to be more particular, prohibition of the sale of its issue took place 15 times and suppression of certain articles 24 times, and this practically means that few days passed without it getting into trouble . . ."

The Japanese are a great people. Their own phenomenal advance of the last two generations is almost unique in history. The cornerstone of their character is loyalty and their outstanding characteristic as a people is the social solidarity that largely accounts for their success. Their high idealism, willingness for self-sacrifice and capacity for organization are remarkable. But even more than the Germans they have a singular incapacity for understanding other peoples. They are intensely reserved, highly sensitive and lacking in a capacity for detached self-criticism.

The Korean has a greater wealth of affection than the Japanese and could be won by a policy of real conciliation, equal justice and growing autonomy, but he will never accept the methods of crushing absorption or autocratic control.

The Japanese are slowly learning at this point. Though they are far behind the large measure of liberty allowed in India and in the Philippines, under the greater sympathy and understanding of Governor-General Saito some advance toward an initial measure of autonomy has been made. Out of thirteen provincial governors five are Koreans. All village headmen are Koreans and nine-tenths of the county magistrates. Viscount Saito now suggests extending the power of the advisory councils to administrative responsibility by a measure of local autonomy in designated areas and municipalities where the Japanese are numerous, where councils will have some financial power. This should prove a wise measure.

3. The policy of economic discrimination against the Koreans in favor of the Japanese is the third indictment of the present régime. Whatever the cause may be, the fact is incontrovertible that many Koreans are losing their lands, although the same is true among farmers in America and in many other lands. More than three-fourths of the Korean farmers must now deal with landlords. Of the landlords about one-fifth rent all their land and own more than half the arable areas of Korea. The Japanese now own from 12 to 20 per cent of the land in the peninsula, [1] yet since the occupation less than 10,000

---

[1] *Rural Korea* by Dr. Edmund Brunner, p. 105.

Japanese families have settled here. In the south about one-fourth of the land has passed out of Korean hands. The Koreans complain that inducements were offered to Japanese settlers with long term loans and easy payments, and that several Koreans, whether as tenants or as holders of mortgages foreclosed, were evicted to make room for one Japanese.

Shimada Saburo and others in Japan with a sense of imperial responsibility protested against the alienation of land in Korea, where tenants, who regarded the grants of royal land, some of them centuries old, as equivalent to ownership, were evicted to facilitate Japanese settlement. The Japanese have naturally captured a large part of the new trade and manufactures assisted by their law that a limited company must have Japanese representation on its directorate. Koreans maintain that every effort is put forth to make of Chosen a producer of raw materials for Japan and a consumer of her manufactures, but that no help is given to their home-made products. They believe that in practice there are two codes of law and of conduct, one for the Japanese, and another for the Koreans. They particularly complain against the discriminations of the Government, the Oriental Development Company, which is coming into possession of enormous holdings and resources, chiefly for the Japanese, and of the Bank of Chosen. They believe that the bank operates for the exploitation of Korea rather than for the development of the Korean people. Thus the President of the Bank, speaking in Japan, said officially: "The Bank of Chosen was floated for the purpose of helping Japanese business interests expand in Chosen and Manchuria. . . . All this has been done out of a desire to do service to Japan's economic cause." [1]

The Japanese claim that Chosen is an integral part of the Empire, and that all his children are equal before the eyes of the Emperor. This is made the ground for the absorption of the Korean people. But Koreans feel that they are becoming divided into possessing and dispossessed children by a continued policy of economic discrimination, as in the case of many Ko-

---

[1] August, 1922, quoted by Dr. Brunner in *Rural Korea*, p. 117.

rean fishermen now deprived of their hereditary privileges. It is here in the economic field that Japan's policy will be judged by deeds rather than by profession.

To sum up the case, it is undoubtedly true that there has been a highly creditable material advance in the Japanese administration of the country, but there seems to be some truth in the threefold Korean contention that the policy of forcible assimilation and absorption has neither been wholly wise nor successful, but has increased the resentment of the people; that the Japanese rule has been too autocratic and dictatorial, and that there has been at least some economic discrimination with the loss of lands by Koreans which might have been prevented. We would lay the blame of the past mistakes not so much to the character of the Japanese people as to the curse of militarism, which is very much the same all the world over. Their economic discrimination also is only part of the acquisitive, profit-seeking, pagan business system which obtains in America and wherever selfish and ruthless capitalism is uncurbed in its power. Treatment of Koreans is no worse than America's economic treatment of the Negro, of child labor and the unemployed.

If we compare the administration of Korea with that of India and the Philippines, Japan's rule would seem to be creditable on the material side. The situation in the three countries, however, is very dissimilar. Korea, for instance, is far more vital to Japan than are the Philippines to the United States. Japan fought two wars largely for Korea, which was once a menace and a danger zone to her, and which she feels must now be incorporated within her empire. She will not lightly consider giving it up.

Both in India and in the Philippines there has been no similar attempt to "assimilate" or absorb or denationalize the people. In both there has been less autocracy and far more liberty, democracy and autonomy. The Filipinos would say that there is little if any economic discrimination against themselves but some legislation discriminating against the Americans and all other foreigners in preventing large alien land holdings. Up to the present there has been a strange absence of bitterness and an almost forced Filipinization of the administration. American officials have been reduced to a handful while the number of Filipino officials has been increased to over three thousand. The Filipinos make all their own laws and have almost complete self-government. In India also, although the British have had a much longer time to develop democratic institutions, there is a much larger measure of self-determination than in Korea.

The Japanese Case

The best Japanese feel keenly the pressure of the Korean problem, just as do the best of the British in India or of the Americans in the Philippines. Some of them have pleaded for dominion status for Korea. Others have said: "Korea is our Ireland. Can you help us to make it our Canada?" Many of them feel that the Koreans will never be satisfied no matter how benevolent their rule. They feel that it is to their credit that a movement to investigate Korean history was set on foot under the Residency-General in 1909, that half of the committee of investigators are now Koreans, and that any Koreans are at liberty to write their own history. The Koreans reply that such a history could never be published without the approval of Japanese censors. They state that of 337 pages of historical texts used in the common schools, only 22 pages are devoted to Korean history covering several thousand years, and that, while 87 illustrations are given of Japan, only 6 are of Korea.

In reply to the point that the Koreans have no political franchise, the Japanese state that the Koreans were not born to a franchise system, that no Japanese in Korea have the vote, while on the other hand, Koreans in Japan have the franchise and in the elections of 1930 51.8 per cent of them voted.

The Japanese admit that the behavior of the police is far from ideal but point out that more than half of the police are Koreans. As for freedom of criticism, they say that the press law in Korea is the same as in Japan itself and governs both the Japanese and Korean press alike. But unquestionably, although the laws may be the same, their administration is far more severe in Korea, as in the case of several editors and critics of the government arrested or imprisoned.

The Japanese admit that tenancy has been increasing among farmers, but they point out that during the period of Japan's occupation of Korea, tenancy has increased in the United States by more than 20 per cent, and that the same tendency obtains in Japan proper. Most of the lands that have changed hands have been those of the larger Korean landlords who have been attracted by the higher selling price of land. The Japanese point to their efforts for the prevention of land amalgamation and for the increase of owner-cultivators beginning with the orders of the Governor-General in October, 1912. State lands were disposed of to 220,505 farmers, most of whom were Koreans.

They point out that they have striven to improve the tenancy system by credit and loans at low rates of interest, by encouraging subsidiary industries and by the promotion of agricultural organizations, culminating in their Revised Tenancy System of 1928. In their "designated model villages" they have provided experimental stations suitable for the improvement of cotton, stock farming, sericulture and cereals. This movement is a valuable and important one as testified to by American experts. By these methods, by their Mutual Aid and Laborers' Trust Societies the yield of rice has more than doubled in twenty years in some villages.

Their rice increase program has made a large volume of rice available for export and for home consumption, to the value of $100,000,000 annually. Their "twelve year program in rice" is calculated to increase production by 40,672,000 bushels, at a value, if the price of rice does not fall too heavily, of $123,000,000 yearly.

Special agricultural courses are provided for graduates of common schools to train leaders in all communities. Institutes are held for the improvement of teachers in agricultural methods and circulating libraries are provided. The teachers are encouraged to visit their pupils and the farmers on Saturdays and Sundays. Agricultural competitions are held, distribution is made of selected seeds and modern agricultural machinery is supplied to members of the various organizations. There are now 621 local credit and cooperative associations with 588,560 members and an aggregate capital of $12,316,500. A definite and genuine movement is on foot to assist tenants to become owner-cultivators. The Tozan organization has loaned over $254,000 to 2,444 farmers at 7 per cent interest to be repaid in ten years, mostly to clear off old indebtedness at exorbitant rates of interest. Some of the Japanese agricultural extension work not only goes far beyond what Great Britain has done in India but in some respects what the United States Government is doing for its own farmers. This whole movement is most creditable.

The Japanese estimate the population of school age at 2,600,000, which is, strangely enough, the exact estimate of the Resident Commissioner of the Philippines, with a much smaller population of thirteen millions in those Islands, as compared to twenty millions in Korea. They claim 471,847 in public schools and 249,000 in unclassified institutions, or a total of 720,847 children, which would be 28 per cent of the children in school.

The Japanese recognize with appreciation the valuable agricultural work of the Y. M. C. A. and the missions, with which the Government is cooperating, and close the statement of their case to the writer with the genuine spirit of these words: "The Koreans are compatriots and brothers. Their welfare is our welfare, their sorrows are our sorrows, their agonies our agonies. Our motto in Korea is 'mutually exist and mutually prosper.' The Government has been facing the needs of nearly twenty million people for the past twenty years or more and has done its best by thorough scientific investigations and research at the cost of self-sacrificing labour, involving a tremendous initial outlay and large recurring expenditure. It has not yet won the full confidence of the people, partly owing to misgovernment in the past, and partly to their slow awakening to their immediate need of improvement, but the helpful spirit and very patient efforts of all directly concerned in these works in country communities are quietly effecting this latter."

Such a spirit on the part of the best Japanese, which is as

genuine as that of Lord Irwin in India, will seek to do the
right thing for Korea in the end.   And where there is a will
there will be found a way, sustained by liberal leaders in
Japan, and by world public opinion.

Japan's Future Policy

While there are many evidences of improvement in conditions, we regret to say that the Japanese and Koreans are still
caught in a vicious circle of hostility.   The policy of forcible
absorption, autocratic rule and some measure still of economic
discrimination drives ninety-nine per cent of the educated
Koreans, including all of the best men, into silent and often
sullen hostility to the Japanese.   As a result the Japanese say
in turn that Koreans cannot be trusted and must be dealt with
by stricter measures.

History would seem to indicate that the Koreans would respond to a liberal policy of growing autonomy, first local, then
provincial and finally central.   Koreans may well be associated with the Japanese in the higher and more responsible
posts and increasingly trusted with larger powers.   More important than growing legal and political autonomy will be cultural autonomy.   The very word "Japanize" is like bitter poison to them.   Instead of trying to force them to be Japanese let
them be themselves.   Let them write their own history, preserve their own language, protect the heritage of their own
culture as in India and the Philippines.   Let them also have
economic autonomy without unjust discrimination.

The Japanese point to their generous treatment of Korean
royalty and nobility.   But one of the bitterest elements in the
Japanese policy was the denunciation of Korean graft and corruption and then loading with titles the worst robbers who had
despoiled their own people, and hounding with spies or re-
warding with prison many of her best patriots, reformers and
deeply religious men.   Japan will find that she can win the
Koreans only by deeds of justice and conciliation.   Her wisest
policy will be with the fewest words to proceed steadily on the
pathway of the policy of autonomy—politically in local, pro-

vincial and ultimately in the central government, as well as in legal, cultural and economic autonomy.

Koreans should not be asked to abandon their hope of ultimate independence, nor should they be suspected or oppressed because of this. No self-respecting Korean, as no true Japanese, could hope for less. On the other hand, the Korean people should not hold themselves aloof in implacable hostility if Japan makes real advances toward genuine autonomy. They should not despise the day of small things. They can have no hope in the use of organized force against one of the strongest and sternest military powers in the world. They should meet halfway every genuine advance of the Japanese toward autonomy. For the present they can only hope to progress one step at a time.

A new day will come both for Japan and Korea. The Philippines will probably gain their independence. India will doubtless win self-determination either within or without the British Empire. Education and enlightened public opinion will beget new ideals among the Koreans. And the Japanese would never dare to educate them if they intended to make them merely contented serfs or economic pawns in the game of their own imperialism. Much more important, a new and liberal Japan is arising. Universal suffrage, the growth of organized labor, the probable development of the proletarian parties, and the education of the students of Japan today in ideals of economic justice, even though they sometimes go to extremes in academic theory in the category accounted by the authorities as "dangerous thoughts"—all these promise well for the future of Korea. Liberals in Japan will in time speak out on behalf of Korea even as a few are already thinking about their future.

Korea's Past

The present relations between Japan and Korea can be adequately understood only in the perspective of their past history. The Korean peninsula at once separated and joined the three great powers that surrounded it—China, Japan and Russia. It was natural that it should become a pawn in the game played by these three. For centuries Korea was a hermit nation avoiding all possible contact with the outside world except with China, whose superior civilization she had borrowed and whose nominal protectorate she acknowledged at times as a vassal state. At an early period Chinese culture and the Buddhist religion were passed on to Japan from Korea. Her shores were sometimes raided by Japanese pirates, and in 1592 Hideyoshi, the Shogun, invaded Korea in order to attack China, devastating the country for more than six years, and embittering the Koreans.

After the beneficial results of the opening of Japan by Commodore Perry in 1854, the Japanese sought in turn to open this Hermit Nation with plans for much needed reform and the maintenance of her independence against the menace to Japan first of China and later of Russia. As we have seen, the Korean court was weak and corrupt, deriving regular income from the sale of public offices.[1] Officials were often entirely unpaid and the buyer of an office had to make his money quickly out of the people before his position was sold again to the highest bidder. The Emperor robbed the nobles, and the nobles fleeced the peasants. The governor "squeezed" his province, the mayor his city, the official the common people. Any wealthy man could be thrown into prison until he bribed the highest official for his release. All habits of thrift were killed and the people still suffer from the effects of this corrupt régime. The respective parties of the King and Queen became divided in fickle intrigue between Japan, China and Russia. From 1873 to 1895 the policy of Japan was for the reform, progress and independence of Korea, maintained against what she felt to be the gathering menace first of China and finally of Russia. Japan stood for independence and reform in Korea against Chinese vassalage, conservatism and corruption.

In 1894-5 the Sino-Japanese war was fought over the question of Korea, resulting, contrary to all expectation, in the com-

---

[1] The Government was a failure but the people were not. As Dr. James S. Gale well says: "The coolie or the laboring man had his ideals of a Confucian gentleman just as truly as the minister or the literati, so that in a large sense Korea could be said to be a land of gentle people. Thus was a law written on the heart that certainly had much to do with steadying the race through long years; and while, from a government point of view, Korea was a failure, she retained certain ideals that placed her among the highly civilized nations of the earth."

plete victory of Japan. China was forced to recognize the independence of Korea, to cede the Laotung peninsula to Japan and to pay an indemnity.

Russia, France and Germany, however, interfered and compelled Japan to give back the Laotung peninsula to China and then proceeded themselves to seize her territory and take concessions from her. Threatened by the advance of Russia in Manchuria, in Laotung which Russia had seized after forcing Japan to release it, and in Korea at her very doors, Japan felt compelled to fight Russia in 1904, in what she regarded as a war of self-defense, just ten years after her war with China. Within a year after her victory over China, Russia had been blocking the reform and independence of Korea, and Japan now fought the largest power in Europe, as she had the most populous nation in Asia a decade before, once more over the issue in Korea.

Americans must remember that the relation both of Korea and Manchuria to Japan is not regarded as similar to the distant and detached Philippines to the United States, but more like California which was taken from Mexico in 1845 in the war provoked by the States. Perhaps, on the principle of abstract right, California should be restored to Mexico, but the Americans would no more consider that question than would the Japanese suggest the independence of Korea over which they fought two wars.

In 1905 Korea became a Japanese protectorate. After fighting two wars because of Korea's inability to defend herself, Japan naturally insisted that this should not happen again. Japan's greatest statesman, Marquis Ito, was appointed resident general in 1906, bringing with him a list of proposed reforms. But these were often blocked under an unworkable dual government naturally unpopular with the Koreans. Finally in 1910 a formal union or annexation was effected. What appeared to be manifest destiny to the Japanese seemed a pathetic blow to the national aspirations of the reform party in Korea.

On the whole, the policy of the Japanese was, as we have seen, materially highly efficient but lacking in sympathy, understanding and conciliation. There have been principally three manifestations of the unbroken spirit of the Koreans against the Japanese. The first was over the mistake of the

Japanese in the matter of the so-called "Conspiracy Case" in 1912; the second was the Korean Declaration of Independence in 1919; the third was the recent student mutiny at the close of 1929 and during the early months of 1930.

Japanese militarists after centuries of isolation, so loyally obedient to a military régime themselves and so lacking in the psychological understanding of other peoples, were ill-fitted for the wise handling of the delicate Korean situation. They naturally erred at first on the side of a stern and sometimes harsh bureaucracy. This was manifest in the "Conspiracy Case." Two burglars, to escape their own sentence, alleged knowledge of a plot of American missionaries and Korean Christians to assassinate the Governor-General, Count Terauchi. Upon their evidence 123 men were arrested, chiefly Christian pastors and laymen, and examined by torture until most of them "confessed" to statements read to them by the police. All these confessions were repudiated in court, but after a travesty of a trial, to save the "face" of the government, six men were sentenced to ten years penal servitude, eighteen to seven years, thirty-nine to six years and forty-one to five years. After the appeal six were still sentenced to penal servitude for periods of five and six years. The pathetic trial became a farce and lowered the prestige of the Japanese régime before the world. It would probably never have taken place under such a humane Governor as Viscount Saito.

The second instance occurred after the leading Koreans, on March 1, 1919, read in the public squares throughout the land their Declaration of Independence, stating the wrongs and grievances under which they were suffering, as the whole people shouted "Mansei," or, literally, "ten thousand years"— "May Korea live forever!" The leaders then peacefully and voluntarily surrendered themselves to the police. Koreans in these gatherings were straightway shot down, whipped, beaten and imprisoned by hundreds often with great cruelty. The Japanese public was stunned by this unexpected manifestation of nationwide resentment against a régime that had ignored the sentiments of the Korean people. But the Japanese press had never been allowed to tell the people of Japan the real condition of things in Chosen which had been ruled by militarists. Shortly before, on January 21, the former Emperor of Korea had died, after living for many years as a sort of State prisoner after the murder of the Queen. In 1895 he had been held back at the point of a sword, while in the next room the queen had been murdered by a gang of Japanese and Korean bullies under the direction of the Japanese Minister, General Viscount Miura, with the complicity of General Kusunose commanding the Japanese troops.   The mourning at the time of the Emperor's death was in reality sorrow at the loss of their independence just when the national spirit had reawakened.   The Emperor's funeral and the reading of the Declaration of Independence were the occasion for a month of ruthlessness.   The Japanese troops were called out and in several cases a number of Koreans were killed, as in a Suwon village where Christians were surrounded, shot down and their church burnt over them.   Many hundreds were imprisoned, often with medieval methods of interrogation and punishment. The writer has personally seen the scars on the tortured bodies of some of these men.   General Hasegawa, true to the military mind, told Japanese journalists that the disturbances were due solely to the Bolsheviks, who have furnished an alibi or a fictitious excuse for most of the political, social and industrial wrongs throughout the world for the last decade.

As a result of the whole "uprising," drastic changes in the administration were demanded, the soldier who had been Governor-General was recalled and Admiral Baron Saito was chosen as probably the best man in all Japan to undertake this difficult task.   The fine spirit and humane temper of his conciliatory administration have introduced a number of reforms which are highly praiseworthy.   There is still, however, a fundamental psychological misunderstanding between the two peoples, which in spite of material progress and the conciliatory attitude of the few subservient Koreans, alienates practically all of the best men and leading patriots.

This was shown in the third manifestation of the unchanged Korean attitude in the recent student mutiny when practically the whole student body of Korea, especially in the government schools, was shown to be deeply hostile to the Japanese.   A trivial incident of an alleged or supposed insult by a Japanese student to a Korean girl led to a series of conflicts between the Korean and Japanese students following October 31, 1929. Students on both sides were injured and the police were called out.   The Koreans felt that the sentence of the courts fell much more heavily on their own than on the Japanese students. This seemed to them only the usual unjust discrimination. As a result a student mutiny or general strike spread all over Korea, the students rushing from the schools and shouting "Mansei" for their oppressed country. This mutiny spread further in January, 1930, until practically all of the middle or high schools of the country were involved in the uprising. There were many clashes with the police, several hundred Korean students were imprisoned and others expelled while most of the middle schools were closed for some weeks. The Japanese officials and police characteristically attribute the whole movement to "a secret Communistic society." It may be flattering to ascribe all such manifestations to Russian intrigue. No one for a moment will deny that there is Communist influence in Korea, but to what does it make its appeal? It appeals to the almost universal resentment against Japanese rule by old and young because of the three indictments previously mentioned. Until the Japanese see and admit this, until they gain the confidence of the leading Koreans and have continued conference with them, until they honestly face these things and alter them, they will continue to meet the growing hostility of the Koreans. Every well-wisher of both peoples will ardently desire a better understanding between the two.

Among others, two forces are today shaping the Korean people. There is the outward, iron framework of the sternly efficient Japanese Government, and the inner spiritual leaven of Christianity working in the most intelligent and progressive community through churches, schools, hospitals, modern institutions and homes. Thirty-five years ago Korea was a corrupt and misgoverned nation, under a retrograde Confucian civilization. The country was asleep, the men were lazy, the women in seclusion. Buddhism had become so degraded, so involved in political intrigue and immorality, that it had been banished from Seoul, the capital. The common people were preyed upon by the superstitions of animism, shamanism, devil worship and sorcery. Human heads impaled upon sticks by the roadside evidenced the irresponsible, autocratic Government, while the unspeakable prisons were filled with young reformers and patriots.

Into this needy country Roman Christianity was introduced in 1784, but some missionaries and converts were put to death or persecuted.   Protestant missionary work began a century later in the form of medical missions in 1884, while evangelistic work was still banned by royal edict.   On its human side the new religion brought its message of the worth of personality and a more abundant life; faith, hope and love in place of despair, self-sacrifice for the common good, and the spirit of liberty in place of bondage.   This seemed to be just what Korea needed.   The new religion rapidly gained ground until the Christian churches of all kinds now include over 360,000, or a little less than 2 per cent of the population.   But the Christian community wields an influence out of all proportion to its numbers.   It is pre-eminently the one educated, progressive and organized community in the country.   The emphasis of early missions was largely theological and moral and had done much to build up the strongest and hardiest independent community in Korea.   But today it has to meet the great economic and social stress of the times.   The Japanese government has wisely cooperated with the new rural and agricultural work of the Y. M. C. A. and the missions in conducting ten-day farm schools throughout the country for improving the economic conditions of the people in cooperative societies, diversified farming, the preparation of soil, seed selection, farm machinery, rice culture, dry farming and stock-raising.   This policy is not only improving their material condition but is getting the minds of the people off brooding upon politics and stimulating them with a new hope of self-improvement.   The Koreans are studying the rebirth of Denmark through her cooperatives and people's schools which were inspired by the church, and observing the rural work of the Young Men's Christian Association in India in organizing cooperative credit unions.   "Model villages" have been developed as an example to the country.   All this points the way to the possibility of growing cooperation between the churches, the government and the people which should all be working together for the economic welfare of the Koreans.[1]

---

[1] In answer to the question, What has the government done for the farmers in your district, one missionary replied as follows: "1. Protected the trees; 2. made roads; 3. secured better average prices for crops; 4. made it possible to buy new things more cheaply; 5. imposed standard im-

The government of one people by another is at best a thankless task and increasingly difficult in the modern world under the steady rise of the spirit of nationalism and the forced retreat of imperialism.   However inevitably unpopular an alien rule may be, the Koreans now have the best modern government that their country has ever known.   While some will become impoverished and perish in the process of transition, a new Korea is being gradually built up under the powerful forces of patriotism, religion, education, law and order.   The future success of Japan in the peninsula will depend, not upon her force nor the growth of her trade, but upon her sympathy and understanding and upon the economic prosperity, the political autonomy and moral character of the Korean people.   In all of these the prospect is hopeful.

---

proved cotton seed; 6. introduced artificial fertilizers; 7. encouraged silk-growing to the profit of the farmers; 8. introduced new food crops for variety of diet; 9. encouraged the bamboo industry; 10. introduced chickens and pigs; 11. maintained an experiment station that is ready to give advice to the farmers who ask for it." This answer is typical of replies received from a number of persons. *Rural Korea,* Dr. Edmund de Schweinitz Brunner, p. 166.

CHAPTER V

We found no subject people in the world today so ready and ripe for independence as the Filipinos—with one important proviso. As we returned recently to the Philippines we noted striking signs of progress after visiting the Islands once each decade during the thirty years of American occupation. If such a division is not wholly arbitrary, perhaps the first decade might be characterized by rapid material progress largely under American leadership in the construction of roads, schools, public buildings, and material equipment. The second period was marked by the advance of the Filipino people in self-government under the trial and error method of an almost autonomous government. Probably the greatest lessons learned during this period were by some of their own costly mistakes. The third decade seems to have been marked by steady growth toward a stable government in almost every department. The Philippine Islands have probably made more progress than any country in the world under foreign tutelage.

The phenomenal economic progress of the Philippines has been so based upon and bound up with free trade with America that, if immediate independence should substitute for favorable free trade hostile tariff barriers against them, it would cause an economic dislocation if not a catastrophe of the first magnitude.[1] It might mean the temporary collapse of their artificially stimulated sugar industry, the failure of their National Bank which is bound up with sugar and is the depository of Governmental securities, an immediate depression in trade, a serious reduction of income accompanied by a heavy increase of taxation, and a lowering of the whole standard of

---

[1] It should be remembered that free trade was imposed upon the Islands not at their request but against their opposition.

living of the people, whose average per capita income is even now only $35 a year.

In the face of these economic facts, what is the attitude of the Filipino people today toward independence? 1. All thinking Filipinos and all Americans without exception desire that *the present situation of unrest and of uncertainty should cease.* The fevered demand for independence which meets with no clear response from America, with the consequent retarding of commercial development and of adequate constructive reforms by the Filipinos themselves, is like the uncertainty before a presidential election in America, multiplied tenfold and continued year after year. This tantalizing and paralyzing uncertainty must terminate. 2. *Every intelligent, self-respecting Christian Filipino in the Islands desires independence;* and these Christians constitute more than nine-tenths of the population. We have found no people in the world so unitedly, so passionately, so insistently desiring independence as the Filipinos.

But if we ask when and how this independence should be granted there is a clear division of opinion. To understand this difference we must realize two facts: 1. No other conquered and subject people were ever given such a large measure of autonomy, such hope and promise of early independence, or were so speedily prepared for it. The result of this artificial stimulation and encouragement on the part of Americans has been the practically universal demand for independence by all parties, all classes, all political leaders. It has become a fever, an obsession. Any political leader who asked for anything less than immediate independence would be considered a traitor to his country and would lose his political head. 2. As we have said, the economic progress of the Philippines has been so bound up with free trade exclusively with America that immediate independence would spell an economic catastrophe for the Islands.

Apart from a half million Moros [1] in the southern Islands who do not constitute a serious minority problem, the united

---

[1] Even the spokesmen of the Moros in the Senate and House have voted with the rest for independence.

nine-tenths of the population who are Christians may be divided into three classes.

1. The bulk of the farming population, nearly ten million people, want their liberty because of the orations they hear every Independence Day and in election campaigns. They know little about the issues involved, but they will "vote right" and follow their leaders when the time comes for voting or for action.

2. Some thousands of the intellectuals, the whole student body, the youth movement and their leaders and orators want always and everywhere, in season and out of season, "the immediate, absolute, and complete independence of the Islands." The spirit of this body is that of the American Colonists in 1776, and their spokesman would be Patrick Henry.

3. Some hundreds of the informed, responsible and real leaders of the Islands in Government and all departments of life want independence as much as the youth just mentioned, but they are in touch with the economic realities and hope to gain independence, not as a sudden catastrophe, but in a way that will benefit the Islands and will be a credit to the United States. This third group is small but it is perhaps more important than the other two combined and probably can carry the others upon any reasonable plan for independence which satisfies themselves. They want to end the present fever of uncertainty. They want independence at all costs and would prefer to have it immediately, even with severe economic loss, rather than to lose it or even to run the risk of its indefinite postponement. But they would infinitely prefer a period of transition that would enable them to reestablish themselves upon a new and sound economic basis upon one of the following plans:

The first choice of many would be the early granting of complete independence at a fixed date of from ten to thirty years from the present. Economically it might be better to have an even longer period, but they all want to enter the promised land of freedom within their own lifetime. This is a passion with many of them who fought against the Americans in 1898. During the period of transition they desire complete internal autonomy in order to be able, along with free trade with America, which is a basic essential with them, to begin to adapt their tariffs and trade relations with other countries, so that sudden independence may not leave them unadjusted in their trade with the rest of the world.

Failing the early granting of complete independence immediately or at a fixed date, most of the Filipinos would prefer the Hawes-Cutting Bill which was favored by the Majority Report of the Senate Committee on Territories and Insular Affairs. This provides for the drafting of a constitution by a constitutional convention for a free and independent government; for a five-year period of test and gradual change in trade relations;[1] this constitution is then to be submitted to the people of the Islands by a plebiscite when they shall vote to accept or reject it; and in the event of an affirmative vote the bill provides for the final withdrawal of American sovereignty over the Islands.

In a striking statement the majority of the Senate Committee on Territories and Insular Affairs, reported favorably on the Hawes-Cutting Bill as follows:[2]

"It is significant that, without exception, every witness of the many who appeared before your committee admitted that the present situation of uncertainty as to the political future of the Philippines should be removed. . . . The reasons are manifest. The Filipino is neither a citizen of the United States nor is he a citizen of a free country. . . . These 13,000,000 people, thrown by a great war into the protective arms of a western nation, find themselves, after a generation, to be in law and in fact neither Americans nor foreigners.

"The initiative of the Filipino is hampered by his status. . . . It appears from our inquiry and study that the uncertainty can

---

[1] During the first year trade relations shall be as at present; during the second year 25 per cent of existing duties shall be levied upon all imports from and exports to the United States; during the third year 50 per cent of such duties; during the fourth year 75 per cent; during the fifth year full duties shall be levied upon imports to both countries. The Hawes-Cutting Bill, S. 3822, Calendar No. 794, 71st Congress.

[2] *Calendar* No. 794, 71st Congress, May 29, 1930, on Philippine Independence.

be removed only if and when Congress shall adopt one of the following courses:

1. Granting immediate independence.
2. Setting a date in the distant future when independence shall be granted.
3. Creating what might be termed a colonial form of government for the future retention of the Philippines.
4. Incorporating the Philippines as one or more States of the American Union.
5. Providing, as in this bill (S. 3822), for the organization of a free government and permitting the Philippine people to determine whether under the new conditions they desire to become independent, and grant them independence. One of these solutions should be adopted by Congress. . . .

"The majority of this committee finds the only possible solution of the problem to be in a proposal to make possible the formation of a free government in the Philippines, to permit the Philippine people to weigh the experiences of their new status, and finally to allow them to express their views as to independence on the basis of their experience. The 'acid test' provided in this bill (S. 3822) is the hardest ever given a nation seeking independence. . . .

"It is insinuated that the Philippine people do not actually desire independence. Not a single witness before your committee could name 10 Filipinos who do not favor independence. The business organizations of the islands, their national conferences, their educators, their government officials, their economists have all declared for independence. The Philippine press, the Philippine public, the Philippine pulpit, the Philippine school, and Philippine industries seem, so far as we can ascertain, to be unanimous in the demand that the United States redeem its pledges to grant to these people the sovereignty to which they aspire.

"This unanimity of opinion in the Philippines contrasts strikingly with the differences among colonial Americans. We were not without many prominent tories during the struggles of our patriots for independence. In the Philippines, however, from the venerable Aguinaldo down to the child in the primary schoolroom, we have not been able to find a Filipino, living in his own country, who is not in favor of Philippine independence. In the face of this attitude on the part of 13,000,000 Filipinos, it would seem that they are entitled to a statement from the Congress of the United States as to what their future status shall be. . . .

"According to the report of the director of civil service of the Philippine Islands, there were on December 31, 1928, only 494 Americans in the civil personnel of the Philippine government, while 19,606 Filipinos were permanently employed under the civil service. Of the 494 Americans, 293 were in the teaching service. There are 30,000 teachers in 8,000 public schools in the Philippines. Of these teachers only 293 are Americans. . . .

"At this date of our supremacy over the Philippines, 30 years after our occupation of the islands, to assert that our granting their freedom would be unwise because of the stimulus it would give to other nations cherishing like hopes, is to validate a theory which will have but little weight with real Americans. We can hardly justify a course which began with the object of establishing a democracy in the Orient and which is to end in colonial control.

"It would seem hardly necessary, after all the discussion that has been had on this subject, to offer proof that we have promised to these people their ultimate sovereignty."

By May, 1931, it was evident that a growing number of more thoughtful Filipinos had begun to modify their demand *for immediate* independence. Senator Juan Sumulong, leading minority member of the Independence Mission to the United States returned to the Islands with the statement that such immediate action was impractical. The Filipino *Tribune* changed front and attacked Manuel Roxas, independence advoate, and advised moderation. Even the Filipino die-hard *Herald* changed its policy and praised the thirty-year plan of Senator Vandenberg of Michigan. The prophecy of the Senator of economic collapse has somewhat sobered at least a few of the agitators. It is not always recognized, either in the United States or the Philippines, that immediate independence would cut off American markets almost overnight and make their exports subject to the automatic application of the American tariff. Our network of treaties with other nations and their "most favored nation" clauses would prevent our making a preferential exception of the Philippines in the event of sudden independence.

As a means of securing one of the above alternatives or of making provision for the period of transition a commission may well be appointed, the Filipino members of which should be chosen by themselves, and the American members by the President of the United States, *provided* the American members are not reactionaries, committed in advance to American economic interests, without regard to the wishes and welfare of the Filipino people.   Such a commission, if rightly chosen, should be able to suggest a wiser and more carefully considered plan than would the great body of Congress, necessarily acting somewhat blindly at a distance.   But the leaders are afraid of what they regard as the repetition of certain previous fiascos, where the cards may be stacked against them in advance.   They ardently long for some early settlement, that will end the present unrest and reach a decision during this period of unprecedented good will and cooperation, rather than to delay until the Philippines are forced into the position of revolt.

Let us briefly note some of the gains of three decades.   This archipelago of 7,083 tropical islands is similar to the northern insular group that constitutes Japan, and about three-quarters of their area.[1]   Potentially rich, with an estimated wealth of some three billion dollars, with only 12.5 per cent of their area cultivated, they have but a scanty population, but are probably capable of sustaining nearly eighty million people.[2] During the last three decades the population has increased from less than 6 to some 13 millions.[3]   While Americans furnished

---

[1] The land area of the Philippines is 114,400 square miles, or about twice that of the New England states.

[2] *Statistical Bulletin of the Philippine Islands,* 1928, p. 197; Census, 1918, III, 8; Forbes, *The Philippine Islands,* Vol. I, pp. 4, 13.

[3] Population Census of 1903, 7,635,426; census of 1918, 10,314,310; estimated 1928, 12,604,000; increasing at the rate of 2 per cent a year, gives approximately 13,000,000 in 1931.   In 1918 there were 9,381,357 Christians and 932,953 non-Christians; 7,790,937 were Catholics, 1,417,448 Aglipayan, 124,575, Protestant, 443,037 Mohammedan, and 508,596 Pagan.   In 1918 3,759,138 were literate; 896,258 could speak English, and 757,463 Spanish. *Statistical Bulletin,* 1928, p. 5.

much initiative and leadership, especially during the first decade, the money for all improvements has come from the Filipinos.[1] The Islands have been self-supporting from the beginning. The first notable advance of the Filipinos was in their rapid training for self-government. At first municipal governments were established, then provincial governments. Next the Filipinos were represented in the Central Government on the Commission and in the Supreme Court; then an elective Lower House composed entirely of Filipinos was established. This now consists of 94 members, 87 of whom are elective. Then the Philippine Senate of 24 members, 22 of whom are elected, succeeded the Commission as the upper house. The Council of State, with only two American members, is composed of the ranking executive officers and the leaders of the upper and lower houses, who serve practically as an advisory cabinet of the Governor-General. There has been a rapid Filipinization of all services. In 1903 there were 2,777 American officials and employees in the Civil Service. Even a decade ago the Americans in the service had been reduced to 58, apart from school teachers, with only eight in positions of political power. There are now 19,606 Filipinos in the Civil Service.[2]

Another impressive advance has been in the department of public health. Upon the arrival of the Americans medieval conditions in hygiene and sanitation prevailed. Epidemics of smallpox, cholera, and plague claimed thousands of victims. Dysentery, tuberculosis, malaria and intestinal parasites were prevalent. Since that time millions have been vaccinated for smallpox without a single death.[3] Plague has been eliminated

---

[1] The only cost of the Philippines for the United States has been the expense of conquest for some three years, the maintenance of military and naval forces, certain fortifications and coastal surveys, small appropriations of $3,451,925 for famine relief in 1903, and for completing the census of that year.

[2] There are 1,165,219 qualified electors and registered voters, 942,404, or 80.87 per cent of whom voted in 1928. The franchise includes all male citizens of twenty-one and over, who can read and write, who own real property to the value of $250, or pay internal revenue taxes of $15 a year. *Statistical Bulletin*, 1928.

[3] Forbes, *Vol. 1*, p. 333.

and cholera checked. Manila, once an unsanitary pest-hole, has become a beautiful and healthy city. By 1928 there were in operation 37 government hospitals and 1,036 dispensaries. The death-rate had been reduced from 30.5 per thousand in 1898 to 17.8 in 1927.[1]

The material advance of the Islands in the last three decades has been phenomenal. The estimated wealth of the Philippines increased from 740 million dollars in 1913 to 2,950 millions in 1927.[2] The total foreign trade of the Islands increased from $34,000,000 in 1899 to over $300,000,000 in 1920, or nearly tenfold.[3] The mileage of first class roads increased from 246 to 3,955. The port of Manila has become one of the safest and best harbors in the Orient. Its public buildings are probably finer than in any city of similar size in the East. Agriculture has been improved. Upon more than two million farms eight million of the agricultural community are settled who constitute the backbone of the community, living for the most part in their own homes. Wages and conditions of labor are better than in any similar country in the Orient. The rapid increase of automobiles is a further evidence of prosperity.

Probably the most notable advance under American occupation is in the field of education. Before the Americans arrived the Filipinos claim that there were 2,160 primary schools, most of which were under ecclesiastical control. Today there are over 1,200,000 enrolled in public and private schools. At the time of the American occupation only about 7 per cent could speak Spanish and only 10 per cent were literate. The whole educational system is now conducted through the English language as a unifying medium. Sixty per cent of the population is now reckoned as literate [4] compared to 7 per cent in India. Their record of literacy is better than some 30 out of 56 independent nations. There are now over a million regis-

[1] Ibid, *Vol. 1*, pp. 351, 359.
[2] *Statistical Bulletin*, 1928, p. 197.
[3] *Ibid*, p. 91.
[4] According to the Census of 1918, 49.2 per cent were then counted as literate.

tered qualified voters and from 80 to 95 per cent of those qualified have voted during the last two decades, compared to less than 50 per cent in some elections in the United States. Although the circulation of newspapers is only 165,000, these are widely read and shared in community reading.

As the contribution of Spain centered in the Church, that of America was typified by democratic education in the public school. The first public school was opened by the American authorities within less than a month of the destruction of the Spanish fleet by Admiral Dewey. So great was their enthusiasm that eight hundred teachers were sent to the Islands on a single ship. By 1902 there were 928 American teachers but since that time, under rapid Filipinization, the number has declined to a third of that total. Probably no people has shown a greater desire and enthusiasm for education. The new Filipino Legislature voted an appropriation of fifteen million dollars for free elementary education, and later in 1924 the sum of $70,000 for a group of American and Filipino experts to make a scientific survey and criticism of the existing educational system. This Board of Educational Survey, under the chairmanship of Dr. Paul Monroe, found that "one of the most remarkable chapters in the history of education" had been written in the Philippine Islands. Defects were found in its mechanical organization, its too academic character and in the fact that 82 per cent of the pupils do not go beyond the fourth grade or spend more than five years in school. By 1924 37.91 per cent of the school population was enrolled, or a little more than one-third of the children, compared to less than one-fifth in India. The estimate of school population to the total population in the United States is 20 per cent. Upon the same basis the Philippines would have a school population of 2,600,-000. Their 1,200,000 enrolled in schools would be 46 per cent, or nearly half, of the population of school age. All children are given practical vocational training in household industries, mechanical trades, housekeeping and agriculture. Physical education, outdoor sports and the spirit of play have been a deeply needed and rewarding contribution. As the writer visited the excellent schools of Manila he felt that the children were getting a better education than he had received as a boy in America. The high schools were particularly fine. If we compare the percentage of children of high school age enrolled in the various countries, we find the following surprising result: United States 27.2 per cent, Scotland 9.1, Japan 8.4, Philippines 7.9, England and Wales, 3.9, France 2.4, Sweden 1.4, Spain 1.1, Italy .7.[1] What other country devotes 28 per cent of its entire budget to education? Certainly none of those just mentioned.

In view of the above facts it is perhaps not too much to say with the report of the Wood-Forbes Mission that: "No people under the friendly tutelage of another have made so great progress in so short a time."

In the light of the total situation, are the Philippines ready for independence? There are strong arguments in favor of this position.

1. *The Filipinos desire independence,* as we have seen, probably more unanimously than any other subject people in the world. They have fought for their freedom since the revolt of 1558, through more than three centuries of attempted revolution against Spanish tyranny. The revolution was fanned to flame from 1892, when the movement became nation-wide. The shooting of their great martyr-patriot Rizal sounded the death knell of Spanish domination in 1896. It is not always known that in the war carried on by American troops for several years to subjugate the Islands, General Bell estimated that one-sixth of the population in Luzon alone, or 600,000 men, women and children perished, at the very time that we were being told officially in America that the Philippines had come to us "unsought."[2]

---

[1] *Survey of Education,* 1925, p. 319. Out of an expenditure of $4.50 per capita for all public enterprises $1.00 goes to education. *Survey,* p. 13. The total number of teachers has increased from 3,187 in 1903 to 26,251 in 1927, of whom only 293 were Americans. The enrollment increased from 160,000 in 1901 to 1,111,509 in public schools, and 86,695 in private schools in 1927. The percentage of illiteracy in Mexico is 62 per cent, in Siam 79 per cent, in Venezuela 72 per cent. The Philippine representatives claim that there is but 40 per cent illiteracy in their Islands.

[2] *The Philippines and the United States* by Storey and Lichauco, p. 121. *New York Times,* May 3, 1901.

The conservative Carmi Thompson, sent out to the Philippines as "the eyes and ears of President Coolidge," reports: "All Filipinos who are interested in public affairs are openly for independence. . . . I believe that practically the entire voting population is for independence. . . . The independence movement is growing all the time." Three visits to the Philippines have confirmed the writer in this view. He has never seen a people so determined upon independence, yet thus far with such an absence of bitterness in their demand. To Americans especially this should make its appeal. They may well remember the words of Froude: "If there is one lesson which history clearly teaches it is this, that free nations cannot govern subject provinces."

2. *In the opinion of the Filipinos America has repeatedly and definitely promised them either ultimate or early independence.* Let us note some of the promises that have been made and ask in the light of them what conclusion the people of these Islands would naturally draw from them.

President McKinley, the man most responsible for the acquisition of the Islands, in stating America's policy, said: "The Philippines are ours, not to exploit but to develop, civilize, to educate, to train in the science of self-government." And the commissioners of the first Philippine Commission were to be the bearers of "the richest blessings of a liberating rather than a conquering nation." President Taft while Governor said: "From the beginning to the end of the state papers which were circulated in these Islands as authoritative expressions of the executive, the motto that 'The Philippines are for the Filipinos,' and that the Government of the United States is here for the purpose of preserving *the Philippines for the Filipinos,* for their elevation, for their civilization, again and again appear." In 1908 while Secretary of War he declared: "The national policy is to govern the Philippine Islands for the benefit and welfare and uplifting of the people of the Islands. . . . What should be emphasized in the statement of our national policy is that we wish to prepare the Filipinos for *popular self-government.* . . . Another logical deduction from the main proposition is that *when* the Filipino people as a whole show themselves reasonably fit to conduct a popular self-govern-ment . . . *and desire complete independence of the United States, they shall be given it.*"   In his message to Congress as President on December 6, 1912, Mr. Taft said: "We would . . . endeavor to secure for the Filipinos economic independence and to fit them for complete self-government, with the power to decide eventually, according to their own largest good, whether such self-government shall be accompanied by inde-pendence."   President Roosevelt in his message to Congress in 1908 said: "I trust that within a generation the time will arrive when the Filipinos can decide for themselves whether it is well for them to become independent or to continue under the protection of a strong and disinterested power, able to guarantee to the Islands order at home and protection from foreign invasion."   Again Mr. Roosevelt said: "The Philip-pines, from a military standpoint, are a source of weakness to us.   The present administration has promised explicitly to let them go, and by its action has rendered it difficult to hold them against any serious foreign foe.   These being the circum-stances, the Islands should at an early moment be given their independence without any guaranty whatever by us and with-out our retaining any foothold in them."

President Wilson became yet more explicit.   In a message to the Filipino people delivered by Governor Harrison, on Octo-ber 6, 1913, he said: "We regard ourselves as trustees acting not for the advantage of the United States, but for the bene-fit of the people of the Philippine Islands.   Every step we take will be taken with a view to the ultimate independence of the Islands and as a preparation for that independence."   In 1916 Congress passed the Jones Law, proposing independence as soon as a stable government should be established in the Islands.   The preamble, which was voted upon separately and passed, was regarded as a promise by the Filipinos.   It reads as follows: "Whereas, it was never the intention of the United States in the incipiency of the war with Spain to make it a war of conquest or for territorial aggrandizement; and whereas *it is, as it has always been, the purpose of the people of the United States to withdraw their sovereignty over the Philip-*

pine Islands to recognize their independence as soon as a stable government can be established therein . . . that . . . they may be the better prepared to fully assume the responsibilities and enjoy all the privileges of complete independence." President Wilson certified the existence of a stable government in the Islands in his message to Congress December 7, 1920, as follows: "Allow me to call your attention to the fact that the people of the Philippine Islands have succeeded in maintaining a stable government since the last action of the Congress in their behalf, and have thus fulfilled the condition set by the Congress as precedent to a consideration of granting independence to the Islands. I respectfully submit that this condition precedent having been fulfilled *it is now our liberty and our duty to keep our promise to the people of those Islands by granting them the independence which they so honorably covet.*" These promises and statements have been eagerly read for thirty years by the Filipino people in the light of America's own Declaration of Independence and the affirmation of Lincoln that "no man is good enough to govern another without that other man's consent."[1] What possible conclusion could the people of the Philippines draw from all these declarations? Is it surprising that after thirty years, they now ask the people of America to fulfill the promises which they have made?

3. *A stable government has been established.* According to the League of Nations a stable government is one which maintains the support of the people. We may add the definition of President McKinley: "A stable government is one elected by the suffrage of the people, supported generally by

---

[1] As if speaking of the Philippines Lincoln said: "These arguments that are made that the inferior race are to be treated with as much allowance as they are capable of enjoying, that as much is to be done for them as their condition will allow,—what are these arguments? They are the arguments that kings have made for the enslaving of the people in all ages of the world. You will find that all the arguments of kingcraft were always of this class: they always bestrode the necks of the people—not because they wanted to do it, but because the people were better off for being ridden . . . Turn it every way you will,—whether it come from the mouth of a king as an excuse for enslaving the people of his country, *or from the mouth of men of one race as a reason for enslaving the men of another race,*—it is the same old serpent."

the people, and is capable of maintaining order and of fulfilling international obligations." In the Islands all Filipino offices are filled by ballot. The Filipinos are noted for their orderly elections. General Wood reports: "All parties admit that the elections were fairly and honestly conducted." [1] The Wood-Forbes Report speaks of the "quiet acceptance by the minority of the results of the popular vote." Law and order are maintained by a small, well-disciplined Filipino constabulary of some six thousand officers and men. General Wood reports: "Conditions of public order have been exellent throughout the Archipelago. There has been no organized resistance to authority." It is difficult to see what more could reasonably be asked of the Philippines in the way of a stable government. And it was never more stable in the matter of law and order, education and the good will of all the tribes, than during the period of almost complete Filipino autonomy. American standards can hardly be demanded at the outset, but certainly conditions are more favorable for stable government than in Mexico and a number of republics in Latin America and even in Europe where the people prize their independence and are gradually working out their own salvation.

4. *Many conditions are favorable for independence.* The people have greater unity than most nations seeking self-government. Although speaking some 87 languages, nine-tenths of the people are Christians speaking three main languages, with a common religion, common ideals and aspirations and now fused by a common sense of nationality. The educated people are all united by the English and Spanish tongues. The Filipinos were the first people of the Orient to be Christianized. They claim that some sixty per cent can read and write, a much higher percentage than in many free republics.[2] One common school system is binding the people together with the rapid spread of education for which the Filipinos display an almost unparalleled desire. What other country spends 28 per cent of its entire budget for education? President Taft said: "There

---

[1] Report of Governor-General, 1922.
[2] According to the Census of 1918, 49.2 per cent were literate. The Wood-Forbes Report estimated the degree of literacy at 37 per cent.

are no tribal relations among Filipinos. There is a racial solidarity among them undoubtedly. They are homogeneous." The administration of justice has on the whole been commendable. Public health is far advanced. "The legislative chambers are conducted with dignity and decorum and are composed of representative men."

The character of the people furnishes a good foundation for lasting independence. They are peaceful, law-abiding, loyal, obedient, home-loving, temperate, hospitable, generous, courteous, artistic and refined in their habits, long enriched by Spanish culture. They are intelligent, quick to learn, with a restless desire for progress. They have proved themselves to be not only orderly but good fighters capable of defending their freedom. According to Governor Forbes the fact that the United States had to send an army that in 1900 numbered 71,528 men, that they had to fight for several years to conquer the Islands, and that they were compelled to spend a total of $376,000,000 for military purposes to subdue and hold these Islands that came to us "unsought," would seem to indicate that they have proved brave fighters.[1]

5. *Race prejudice, social segregation and exclusion,* both in the Philippines and in California have given the Filipinos a yet deeper determination to be independent. The traditions of a once free people after four centuries of Spanish and American rule have left them a proud and sensitive race. The Filipinos believe that there was less race prejudice and more social equality manifested by the Spaniards than by the Americans. As Sir John Seeley pointed out in Britain's rule of India: "Subjection for a long time to a foreign yoke is *one of the most potent causes of national deterioration.*" The steady pressure of an Anglo-Saxon "superiority" has produced the inevitable reaction of a painful complex of inferiority on their part. There are clubs and places where the Filipinos in their own country are excluded and others where they are not wanted and simply ignored or frozen out. The treatment of Filipino laborers in California has widely accentuated this racial feel-

---

[1] Forbes, Vol. I, pp. 109, 242.

ing. We attended a student indignation mass meeting at the University of the Philippines and a memorial service in Manila for the Filipino killed in the riot in Watsonville, California, early in 1930.   In the latter service many were in tears. The audience manifested great restraint and a strange absence of bitterness, but the deep sentiment of the gatherings was unmistakable. The Filipinos feel that they are not wanted as American citizens, and that they are excluded from any full or equal brotherhood either in America or in their own country. They do not wish to intrude upon Americans, nor upon their society or clubs where they are not wanted in the Islands. But as any self-respecting race would be, they are all the more determined to be free from a "superior" and galling foreign domination. Should America finally break her promises and try to hold them in unwilling subjection, the Philippines will probably become embittered and they will fight to the death against any race that would seek to enslave or exploit them.

One cause of racial antagonism in the Philippines, as in India, is such a book as Katherine Mayo's *Isles of Fear.* If coupled with her *Mother India,* it is difficult to recall two books more cruelly unfair or that have produced more racial antagonism, of contempt on the one side and resentment on the other. These books would furnish an interesting study in psychoanalysis. Both show the same horror—or fondness—for sex perversions, usually testified to by some unnamed and inaccessible witness. The heroes in both books are the foreign rulers. The villains are the contemptible "natives." Miss Mayo stoutly champions the brave Moros and the hardy village peasants, but through her more than 340 pages she pours her wrath and contempt on all educated Filipinos who dare to aspire to independence. Her chief informer stated to the writer that he had furnished individual cases upon which she made her sweeping generalizations "as a prosecuting attorney" whose business it was to convict and not to admit anything good on the other side. The following quotation is typical of her book: "These people have no character and no consciousness of what truth and honor mean. Their old religion has been taken away. Nothing has been put in its place. They have nothing to build character on.   And you cannot properly call them immoral for they have no moral idea at all." [1]

In this connection the writer desires to record his own testimony.   After many years of residence both in the Orient and Occident, frankly he has been profoundly impressed with the Filipino people.   If they have no character he never saw it in any people.   That is not to say, of course, that all people can be judged by the same inflexible standards.   Probably the Filipinos will never aspire to rise to the moral standards of Chicago while under the rule of its worthy ex-mayor, "Big Bill" Thompson, and of its gang warfare, nor to the political practices of Pennsylvania nor of Tammany Hall, nor of the Ohio Gang nor of Teapot Dome.   But perhaps these "lesser breeds without the law" [2] may have more modest standards of their own.   The Filipinos have a powerful appeal.   After living with them, one could quite understand Lord Byron devoting himself to the cause of freedom for Greece when Athens was "but a collection of mud huts."   One could quite understand many an American in the future risking his life, or if needs be going to prison, that these people should have their human rights.

It is not generally realized in America that there exists in the Philippines today something very like the spirit of 1776 in the American Colonies.   They celebrate Washington's birthday as *their* independence day.   They are reared under an educational system that Americans have installed, where they are taught the principles of Washington, Patrick Henry and Abraham Lincoln.   No subject people in history was ever thus drilled by their conquerors in the expectations of their own liberty, nor so rapidly prepared for it.   It has become an all absorbing and consuming obsession.   They can think of nothing else.   They are continually upset by this fever of a burning demand for independence which has possessed almost

---

[1] *Isles of Fear,* p. 197.   This characteristic statement is by "a distinguished citizen of the world.   His one flaw as a witness lies in the fact that his name must be withheld."   He further testifies that "the sole motive that will influence the Filipino is vanity."

[2] It was concerning America in the Philippines that Kipling wrote these lines of *The White Man's Burden.*

the entire nation.   No other logical conclusion is to be thought of.   Nothing less will ever satisfy these people.

Opposed to the case for independence certain arguments are presented such as the following:

1. *The United States needs the Islands as a commercial, military or naval base.*   This has frequently been maintained from the time of Admiral Dewey to General Wood and Carmi Thompson.   Senator Lodge said frankly: "We make no hypocritical pretence of being interested in the Philippines solely on account of others . . . While we regard the welfare of these people as a sacred trust, we regard the welfare of the American people first.   We believe in trade expansion." [1] President Roosevelt, on the other hand, maintained that "the Philippines from a military standpoint are a source of weakness to us."   They are the Achilles' heel of an otherwise compact and relatively isolated nation.   Secretary of War Weeks estimated the annual military cost of the Philippines to America at $12,000,000.   Although, as we have seen, the Islands have been entirely self-supporting, the total spent to date for military purposes, for the conquest, fortification and holding of the Islands against their will, is estimated at a total of $750 millions.[2]   At a distance of more than six thousand miles from the United States, the Islands could hardly be successfully defended from a determined attack from Japan, Hongkong or Singapore.

The independence of the Filipinos cannot be studied in isolation.   They are a part of an Asiatic and a world-wide movement.   A rising tide of nationalism is sweeping over Egypt, Syria, Palestine, Iraq, India, China, Korea, Japan and almost the entire Orient.   Little Holland, Belgium and Britain hold empires from fifty to more than a hundred times the area of the mother countries.   Perhaps they might plead the need of raw materials and imperial possessions.   But what possible excuse has America, possessing approximately one third of all the wealth of the world, with much of Europe in her debt?   If Americans cannot turn back this advancing tide of imperial-

---

[1] Address at Republican National Convention.
[2] The American *Manila Daily Bulletin,* Feb. 1, 1930.

ism, if they cannot keep their promises, or respect the right of other peoples to the same liberty and independence for which they fought, who will do so?

2. *It is said that the Islands could not defend themselves* nor maintain their independence against Japan and other nations. Judged by certain difficult standards there are only four or five of the great world powers capable of defending themselves. Yet there are some sixty independent nations which do exist and maintain a stable government, many of which could not offer half the resistance that the Filipinos did to the American army. Does the safety of Denmark depend upon the size of her army and navy? Does the stability of the Dutch East Indies depend upon their armament? Japan and the independent Philippines would both belong to the League of Nations whose members under the Covenant "undertake to respect and preserve the territorial integrity and existing political independence of all members of the League." The four-power pact of the Pacific Arms Conference, to which Japan is a party, offers additional protection to the Philippines. [1] Britain, Holland, France and the United States would be unwilling to have Japan annex the Philippines. Premier Hara said: "When the United States decides to give the Philippines their freedom, the Japanese Government will be the first to sign an agreement for their neutralization." Such an agreement, signed by Britain, France, Japan and the United States and backed by the League of Nations, would furnish more protection than many other stable republics possess.

3. *The economic backwardness of the Islands* is a much more serious objection. After the Payne Tariff Bill which gave to the Philippines practically free trade with the United States in 1909, there was a marked development in industry, commerce and in the income of the Islands. Their trade multiplied fivefold within twelve years and nearly three-quarters of this trade was with the United States. Within twenty

---

[1] President Coolidge wrote: "As a result of international arrangements negotiated by the Washington Conference on Limitation of Armament and Problems of the Far East, the position of the Filipino people has been greatly improved and assured." Letter to Mr. Roxas, Feb. 21, 1924.

years imports from the United States increased 1643 per cent between 1908 and 1928, from $5,040,734 to $87,858,067. [1] The sugar industry was developed until it is their chief source of income. If now, under pressure of the sugar interests in the States, the Philippines were suddenly cast adrift and a tariff barrier erected against their raw products and infant industries, with no provision for any readjustment or period of transition, the result might be disastrous for the Philippines and discreditable for America. Ninety-six per cent of all the sugar exported from the Islands now goes to the United States. As one leading Filipino editor said: "You came here against our will. You conquered us and remained by force. You wound yourselves round our whole economic structure until we are artifically dependent upon you and we cannot now suddenly stand alone."

Any reasonable period allowed for making a transition in trade and tariffs with other countries would enable the Philippines to make a successful adjustment. If America gave Spain as an enemy a decade of equal priviliges with the United States in the Islands, during a transitional period, could she not make adequate provision, not only for a friendly people, but for her own daughter? To place this child as a foundling on the world's doorstep would hardly be in accord with the lofty idealism proclaimed and the promises made to the Filipino people for three decades. On one thing, however, we found the people united. Upon certain terms they all want independence. They would rather be free though poor, than prosperous and dependent. But their thoughtful leaders are deeply concerned that the terms of transition shall be favorable and that they shall not be suddenly cast off on careless impulse, nor their independence flung at them by the pressure of the sugar interests in America.

The economic position of the Philippines is sound, but from the standpoint of unfriendly legislation in the United States, precarious. They have a wealth of potential tropical resources, but owing to their fear of large foreign capital mort-

---

[1] *Statistical Bulletin*, 1928, and preceding years.

gaging their future independence, these are largely undeveloped. Most of their trade is in the hands of Chinese,
Americans and foreigners. Spain for centuries taught the
people to despise the world that now is, and to aspire to the
white collar jobs of the "gentleman" rather than to the industrial efficiency later developed in America. Filipino students are now entering the practical pursuits and there is
evidence that these people can in time stand on their own feet
against all comers in industry and commerce as well as in agriculture. They will doubtless rise to the situation as did the
Turks whose business had been in the hands of Armenians
and Greeks. Independence furnishes a strong stimulus and
spirit of victory to a free people as in the case of Turkey,
Greece, Poland, Czecho-Slovakia, Finland and many other
countries. But at present the Filipinos are economically in
the difficult stage of adolescence. They need the cooperation
of a wise parent, not the cynical unfriendliness of paternal
exploitation.

The writer left the Islands with the conviction that no
people in the world today is so ripe and ready for independence, as are the Filipinos, provided a period of transition is
allowed to enable them to adjust their trade relations. We
repeat that we know of no country in the world that has made
a better record in preparing a people for freedom than has the
United States. Unless one believes in a future world of ruthless imperialism and of permanently enslaved nations ruled by
force against their will, the Philippines are going to gain their
independence. Either it will be upon early, honorable and
favorable terms, or upon conditions of hostility, bitterness and
much suffering. That decision rests with America. But—
the Philippines are going to be free.

The Economic Situation in the Philippines

The Philippines are potentially rich. Their 20,260 miles of
coast line are almost twice that of the United States. The
seven thousand islands abound in tropical forests containing
the finest cabinet woods and commercial timber near the coast
and covering 86,003 square miles, or 73.7 per cent of the entire

area, greater in extent than New York and four of its neighboring states. [1] Some 87.4 per cent is still undeveloped public land, with only 12.5 per cent as yet cultivated.

No adequate surveys of mineral deposits have yet been made, but it is known that iron, gold and copper have been found and mined. But neither mineral oil nor coal in commercially available deposits has been discovered.

Agriculture is the chief resource of the Islands. A fertile soil, favorable climate and rainfall and abundant rivers for irrigation and power, constitute the economic basis for the future. The occupied land is well cultivated in terraced rice fields, sugar cane, cocoanuts, Manila hemp, corn, bananas and tobacco. More than 1,500,000 acres in the southern Islands are available for rubber plantations. Although there are at present sixteen relatively small plantations, the uncertain political future of the Islands, the restrictions to small holdings of land by the Filipino Legislature, [2] and the general depression resulting from over-production of rubber in the world market have discouraged the larger development of this industry in the Archipelago.

The manufacturing and industrial development of the Philippines is as yet insignificant. There are at present only some 8,354 factories employing 143,464 men, producing annually $178,047,216 in manufactured products. Wages in the city vary from 50 cents to $1.50 a day and in the country average 49 cents. The standard of living of the laborer in the Philippines is higher than in neighboring Oriental countries. In Java, for instance, wages are from 10 to 20 cents a day.

The expenditures under the Spanish and American administrations were in marked contrast. In the last year preceding the insurrection of 1896, the Spanish allocated nearly 50 per cent of the budget to the army and navy, nearly 10 per cent to the ecclesiastical establishments, and less than 5 per cent

---

[1] U. S. Department of Commerce, Commercial Survey, The Philippine Islands, 1927, p. 61.

[2] An individual may acquire 356 acres of public land by purchase, and a corporation a maximum of 2,530 acres, provided 61 per cent of its capital stock belongs to the citizens of the Philippine Islands or the United States. Commercial Survey, *The Philippine Islands,* p. 26.

to education, public works, etc.[1]   Contrast with this the budget for last year under American occupation.   For the American army and navy nothing; for law and order, Philippine Constabulary, etc., 7.8 per cent; for public education 28.7 per cent; public health 8.9 per cent; for industrial operation, encouragement of agriculture, commerce, roads and other economic development 25.1 per cent.[2]   Much of the Spanish budget was devoted to keeping the people in subjection; almost the whole of the present budget is for constructive purposes, and all for the welfare of the Filipinos, voted by their own Legislature.

The Philippines are poor and their administration is economical.   The Governor-General receives a yearly salary of $18,000, the President of the Senate $9,000,[3] various Americans in important offices from $3,000 to $6,000.   The Insular per capita taxation is only $2.30.   The annual budget in 1930 was $38,826,345.   Since 1920 the trade of the Islands has varied from $175,780,943 in the post-war depression, to $300,-000,000.   The principal exports in order are sugar, hemp, cocoanut oil, copra, and tobacco..   The principal imports are cotton, steel, mineral oils, rice, flour, meat, automobiles, silk and coal.

During the Democratic administration of Governor Harrison, from 1913 to 1920, the Government of the Philippine Islands entered business to a considerable extent.   They invested their funds in a National Bank, sugar centrals, a railway, cement factory, hotel and other business enterprises. Unfortunately, when Governor Harrison arrived he was confronted with a serious financial situation in Government finances.   This was followed later by the post-war world-wide depression and many bank failures.   The National Bank was placed in charge of a man who proved to be both inexperienced and dishonest.   There was evidence of incompetence, reckless

---

[1] Forbes, Vol. I, p. 247.
[2] *Budget for 1930, Philippine Islands*, p. 26.
[3] The Viceroy of India receives $90,000, the Governor of the Straits Settlements, $60,000, of Hongkong $35,000, of Ceylon $35,000. *Budget for 1930*, p. 35. Nicholas Roosevelt, *The Philippines*, p. 260.

speculation and misappropriation of funds for which the President, General Concepcion, served a term in prison. An American named Miller, head of the Shanghai branch of the bank, absconded with some millions. All of these things were duplicated during the panic in the New York Stock Exchange in 1929, but they were not suggested as evidence of unfitness for self-government on the part of Americans, and they are not necessarily so on the part of Filipinos.

The failure of the National Bank was, however, a heavy blow to Government finances. For several years now the bank has been making a profit and is slowly repaying its liabilities. Several of the other business ventures are also making an annual profit.[1]

Past History of the Philippines

While some may not wish to dwell upon the past, there is no other way adequately to understand the present situation in the Philippines than by a brief review of their history. The Filipinos are prevailingly a Malay people, but of mixed race modified by migrations from China, Japan and India. From about 200 to 1325 A. D. they belonged to the Hindu-Malayan empires set up throughout the Indies, and were enriched by the culture of both India and China. They were pagans but largely converted to Islam in the southern islands. Magellan's fleet discovered the Philippines in 1521 in his memorable voyage, seven times longer and far more hazardous than that of Columbus, during the former's first circumnavigation of the globe. The Spaniards promptly claimed possession of the Islands for the King of Spain but the Filipinos offered stout resistance, killing Magellan and many of his men in battle, so that of his proud fleet of five ships but one ship and eighteen men returned to Spain.[2]

---

[1] The losses of the National Bank in fixed deposits and capital stock were written off of $39,975,965. *Auditor's Report*, 1929, p. 11. The Manila Railroad made a profit of $2,053,744, the Manila Hotel of $58,769, and The Cebu Cement Co. a profit of $215,064 during the last year of operation. *Auditor's Report*, 1929, pp. 353–360. It should be remembered that there were bank failures all over the world and especially in the Far East during the depression of 1921 and 1922.

[2] Blair and Robertson, Vol. XXXIV, p. 143; Forbes, Vol. I, p. 30.

The permanent conquest and occupation of the Islands began in 1565 with Legaspi and the Augustinian friar, Urdaneta. The monument of these two men stands today with sword and uplifted cross in beautiful Manila and is typical of the best that Spain had to give the Philippines through State and Church. The record of Spain for 377 years was on the whole creditable and of great benefit to the Islands. The warring tribes were welded into a fairly homogeneous people, nine-tenths of them were converted to Christianity, with increased health, population, prosperity and civilization. Under her one hundred and twenty-two Governors-General, Spain brought a ripe culture to the Islands.

The greatest contribution under the Spanish régime was made by the Church, which became the most potent factor for good in the history of the Philippines. Following the first friars, the Augustinian, Franciscan, Jesuit and Dominican orders poured into the Islands many of their best men who traversed sea and land with untold hardships and heroism to make converts and to educate and uplift the people. Typical of all the orders was the high educational work of the Dominicans in the College of St. Thomas, established in 1611, long before the landing of the Pilgrim Fathers or the founding of Harvard. Equally fine was the scientific and health work of the Jesuits. When the call came for volunteers to work among the lepers every Jesuit priest responded. The Franciscans, often in the spirit of Francis of Assisi, carried on their self-denying missionary labors.

But gradually their native ability, backed by the authority of King and Pope, gave the friars a dangerous monopoly of power, both spiritual and secular. They became the municipal rulers, immune from trial by civil courts, possessed of great wealth and of one-tenth of the best lands of the Islands, with the power almost of life and death over their heavily taxed tenants. Abuses grew in the Church and there was no authority that could check them. The Inquisition with its irresponsible tyranny was established in 1583. Monopoly of power led to luxury and corruption until finally an agrarian war was threatened and the uprising of the outraged tenants and peasants demanded the expulsion of the friars from the Islands. The rival power of the religious orders led to jealousy and division between themselves and between Church and State. Many celibates, far from home and tempted in the tropics, "who had meant to be heroes found themselves enmeshed in immorality."

The State in its unbridled power had imposed forced labor and heavy taxes upon the people, non-compliance being followed at times by invasions, torture and death. Against these practices the best minds of the Church protested to the Spanish monarch, but the oppressed peasants and intellectuals became finally more indignant against the abuses of the Church than of the State. The Filipinos were treated as inferiors and contemptuously called Indians, natives, or monkeys. The people finally demanded the expulsion of all the orders and when captured during the revolution many of the friars were beaten and some were cruelly tortured and put to death.

Although untold good had been done by countless high-minded and consecrated men, the fact remains that after a fair opportunity for more than three centuries, both in Mexico and in the Philippines, the masses in both countries were left in ignorance, superstition, poverty and oppression, and in both countries they had risen in revolt. At the time of the American occupation the population of the Philippines was less than seven millions, of whom few were educated and only seven or eight per cent could speak Spanish. Tuberculosis carried away some 50,000 people a year, smallpox 40,000, malaria some 35,000 and cholera as high as 100,000. There was almost no freedom of press or speech and little civil or religious liberty. Spanish rule at the end spelled tyranny and the people were rising in increasing revolt.

Indeed if one peruses the fifty-five volumes of Blair and Robertson's *Philippine Islands* they seem like one long record of revolt and revolution against wrong and injustice. Among literally hundreds, a few of the principal uprisings may be mentioned:

1521—Resistance to Magellan in which he and many Spaniards were killed.

1558—Revolt to expel the Spaniards from the Islands.

1574—Revolt of several chieftains and districts.

1649—Widespread uprising against forced labor.

1601, 1621, 1622, 1639, 1649, 1650 and 1661—Insurrections in northern Islands and attempts to found a native government.

1718, 1744, 1745-46, 1762-64—Revolts and uprisings put down with great bloodshed.

1744—Revolution in Bohol, lasting three-quarters of a century.

1807—Uprising in Northern Luzon demanding constitutional rights.

1813-1814—Revolt after abolition of Philippine representation in Spanish Cortes.

1841—Revolt of a Filipino brotherhood led by a student of theology, de la Cruz, put down with bloodshed.

1872—Revolt of laborers followed by execution of Filipino priests and leaders.

1888—The first popular demonstration against the Friars.

1892—A widespread, systematic Filipino campaign for freedom.

1896—Revolution on a nation-wide scale. Execution of Rizal, patriot, reformer and martyr that "sounded the death knell of Spanish dominion."

1897—Growing revolution under Aguinaldo throughout the Islands, surrounding the Spaniards in Manila, declaring independence of Spanish rule, and proclaiming the first Philippine Republic.

August 13, 1898—Capture of Manila by American forces.

Feb. 5, 1899—War against Americans, who employed over 70,000 troops and fought for three years to subdue the Islands.

No unprejudiced person could read through the fifty-five volumes of Blair and Robertson's history, especially of the growing spirit of revolution during the last century of Spanish rule, or Storey and Lichauco's account of the three years' insurrection against American occupation, and question that these people have passionately desired and demanded independence, and that they have been fighting for it for over four hundred years, first by forcible and now by peaceable means. No one can read the record impartially and deny that the Spanish occupation resulted in outstanding good but also in intolerable evils.

In 1897 General Aguinaldo had issued his proclamation declaring the independence of the Philippines, at the same time that the people in Cuba had been driven into revolt against Spanish tyranny and cruelty there. In 1898 the battleship *Maine* was blown up and the United States declared war on Spain. Two months before the sinking of the *Maine* Admiral Dewey, when in the Gulf of California, had planned to take Manila.[1] At the battle of Manila Bay on May 1, 1898, Admiral Dewey sank the entire Spanish squadron and three months later, on August 13, the city of Manila was captured by the Americans after a brief bombardment.

Both the American forces under General Otis and the Filipino insurgents under Aguinaldo had surrounded Manila and both sought to take it from the Spaniards. The Filipinos, resenting the American intruders as they had their Spanish conquerors, had apparently determined to provoke an attack on the part of the Americans, though the war was begun by the fire of the American troops upon the insurgents.[2] The Americans attacked and killed some three thousand Filipinos in the first day's fighting, General Otis reporting that the engagement "was one strictly defensive on the part of the insurgents and one of vigorous attack by our forces."[3] He refused Aguinaldo's efforts to prevent further hostilities and said that the war must go on "to the grim end."[4] The war was begun by the Americans on February 5, 1898, and was carried on for two and a half years with great vigor. At home President McKinley was saying "forcible annexation . . . cannot be thought of; that, by our code of morality, would be criminal

---

[1] Dewey sailed December 7, 1897 for Hongkong to prepare his squadron for the capture of Manila two months before the sinking of the *Maine*. See Dewey's *Autobiography*, p. 168; also Roosevelt's *Autobiography*, p. 231.

[2] Worcester, Vol. I, pp. 145–151 and Storey and Lichauco, *The Philippines and the United States*, p. 92.

[3] Otis' *Report to the War Department*, 1899, p. 99.

[4] *Congressional Record*, Jan. 11, 1900; *Proceedings of the Senate*, p. 770.

administration made strenuous efforts to fulfill the promises of self-government and preparation for speedy independence.

Unfortunately the record of the Governor's private life did not sustain the high standards maintained in previous administrations. Even his Filipino friends admitted many of his personal mistakes in judgment and policy. These, however, should not be charged to the Filipino people. It was during the Harrison régime that the disastrous commercial adventures were made in the National Bank, etc. Despite these losses there was a steady advance in relations of good will in the system of popular education, the successful conduct of national and local elections and an improvement in many of the economic conditions of the country. Governor Harrison maintained that "the extension of self-government and spread of democracy may in themselves have impaired somewhat the efficiency of administration," yet "that disadvantage has been more than offset by the gain in contentment of the people, the growth of respect and friendship for the United States, and the valuable lessons in self-government secured by the Filipinos."

Probably a neutral observer from another country who was neither a partisan Republican nor Democrat would agree to both sets of facts. There was a slump in the efficiency of many departments. There was also a notable advance in lessons learned in self-government and a more kindly and cooperative attitude on the part of the Filipinos than under any previous administration.

There are certain factors that are shaping the Philippine Islands today. Among these creative and constructive forces might be mentioned the following: the educational system, the Roman Catholic Church, the Protestants, the Masons, the Americans and the Filipino people. Of the educational system and its splendid contribution we have already spoken.

Of the Catholic Church Governor Forbes writes: "It has been one of the most potent determining factors—perhaps *the* most potent determining factor—for good in the history of the people."[1] It gave to the Filipinos the Christian religion, spir-

---

[1] Forbes. Vol. II, p. 50.

itual teaching, moral standards, the saintly and self-denying lives of many of its priests, especially in the earlier days, the uniting force of a common heritage, the uplift of womanhood, the higher standards of the first nation of the Orient to be Christianized.

The *Catholic World* makes the sweeping claim: "When all is said, the success of the Church in the Philippines is as great as the circumstances would permit, and infinitely greater than Protestantism or any other religion has made in any other mission field."[1] But Catholics as well as Protestants know the evils that had gradually crept into the system. The friars who had taken the vows of poverty, chastity and obedience found themselves possessed of a tenth of the best land of the Islands, with vast wealth and political power. To settle the problem of this friar land, Governor Taft visited Rome and after months of negotiation, paying more than double the price fixed by the government appraiser, negotiated for the purchase of a part of it, or 410,000 acres, for $7,239,000. The more than one thousand friars whose expulsion the people had demanded were reduced in five years to 246.[2] When Mr. Taft failed to secure the immediate eviction of the friars, a Filipino priest of the Roman Church, smarting under the indignities and humiliations of the people, organized a schism of some two million members to break from the Roman Church in 1902. He took a rational, modernist, independent and nationalist view and by 1905 claimed five million followers. With the court decision which gave the church buildings to the Roman Church and the political and unspiritual character of the movement, it rapidly waned until in 1918 it had but 1,417,448 followers.[3]

The places of many of the Spanish friars were taken by American priests with an entirely different political outlook

---

[1] *Catholic World,* October, 1898, p. 122. Laubach, *The People of the Philippines,* p. 83.

[2] Of the 1,142 friars in the Islands in 1896, 40 were killed, over 300 were held prisoners, others fled from the Islands. Several were tortured by infuriated mobs. Laubach, *The People of the Philippines,* p. 114.

[3] *Census,* 1918, *Statistical Bulletin,* pa. 5. The Roman Catholics numbered 7,790,937 with over 75 per cent of the population, the Aglipayanos 1,417,448, the Protestants 124,575.

and tradition. They adopted a policy of Filipinization with many of the clergy and some of the bishops drawn from the people. Forced to face the challenge of the Protestant Churches, the Aglipay schism, the public schools and American ideals, the Church has striven earnestly and successfully to put its house in order. The Roman Church is much better than it was in Spanish times; just as the Catholic Church in the United States is today, if compared to conditions that prevailed in Mexico after it had had despotic power there for more than three centuries. Robertson admits that "the competition has served a good end for Catholicism." [1]

The Protestant missionaries who began to arrive in 1899 found a wide open door. Their influence spread rapidly and by 1918 the churches included 124,575 members. The entire community may be nearly three times that number at the present time. The Protestant movement brought in the open Bible which previously had been kept from the people. It emphasized lay leadership, the spirit of liberty, individual initiative, popular education and moral reform. Its missionary spirit places before the Filipinos the responsibilities of the first people to be Christianized in the Orient. Its emphasis on freedom gives leadership to the independence movement among its pastors and laymen. Its Filipino leadership, self-support and evangelistic zeal make it one of the constructive forces in the Islands today.

The fraternal order of Masons has also been a strong and silent agency for progress in the Islands. Spanish and Portuguese Masonry was introduced into the Philippines in 1856, at first among Spanish liberals and later as a rallying center for liberty-loving Filipinos. So rapidly did the movement increase that "all secret organizations" were forbidden in 1888 and no man dared speak his mind. Banishment, imprisonment or death became the lot of the reformer. But the movement could not be crushed and both in Spain and in the Philippines it became the haven of lovers of liberty and justice in the darkest times. Even today, against any menace of the old

---

[1] *Catholic Historical Review*, 1917, Vol. III, p. 387.

tyranny reasserting itself, the Masonic order would be the first bulwark, aided by liberal Catholic laymen.

Enough has already been written to show the contribution that Americans have made to the development of the Islands. Comparing the administration of the British in India with that of the Americans in the Philippines, we believe that British rule in India has been perhaps the finest instance in history of the government of one people by another, but that the Americans have furnished the most striking example of the rapid development of a people for self-government in the interests of the people themselves. The characteristic of their régime has been American efficiency and Filipino autonomy. If carried through to its logical conclusion it should furnish a powerful example against western imperialism. America has furnished, on the whole, able and sympathetic men in the civil administration of the Philippines. She did not develop many of those great statesmen and distinguished representatives such as characterized the Indian civil service from Lord Macaulay to Lord Curzon and Lord Irwin in India. She lacked the ripe culture of Britain or of ancient Spain. But she furnished what perhaps was even more useful for the Filipinos themselves, and they are not ashamed today to say, with all self-respect, that they are grateful. It is devoutly to be hoped that this experiment in nation building may be brought to a successful conclusion before gratitude and cooperation give place, as they have so often in history, to bitterness and hatred. The Anglo-Saxon sometimes has the unhappy faculty of doing the right thing in the wrong way when it is just too late.

Finally, may we close with the mention of what seems to us to be the chief constructive force in the shaping of the Islands whether in the past, the present or the future—the Filipino people themselves. They are, of course, far in advance of the simple, undisciplined Malays of the backward islands of the Indies. They are a fine people; they may become a great people. The future lies in their hands and they want to shape it for themselves. The foreigner has undoubtedly helped them much, but he has also inadvertently hindered them, as fond parents often hinder their children.

These words are written as the Islands fade from view in the distance. Our last sight was of Fort Santiago and the Luneta where patriot-martyr Rizal was shot by a Spanish firing squad in 1896. Undoubtedly the tendency to hero-worship and apotheosis has already been at work, as on the tradition of Washington and Lincoln. But this man seems to gather to himself and to incarnate the spirit of the Filipino people, both in their brave struggle for liberty against Spanish tyranny in the past and in their hope of complete national independence in the future. The picture of the last decades of Spanish rule is vividly portrayed in his realistic novel *Touch Me Not,* translated into English under the title *The Social Cancer.*

The brief period of partial liberty under the Spanish Republic in 1869 had been succeeded by the forces of reaction and the vengeance of the friars. In 1872 three Filipino priests and patriotic laymen were tried and tortured to death. Martial law followed with the arrests of suspects and wholesale deportations, resulting in colonies of exiles. Liberal Filipino youth escaped to Spain and founded *La Solidaridad,* a paper like Garrison's *Liberator.* One of the leading contributors was the young genius, José Rizal. He was brilliant and versatile —a physician and oculist, painter, sculptor, poet, novelist, linguist. It is doubtless something of an exaggeration to say he "felt at home in fourteen languages," or to say with William Dean Howells that his novel *Touch Me Not* was the greatest book written in any language in fifty years. But it was the *Uncle Tom's Cabin* of the Philippine Revolution. Rizal's novels were condemned by the friars and thereby widely advertised. They were passed secretly from home to home. They exposed at once the tyranny of Spain, the corruptions of the friars, and the slave mentality of the people under their rule. "The Filipino people had found their soul." Rizal was an idealist, almost a pacifist, who longed to be loyal to Spain. When he returned to the Islands he was arrested and sent into exile, thus silencing the one Filipino who stood absolutely for peace. In exile he became the idol of his people. In the confessional a plot was exposed of a secret society, the

Katipunan. The Archbishop demanded "fire, sword and wholesale executions." Six hundred prisoners were thrown into the dungeons of Fort Santiago. Governor Weyler, after his ruthless methods in the Philippines, was now trying to crush insurrection in Cuba by the terror of his cruel concentration camps. General Aguinaldo issued his proclamation for independence and was leading the revolution among the Filipinos. The Spanish Governor had already deported 1042 persons but the friars demanded blood. Rizal was one of the first victims. After exile, repeated arrest, and imprisonment, he was given a farcical trial with his arms tied behind him and men clamoring for his life. On the morning of December 30, 1896, he was taken out to be shot. His alcohol cooking lamp which he left with his sister was later found to contain a poem of farewell to his people, which fell like a kindling flame upon their hearts after his death.

He asked to be permitted to face the firing squad but even this was denied him, though he tried to turn and fall face forward after the firing. "The volley that brought death to Rizal sounded the knell of Spanish dominion in the Philippine Islands." But it did more. It gave the Filipinos a deathless ideal of liberty such that they will be almost as unwilling to live permanently under American benevolent paternalism as under Spanish tyranny. Surely no Anglo-Saxon, after the Magna Carta, no American mindful of the Declaration of Independence, can fail to understand the soul of a people who in the person of Rizal say with one voice—the *Philippines shall be free.*

CHAPTER VI

TURKEY'S NEW REPUBLIC

Upon our return to Turkey we found a new Republic in place of the tottering Ottoman Empire that we had known, the massacres of "Abdul the Damned" which we had followed at Adana, and the last of the Sultans whom we had seen at Constantinople. The awakening of Turkey during her Renaissance of the last generation, her recovery from defeat in the World War, the establishment of the stable and successful Turkish Republic, and the sweeping reforms carried out during the last half decade have astonished Europe and sent a thrill of hope throughout Asia, almost approaching that occasioned by Japan's victory over Russia in 1905.

Merely to catalogue the principal reforms undertaken makes an imposing array. At the risk of oversimplification we may divide these into secular and religious, those involving the construction of a new order and those incident to the destruction of the old. Among the constructive secular reforms we may note briefly the following:

1. *The new spirit of nationalism,* the new Republic and the new Parliament have taken the place of the medieval Sultan and the decaying Ottoman Empire. Turkey, which was so long the dread of Christendom and the "Sick Man of Europe," has become a challenging example to the now awakening East. The old theocracy of the successors of the Prophet has been displaced by a growing democracy under the new President. Upon the ruins of the old empire of Abdul Hamid, after five years of heroic struggle, from 1918 to 1922, a young republic was founded upon Western ideas and the principles of the French Revolution, supported by growing public opinion and the national spirit of modernism. In contrast to the autocratic spirit of her former Sultans, behind the seat of the new

207

President of the Grand National Assembly of Turkey in 1923 there hung the Turkish inscription: "Sovereignty belongs to the people."

After thirty centuries of warfare about these strategic straits and thirteen centuries of strife between Moslem and Christian, and between the intrigues of degenerate Turkey and the ruthless imperialism of the Western Powers, the world is apparently now witnessing a new and stable peace in the Near East. There is even a rapprochement and friendship between Turkey and Greece, a new cordiality between Kemal Pasha and Venizelos, with Turks and Greeks cheering each other for athletic victories in the Balkan Games. This is a remarkable achievement in view of the strife of the past and the recent war between these two peoples, with savage atrocities on both sides.

2. *The new alphabet and resultant changes in language, literature and printing* marked the most sudden and dramatic of the new reforms. After some months of preparation and warning, on a single day, December 1, 1928, the old classic Arabic alphabet that bound Turkey to the past and to the East was swept away and forbidden, and the new Latin characters or Roman alphabet used in America and over most of Europe were finally adopted. On November 1, 1928, Mustafa Kemal Pasha, as President of the Turkish Republic, opened the second session of the Third Grand National Assembly by an address upon the new alphabet, pointing out the importance of the reform and its far-reaching advantages to the country. His speech was broadcast over Turkey. At the close of the address, Parliament resolved itself into a special committee to deal with the Alphabet Bill and it was finally passed into law by the unanimous vote of the House without modification. After January 1, 1929, all departments of the government, all business administration, all books, newspapers and periodicals might use no other script. All shop signs and street names were to be completely latinized; all official communications and formalities connected with the government must employ only Latin characters. The Assembly and Law courts were given one year in which to effect the change in their reports and

records. On the historic point of Seraglio, where emperors and sultans had ruled for sixteen centuries, the President announced the adoption of the new alphabet and the campaign for literacy. The Turkish races of Russia also adopted the western letters. This is the more significant when it is remembered that there are twice as many members of the Turkish race in the Russian and Chinese republics as in Turkey itself. Where Enver Pasha failed to conquer the eastern Turks by the sword, Kemal Pasha is now conquering them by the pen. The new letters will link Turkey with the whole modern world in its life and literature.

Such a bold and costly innovation, involving great difficulty for the educated classes, would have occasioned a storm of opposition in almost any other country. It would have been impossible, for instance, amid a conservative and individualistic people like the Chinese. Yet such was the faith in the President, and the spirit of the New Turkey, that the nation was willing to go to school at the Gazi's [1] bidding with real enthusiasm. During our recent visit the people pointed proudly to photographs of the President himself teaching classes in the new script. When a backward people, hitherto noted for their conservatism and medievalism, can willingly apply themselves to mastering a foreign script so radically different from their own, which had been read from right to left, anything may be possible in the future. By such heroic changes Turkey has both amazed and encouraged other Oriental peoples.

3. *The new education* followed logically the adoption of the new characters. Adult schools with day and night classes were at once established. One Turkish journal estimates that under the old régime 90 per cent of the people were illiterate but that 43,000 were in attendance in the popular schools in Constantinople in 1931. Wholly illiterate persons began to study the new characters in their shops and homes; vendors studied them in the streets while exhibiting their wares. Turkish optimists claimed that nearly half the population began to

---

[1] Gazi or Conqueror, the title formerly given as "Conqueror of the Infidels" to successful generals and successors of the Prophet.

learn the new characters and that already one-fifth of the people could begin to read newspapers and books in the new style, although the estimates were doubtless too high.

A new national system of education was organized to supervise all schools based upon the educational systems of the West. History, science, philosophy, modern languages, together with practical subjects designed to aid agriculture, industry and commerce, held a prominent place in the curriculum. Physical training and athletics have become popular. Many modern primary schools have been opened during the last six years. European and American systems of education are being applied and foreign teachers employed. Anglo-American texts are being adapted or translated. As in Japan and the Philippines education has been given a central place in the policy of the government. It will mean much for the future when all Asia goes to school and seeks to draw the best from the cultures of the Orient and the Occident. The Turks enthusiastically hope to become a literate nation within a decade of the adoption of the new alphabet, but it will doubtless require a much longer time.

The new education was a creative and far-reaching reform. The sultans had long neglected Moslem learning while the Christian communities had prized education and captured trade. They had seized upon the advantage of the education provided by foreign schools, American, French, German and Italian; while Moslems, as in India, had become an educationally backward community. Now all this has been changed. The government quickly opened new primary and secondary schools as well as technical and commercial colleges. Kemal Pasha misses no opportunity to emphasize the importance of education, to avoid the Turk's past error of leaving a monopoly of learning, commerce and industry to the subject races.

In many places the people themselves have opened popular schools at their own expense. Reading rooms are being opened. The Government hopes in time to open schools in all villages that are without them. At the recent congress of teachers held in Angora it was decided that there should be one brief course in Turkish literature but that there should be full courses in Western classics and the history of Western literature.   This will open vast streams of influence in Turkey.

4. *New codes of law* have taken the place of the old Moslem Sheriat law, one based upon the Swiss Civil Code, one upon the German Commercial Code and a third upon the Italian Penal Code.   New methods have been applied to the courts. Many of the old Turkish courts were religious tribunals; the new courts are occidental even to the dress of judges and counsel.   The spirit that is behind this change implies that new laws will in time mean new life.   A rule of law when finally realized under a constitutional government will mean a transformation of conditions in the Near East.

5. *A new womanhood* is appearing in Turkey, resulting partly from the new laws and system of education.   Women are being emancipated from the ancient custom, based upon the teaching of the Koran, which forced them to veil themselves in public, to be segregated in the women's department or harem in the home, and to occupy secluded and inferior places set apart for them in public conveyances and buildings.   The streets of the cities today are filled with unveiled Turkish women, and they now mingle freely with men in society.

The new Swiss code took the place of the old Islamic family law providing for polygamy and easy divorce, which had degraded and wronged women for centuries.   This law will mean the final social unification of the Turks with European nations and will give the Turkish family the kind of stability which is in accordance with the Western ideal.   The Swiss code will probably prove to be the Magna Carta for Turkey's new womanhood.   Women can now claim a secure place of equality and companionship in a monogamous home.   The spirit of the new Turkey swept away the corrupt harem and the eunuch system.   Polygamy has been condemned and subsequent to a certain date entrance into polygamous relationships has been declared illegal.

In old Turkey women had no security.   If a husband tired of his wife he had but to repeat three times a declaration of divorce in a single sentence and the marriage was dissolved and the home ended.   Women were thus left defenceless

under the old laws.[1] Today a woman may choose her own
husband.   The couple are married in the town hall and both
sign the marriage documents in the presence of the mayor.
Divorce can only be decided by a court of law as in Switzerland.   A revised Islamic law providing license for men by
easy divorce would have brought new Turkey nearer to Russia but would have left her without this foundation stone of
the stable monogamous family.

A new law now gives women the right to vote in municipal
elections.   They are already candidates for the city boards
and will eventually run for Parliament.   Under the old régime
woman had but limited influence even in the home circle and
none at all outside of it.   She played no part in the affairs of
the nation.

Women have now gained permanent educational rights that
can never again be lost.   Education for girls quickly became
popular.   Foreign schools and colleges for girls were filled
and the University of Constantinople became coeducational.
Turkish girls may now study for any profession they choose.
A few are active in business.   Thousands of them are working
in factories and mills.   The emancipation of Turkish women
in the last two years will add thousands of clear brains and
healthy arms to the creative and productive capacity of the
nation.

In the cities women have entered into the professions of
teaching, law, medicine and various forms of social service.
Writing, lecturing and agitation for reform have been successfully undertaken.   In the country their old life will continue
until the coming of modern agriculture, which will in time be
influenced by the advance of collective and industrialized
farming near at hand in southern Russia.   Probably nine-

---

[1] Mohammed's law of marriage and divorce read: "Marry what seems
good to you of women by twos or threes; and if ye fear that ye cannot
be equitable, then only one, or what your right hands possess (female
slaves). . . . Divorce may happen twice. . . . Then keep them in reason
and let them go in kindness. . . . But if he divorce her (a third time)
she shall not be lawful to him after that, until she marry another husband."
The Koran, Chapter II, verses 226, 230; Chapter IV, verse 3.

tenths of the women still belong to the poor, hard-working class, but the spirit of emancipation is alleviating their lot, if not yet lightening their work. In the cities at least women have been freed from the confinement and subordination of centuries.

Many of these modern practices are in direct opposition to the teaching of the Koran and the practice of Mohammed. New laws, new education, new customs, new home life, a new place in the national economy will gradually produce a new womanhood for Turkey.

6. *A new manhood* and a new faith in the common man are appearing in Turkey. The stolid peasant is now recognized to be fit for something more than gun-fodder to fight in continual wars, or as a possible source of exorbitant taxes wrung out of his poverty to supply luxury-loving sultans with revenue. The new democracy is beginning to reveal the worth of the individual man, his rights and duties, his possibilities when educated and developed.

The new Western dress, the discarding of the fez, once a mark of privilege and a sign of loyalty to Islam, for the Western hat, are but outward symbols of a more significant inward change. It marks by a dramatic gesture the abrupt turning of Turkey from the East to the West, from the past to the future. In intention it marks the putting off of the old and the putting on of a new way of life.

The new Western calendar was adopted in 1926. A new census was taken in 1927, carried through like that of India in a single day. The census returned 13,660,275 as the population.

7. *The new era of building* is typical of the new Turkey. Over $100,000,000 has already been spent in the creation of the new national capital at Angora with its imposing buildings. The Parliament buildings, the Agricultural Bank, the Ministry of Health and Social Welfare, the Rockefeller Institute for Sanitary Research, the government offices, modern hotels, homes and institutions have a direct bearing upon the living standards of the nation.

Scores of villages, which were destroyed by the armies of occupation, have been rebuilt with local means and without foreign loans. Over Constantinople there still broods something of the spirit of the past. The walls of old Byzantium, the seraglio of the sultans, the whole setting of that ancient center of corruption and intrigue cannot be changed in a day. But in Angora Turkey has made a fresh start. Here one finds the symbol and epitome of the dynamic new Turkey. Like the new yet ancient capitals of India at Delhi and of Russia in Moscow, Angora is a more impregnable military center than the older capital by the sea, and a safer radiating center for the new nationalism. In place of the decaying splendor and degenerate ease of Constantinople, Angora represents the spirit of creation, of hard work, and of self-reliance of the new Turkey. The old destroying Turk, as a soldier or corrupt official, is giving place to the creative pioneer. He has sternly left the soft palaces of Constantinople with their oriental luxury to build his new city set on a hill, and to make this wilderness blossom with his new dry farming. Here on every side rise the modern buildings with the speed of a Western boom town, yet with the permanence and beauty of a modern city. Doubtless too much money has been invested in this façade of stone, bricks and mortar. Perhaps it would have been better to have lived in more stoic simplicity and to have first built up scientific agriculture and industry as in Russia. But the very buildings are typical of the progressive, indomitable spirit of the new Turkey which will in time permeate the whole peninsula.

Today in Angora it is not the ancient Hittite, Greek or Roman ruins and influence that pervade the place, but the spirit of Henry Ford and modern industrialism. As Arnold Toynbee says: "Americanism expresses the feel of Angora today . . . in Ford cars and in four story reinforced concrete buildings; but what is important and interesting is the spirit that these things embody, and that is the spirit of the pioneer . . . The pioneer spirit of America is just what Turkey needs, for it is this vital element that was lacking in the life of the Turkish people before. There used to be a saying that 'grass

does not grow where the Turkish horse-hoof has trod.' " [1]
The old Turk was a destroyer; the new Turk is a builder.

8. *A new agriculture, industry and trade* mark the modern
economic era despite Turkey's very limited natural resources.
Home industry has been encouraged by a system of protective
tariffs.   Sugar factories, textile mills, cement works and
other factories aim to meet the basic economic needs of the
country.   The Government has recently encouraged the production of wheat, sugar and cotton.   Coal mines have been
opened on the Black Sea within 150 miles of Constantinople.
New railways are being built to open up Turkey's resources
of copper, silver, lead and chrome.

On October 29th the Turks annually celebrate the anniversary
of their young Republic, founded in 1923.   Politically they
have accomplished much but economically their problems are
still grave.   The new government was left with a legacy of an
enormous public debt under foreign control.   War had reduced the man power of the nation and had expelled the non-
Turks with their business skill and capital.   The new political
independence led to a series of economic mistakes.   The transfer of some 400,000 refugees of the Turkish minority from
Greece was not conducted with the same ability as that of the
Greek refugees to their homeland, and there was much needless
suffering and privation.

It was long supposed that the Turk, hardy soldier and
sturdy peasant though he was, could never succeed in any economic field, as the business of Turkey had always been conducted by the shrewder and more practical Greeks and
Armenians.   But once the latter were excluded from the An-
atolian peninsula and populations exchanged the Turk developed in practical ways most commendably.   Yet there is
still the inheritance of the old inefficiency, slackness and pro-
crastination.   Massed inertia will be slow to move, for there
has not been the volcanic upheaval and drive of the Russian
revolutionary spirit to change Turkish psychology.

Agricultural machinery is little used and production is at
low ebb.   Although primarily an agricultural nation, only a

---

[1] *The Nation and Athenaeum*, Sept. 28, 1921, p. 820.

fifth of the land is under cultivation, and that often with depleted soil and without fertilizers. Their primitive agricultural methods, plowing with an implement little better than a crooked stick, threshing with sledges dragged over the grain, leave them as an agricultural people still backward.

The Government has established several endowed agricultural schools in various centers and within its inadequate budget has made heroic efforts to introduce modern methods to aid the farmer. The President's farm near Angora, with its modern tractors, furnishes a model. The Turks have shown enterprise and met with success in their export of figs, tobacco and cotton. Production in the economic zone of Smyrna has shown progressive increase. The raisin and fig crops are increasing. The production of wheat and other cereals is steadily rising so that the importation of wheat into this agricultural country should soon cease. The Government is giving increasing attention to the development of agriculture as a chief source of the nation's real strength.

Industry and trade are even more important than agriculture in the modern world and Turkey has made earnest efforts in this field, though with only a fraction of the possibilities or herculean achievements of Soviet Russia. The natural inheritance of suspicion of foreign financial interference left Turkey without adequate capital. Nevertheless, this created a new spirit of self-dependence and self-help in the Turk. The Government nationalized several industries on a monopoly basis. The former monopoly on salt was followed by the tobacco and cigarette-paper industry, the manufacture of matches, alcohol and liquors, and the subsidizing of the sugar industry. Infant industries have been encouraged in canning, paper, porcelain, olive oil, textiles and jute. With over half the revenues, however, claimed for the public debt and defense, all constructive advance in economic, educational and social fields is hampered. Credit and capital are the monopoly of the few. Turkish commerce and export trade are without organization. Only about two per cent of the population controls the political destinies of the country. Incomes of the professional classes are diminishing. Foreign capital has been largely driven out and the country is suffering for the lack of it. In her material welfare Turkey is not only poor and undeveloped but not working sufficiently along modern lines.

9. *New roads and railways* are opening up modern Turkey. The Ottoman Empire had built some 1,242.7 miles or 2,000 kilometers of railway in 50 years entirely with foreign capital. The new Turkey, during the last decade, has built an equal amount with Turkish capital. There are now 3,063.2 miles in operation, while seven new lines covering 1,391.8 miles are projected and will be built within five years. Many of the railways are for military requirements but the new roads and highways are to meet the economic needs of the farmers.

In addition to the above constructive secular changes there have been certain religious reforms in the program of the new Republic:

1. The position of the Caliph of Islam, as the religious and political head of the entire Mohammedan world, had been held for centuries by the Sultans of the Ottoman Empire, as successors of the Prophet Mohammed and defenders of the Islamic faith. The abolition of the Sultanate in November, 1922, inaugurated a long series of reforms. After the abject degradation of the Sublime Porte before the foreign powers, the Sultan was accused of high treason and was summoned for trial. He fled for his life on board a British battleship. After abolishing the Sultanate, the Nationalists boldly abolished the Caliphate on March 3, 1924, and the following month adopted the new Constitution of the Republic. Turkey now surrendered her position as the center of Islamic authority, both temporal and spiritual, for a Western political nationalism, and left the disintegrated Islamic world without leadership or unity, thus removing the barrier which separated a hostile Pan-Islam from the Christian world. This has tended to turn militant Moslems from the thought of a holy war to the tolerance of peace and cooperation in a friendly society of nations. The reactionary and fanatical portion of Islam has naturally viewed these sweeping changes with silent hostility.

2. The Islamic Church and State, as we would call them in the West, were now separated for the first time in Moham-

medan history.   Islam was a theocracy in which the civil ruler
was also dictator in matters of religion.   The whole machinery
of government had been built around such a central autocracy.
The new Republic, as a theoretically democratic state, was now
created in place of the autocratic theocracy.   The greatest
obstacle to progress in Turkey had long been its slavish submission to the literal legalism of Islam and to the tyranny of
custom.   All this was swept away.

3. Church and law also have been separated for the first
time, at least technically and legally.   There are now no recognized religious courts, and religious questions are supposed to
be excluded from the civil courts, on the ground that the state
has nothing to do with religion.   This rules out the Koran, the
Sheriat, and religious tradition from all legal proceedings.
Even the oath in court is no longer taken on the sacred books,
nor in the name of God.

4. Church and school, religion and education, are now separated.   Schools for boys were formerly connected with the
mosques, presided over by an often ignorant hodja.   These
schools have been completely abolished.   The old hodjas with
their powerful reactionary influence are forbidden to wear the
white turban or pose as teachers unless they pass an examination in the topics taught in the secular schools and hold teaching
certificates.   Religious instruction has been abolished both in
Turkish and foreign schools.   Instead, home atmosphere, education and voluntary religious worship on the part of the individual are considered sufficient means of religious development.

5. The dervish sects have been prohibited and their property
confiscated by the government.   These emotional and zealous,
though often reactionary, dervishes were frequently the defenders of the faith most ready to take up arms on behalf of
the old religion.   Mohammedan monasteries, cloisters and
mystic institutions have now also been prohibited. Religious en-
dowments have been nationalized to some extent and Turkey
has become a severely secularized state.   It was felt that no
progress could be made and no reforms would be secure if the
people remained under the influence of religious fanatics.

6. Religious liberty has been declared for all Turkish subjects. In treaties made with England, France and other counries, it is declared that: "All inhabitants of Turkey should e entitled to free exercise, whether in public or private, of any creed, religion or belief, the observance of which shall not be incompatible with public order and good morals." Atrocious massacres of Armenians, as under Abdul Hamid, are probably a thing of the past. Complete religious liberty, as understood in England and America, will probably be a slow growth in Turkey, but it is proclaimed at least in principle. Missionary colleges and schools may conduct chapel exercises and religious worship for Christians but Moslems are not permitted to attend. Foreign schools are allowed to give instruction to their Christian pupils in their religion if they obtain the consent of their parents. In certain Turkish schools two hours a week are devoted to instruction in Islam from the most novel textbooks, which are a strange compound of modern nationalism, patriotism, and a diluted and newly tolerant Mohammedanism.

The Koran, hitherto so sacred that its truth could only be expressed in Arabic, has been translated into Turkish and widely circulated and studied, but with more enlightened criticism and less blind dogmatism. The statement that "Islam is the religion of the State" has been dropped from the Constitution. The apparent aim of the government has been to free the religious spirit from the restrictions of superstition, dogmatism and tyranny and to develop individual liberty.

Turkey's Past

To appreciate the significance of the present reforms, we must briefly recall the background of Turkey's history. The Turks had captured Constantinople in 1453 from the degenerate Byzantine rulers, thenceforward holding the gateways and trade routes to Asia, forcing the European maritime nations to discover new sea routes and thereby a new hemisphere. It is hard to realize that for two centuries the Turk had threatened European civilization, being the aggressor against the Germans and Magyars, until finally turned back in

1683 at the second siege of Vienna by the Polish leader Sobieski.

In revolt against the corrupt and degenerate Ottoman Empire under Abdul Hamid, the Revolution of the Young Turks in 1908-1909 had abolished the despotism of the Sultan and promised a democratic constitution. Although they introduced many reforms, they betrayed their trust by instituting a tyranny almost as great as that of Abdul Hamid himself. It was left for Mustafa Kemal to carry out the reforms which the Young Turks had promised but had not fulfilled. Revolting as a young radical against the unspeakable régime of Abdul Hamid, he became an enthusiastic Young Turk in the revolution of 1908 with experience in battle, imprisonment and exile. He became a military hero in the Balkan Wars. Later as a young general he won fame by defeating the British forces at the Dardanelles at the first Anafarta landing.

Turkey's strength had been drained and her man-power depleted by the long period of internal corruption of the Sultans' rule and by incessant fighting.[1] After Turkey's defeat in the World War, Constantinople was occupied by the Allies, the French took Adana, the Italians occupied Adalia, and on May 15 Smyrna was occupied by a Greek army under the protection of Allied and American guns, financed by the government of Lloyd George.[2]

It was Kemal Pasha who formed the new Nationalist Party and called the national convention at Angora when he was made commander-in-chief of the army and head of the state. Here the National Pact was adopted which became Turkey's Declaration of Independence. The Turkish soldiers, after a dozen years of war and defeat, gathered at Angora like the battered troops of Garibaldi, or of Washington at Valley Forge,

---

[1] In the war with Italy in 1911–1912, the first and second Balkan Wars in 1912–1913, and the World War in 1914–1918.

[2] On March 15, 1920, British and Allied forces under General Milne had seized the public buildings, proclaimed marshal law in Constantinople, arrested members of the Turkish Parliament and deported them to prison in Malta. Undaunted, Kemal Pasha called the National Assembly which declared Turkey's independence of foreign nations and of the Ottoman Government which had sold itself to foreigners.

and they fought as bravely. The Greek advance in the war of 1919-1922 had been marked by atrocities and a reign of terror.[1] After the Greeks were defeated before Angora in 1922, they retreated, burning Turkish villages as they did so.

It was due to the leadership of Mustafa Kemal and the loyal Turks who gathered about him that they turned back the tide of the Greek invasion which was so powerfully backed by British finance and expelled by force or diplomacy four foreign armies which were on Turkish soil—the Greek, British, French and Italian—won a sweeping diplomatic victory over the Allied powers in the Treaty of Lausanne in 1924, and began to build a progressive, nationalist, modern state on the ruins of a decaying empire. No wonder he was affectionately acclaimed the Gazi or Conqueror by his loyal and admiring people.

The Gazi is a short, thickset man with piercing black eyes and an intense, earnest look. He has proved himself a real soldier and statesman. His chief diversion is found in his horses and his farm, but he also fancies tennis, billiards, jazz dancing and poker playing. The Puritan element that has been so powerful a factor in the lives of so many reformers has been entirely absent in his training and character.

The character and policy of the Gazi were shown in the recent Menemen affair, when he dealt swiftly and ruthlessly with religious fanaticism. On December 23, 1930, a Moslem named Dervish Mehmet, who called himself the Mehdi, together with five armed companions appeared in the town of Menemen and tried to incite the population to join with them in shouting, "We want the Sheriat Law." A considerable crowd gathered, many of whom seemed to be in sympathy with the dervishes. A young student officer named Kublay Bey interfered, warning the dervishes that they were committing treason. They promptly shot him and hacked off his head. Finally gendarmes shot Dervish Mehmet and one of his companions and arrested many others. A court martial was ordered and for weeks the newspapers contained little except reports of the affair. These dervishes were of the Nakshibend

[1] *Report of Inter-Allied Commission on the Greek Occupation of Smyrna,* October 12, 1919; *Turkey,* by Arnold Toynbee and K. P. Kirkwood.

order and it was believed that they were incited in some measure by an aged Sheikh of the order who lived in Constantinople. On the 4th of February twenty-eight of these men were executed. Seven other men were sentenced to twenty-four years in prison. Others were condemned to serve fifteen years.

There was indication in the affair that if the reactionary dervish forces once got the upper hand hell would be loose in the land. The Gazi evidently decided to take this as an occasion for very effectually and completely squelching any demonstration of dervish activity. The whole incident was used as a piece of gigantic propaganda to show the whole country that at least the dervish type of Mohammedanism is inimical to the Republic and will be treated with no mercy. Parades were organized among students and meetings were held to stir the youth of the land to an appreciation of their part in making secure the principles of the lay Republic. The Government is quite obviously placing its hopes upon youth, as in Russia and Italy. The Menemen affair was probably a flaring up of religious fanaticism and not at all an organized attack against the dictatorship, but the incident was used as a means of striking another blow at the old Moslem mentality of the past.

In May, 1931, the newly elected Turkish Parliament, consisting of ninety-seven per cent members of the Gazi's party, elected him President for the third time without a dissenting vote.

The character of Mustafa Kemal is reflected by his followers, the Kemalists, and by the whole spirit of the new Turkey. It is virile, fearless, progressive, absolutist, but peaceful in relation to foreign powers. The driving force and loyalty of the new patriotism is Turkey's largest asset. If there is any truth in the contention that each country has the government it deserves, Turkey is no exception. If it is a one-man government, the majority of Turks are content with their measure of growing responsibility. A soldier himself, the Gazi has increased the civil control of posts originally given to his trusted military officers. His desire for peace was shown during the Mosul crisis with Great Britain in 1925-1926. Yet he has demanded that nearly half of the budget should be spent for military defense. He has held aloof from the League of Nations, maintaining an independent stand, steering a middle course between the two great powers of Britain and Russia. He has no use for Communists and has shown no hesitation in hanging them when deemed necessary, yet he has manifested a desire to develop friendly political and trade relations with Soviet Russia to the mutual benefit of both countries. The Gazi will tolerate no effective Communist propaganda in his nationalistic state, and the Russians seem to accommodate themselves to his policy, using Constantinople only as a center for their Near East propaganda, but not troubling Turkey itself. They apparently desire a friendly Turkey that will be amenable in time of crisis with her neighboring frontier, her open sea and ports.

In all fairness it is necessary to consider some of the limitations and shortcomings of the new régime in Turkey. The government is a dictatorship in the midst of a growing democracy. Although perhaps a necessary evil, dictatorship is none the less an evil. When as a student of the French Revolution the Gazi, together with the Nationalists of Turkey, accepted the principle of popular sovereignty, it could not be in the sense of the ripened democracy of Abraham Lincoln. It was not the hard-won victory of a people but the ideal of a few leaders for the former subjects of a theocratic Sultan and Caliph, whose highest virtue had been Islam or submission.

At first the enormous prestige of the Gazi gave him all the powers of a dictator like an Oriental Cromwell or Napoleon. Such a dictatorship inevitably aroused criticism, and quite naturally, in the supposed interests of the country against all foes, the Kemalist dictatorship began to shackle the Turkish press. From December, 1923, special Tribunals of Independence were instituted, like the French Committee of Public Safety, or the Russian Cheka, for trials on charges of treason. These naturally became, as in Russia and Italy, a kind of political inquisition, arresting editors and intellectuals, suppressing outspoken journals, and smothering opposition, under an enlightened and progressive despot. As both the creator and leader of the Popular Party, the Gazi could easily dominate Parliament.

In March, 1929, the law of Maintenance of Order was abolished.   This law had made possible a party dictatorship and a suppression that amounted almost to a reign of terror for the opposing minority from 1925 to 1927.   Far too many "plots" have been discovered and summarily dealt with.   There is real need of the development of a genuine democracy in Turkey. Only on April 30, 1924, the new Constitution was promulgated. The Prime Minister, Ismet Pasha, apart from the Gazi the finest political mind in Turkey, reasonably suggests that a period of twenty-five years should be allowed for the Turks to become "a civilized people."   The period when it is thought that favorable opinion must be maintained by exclusively optimistic reports or propaganda must give place as rapidly as possible to constructive, critical realism.   One man alone cannot reform a nation.   The reason why some daring reforms have been accomplished with Turkey still lagging behind in other practical matters is thus expressed by one editor: "We have a great man capable of solving great problems, while the machinery for small matters is entirely out of order."   This can and will be gradually built up by slow growth, but the heart of Turkey's real reform will not be spectacular like the changing of the fez or the alphabet.   Men's hearts and habits change but slowly.   Russia, Japan and other countries show that even the ideas, habits and psychology of a people can in time be changed.   Turkey, like Russia and Italy, is suffering from over-centralization in this necessary and temporary transitional period.   She has good reason to dread foreign interference, but she has not as yet shown the same willingness to avail herself of foreign technicians as the new Russia or Japan.

Another sign of autocracy is the treatment of minorities. The non-Turkish subjects have all the duties of citizens without their privileges.   They pay the same taxes and serve in the army, but are practically excluded from Parliament and from public office.   Greeks and Armenians for the most part have been removed from Turkey, and are mostly confined to the city of Constantinople as a sort of ghetto.   The Minister of Justice said: "Friends and enemies alike should realize the fact that in this country the non-Turks shall never enjoy equal rights with the Turks." [1]   In many respects their condition is worse than it was a generation ago.

A typical and costly example of autocracy and exclusive Turkish nationalism was the expulsion of the Greeks and Armenians from Anatolia.   It is true that the Turk has improved since he has been compelled to stand on his own feet.   Politically a gain in unity, it was an economic loss to expel the Greek and Armenian artisans and business men.   Turkey may lose as France did permanently after the expulsion of the Huguenots, and Spain of the Moors.   Such are the inevitable handicaps of autocracy.

The old Ottoman Empire was based on the recognition of the political and economic privileges of the European Powers and on the separate ethnical and religious status of the non-Turkish races.   The two fundamental aims of the new Turkey are its political and economic independence, after centuries of outside interference, and its creation of a homogeneous Turkish nation.   For generations the Greek and Armenian Christian communities had been used as pawns by the intrigue and military designs of the great powers such as Russia, and had meant for the Turks control from without by European nations and endless internal trouble.   The latter came to a head in the fanning to flame of religious fanaticism by the atrocious Armenian massacres permitted under Abdul Hamid.   It seemed best to many neutral observers once for all to exchange populations between Greece and Turkey.   Painful as was the process, resulting in privation and terrible suffering for many of the refugees and migrating inhabitants, both Greece and Turkey are now more peaceful and prosperous and have profited by the exchange.

It is difficult for the Westerner to understand the strength and the novelty of the new nationalism in Turkey.   The veteran editor, Ahmet Ihsan Bey, in his memoirs traces the birth of the new nationalism to 1898, its activity in the revolution of 1908, its revival in full strength under the Gazi.   In his boyhood, as the son of a Turkish official, this editor says they depended upon Greeks as physicians, pharmacists, shopmen,

[1] Mahmoud Essad Bey in the *Stamboul,* July 28, 1928.

grocers, carpenters, barbers, peddlers, boatmen, and other work-men. They turned to Armenians as bankers, shopkeepers, tailors and money lenders. The Turks were government offi-cials, military officers, soldiers or dervish chiefs. "All of the Turks looked down upon and hated commerce, business and industries. . . . One could not see any Turk at the railroad stations, at banks and other business centers. Even the print-ing press, book business, publishing of papers and magazines were all in the hands of non-Turks." ´

The former Minister of Justice Mahmut Esat Bey, who introduced the Swiss Civil Code, says: "Vineyards, gardens, even mountains and plains, real estate and personal property, the whole economics of the country, were they not in the hands of those who were not Turks? Today all these have passed into Turkish hands. And this is the fruit of the policy of the People's Party." It is perhaps natural that the new national patriotism and pride of the Turk should somewhat turn his head. The Minister of Justice adds: "The Turk is the lord of this country. Those who are not real Turks have just one right in the country of the Turk, that is to be either servant or slave."

Shortly after this insolent speech, which would have denied economic justice to Greek and Armenian citizens who were left in Constantinople, the resignation of this minister and indeed of the whole cabinet was called for. It is not strange that the new nationalism in Turkey should take the same naive, boastful and provincial forms that are so familiar among all other "pe-culiar peoples." Members of the Faculty of Medicine, after examining a thousand skulls and skeletons, found that "the Turks are the most perfect and highest of all the races in Turkey regarding ability and other characteristics." [1] Another author modestly states that: "The root of all tongues is Turk-ish; that Turkish civilization is earlier than all other civiliza-tions; that the foundation of Greek civilization is Turkish; . . . The Turks established the first democracy thousands of years

[1] *Milliyet,* May 19, 1930.

before Christ; the first parliament was Turkish . . . Our Great Savior, the Gazi, made Turkey; now he will make the Turks." [1]

However shortlived, the formation recently of the new Liberal Republican Party marked a milestone of advance in the Turkish Republic in the matter of democracy. Up to that time but one party had been permitted as in Russia and China, the People's Party of the Republic of which the Gazi was the titular head and the Prime Minister, Ismet Pasha, the active president. After repeated conferences with the Gazi and doubtless with his permission, Fethi Bey, a former Prime Minister, addressed a letter to the President on August 9, 1930, openly accusing the Party in power with having mishandled the government and thereby increasing the economic distress of the country. He asked permission to form a new party. This was granted by the President in his reply. The two letters throw light upon Turkey's present internal situation. Fethi Bey speaks of the prevailing dissatisfaction in the country over the financial and economic distress owing to shortcomings of the government officials. He finds the cause "in the fact that the Grand National Assembly is composed of only one Party. In fact since the members of the Party have refrained from criticizing their own Cabinet, free discussion in the National Assembly has diminished and the government has remained in a condition that can be called irresponsible."

The principles of the new Liberal Party were stated as republicanism, nationalism and laicism, or secularism. Its aims showed their opinion of the country's needs. These included liberty and security, reduction of the heavy taxes, public economy, stabilization of the currency and encouragement of foreign capital and trade, less government interference in economic enterprise, strengthening the Agricultural Bank with loans at low interest for peasants and farmers, the development of domestic arts, crafts and industries, greater government efficiency, the elimination of bribery and abuse, the reform of the courts, friendly relations with other countries and with the League of Nations, direct elections and full political rights for the womanhood of Turkey.

[1] *Cumhuriyet,* June 19, 1930.

In the President's reply to Fethi Bey on August 10, he said: "The free discussion of national affairs both in the National Assembly and before the nation . . . is a system which I have strongly favored from my youth . . . I count it as one of the fundamentals of the Republic that there should be a new party . . . I will lay no barrier in the way of the carrying on of your party."

The new party appeared to thrive for about three months. Although there were not really free elections and few dared to vote the new ticket, a few members were permitted to be elected to Parliament by Ismet Pasha.   A new spirit of healthy criticism appeared, so much so, in fact, that at one time it appeared that there might be a landslide in favor of the new party.   But when Fethi Bey found that his party was forced into opposition to the Gazi, he dissolved the party.   The position of the President is sacrosanct like that of the King of England.   He is at once the head of the government and yet above it and beyond criticism.   All this possibly indicates a wise handling of the situation on the part of Mustafa Kemal, bringing forward one reform at a time, or as fast as he thinks the people are ready for it.   Even this shortlived second party did much good and opened the door wider toward a much needed steady democratic advance.

Religion in Turkey

The Government's attitude to religion in Turkey is problematical.   Many have interpreted its position as an effort to destroy Mohammedanism.   Its drive to break the reactionary power of Islam with its stultifying control over life and to establish a purely secular or lay state was unmistakable.   Expelling the dervishes and mendicant orders, forbidding their meetings, confiscating religious property, crippling the power of the hodjas, closing the mosque schools and discarding the fez were all signs of the times.   The cynical attitude of many of the leaders held up religion to ridicule and as a result youth often becomes indifferent or contemptuous.   The Turk is naturally somewhat slothful, not deeply spiritual and perhaps the least earnest of all Moslem people. The younger generation now begins to discard religion as an outworn superstition.

The Government has been indicating its own attitude in its textbooks and in its inspired articles that the whole system of Islam has been a harmful and reactionary foreign influence, Arabic and essentially non-Turkish, and that Turkey must now face West for its new inspirations. The *Politica,* the Gazi's personally controlled evening paper, recently carried a long series of articles for two months under the title "How the Turks Became Mohammedans, or An Inside Picture of the Arabic Sultanate." These articles violently attacked the whole Arabic system and left the impression that the Arabs were a good people until they accepted Mohammedanism, then they became corrupt, developing the passions of avarice and murder.

Literary men are encouraged to find the source of Turkey's greatness in the pre-Mohammedan period when the Turks were said to have a really wonderful civilization which included many of the later discoveries of classic Greece and modern Europe, but a continued subtle attack is being made upon Islam. In some respects the goverment has left the Moslem community less free and independent than the Christians. In part they are "chained to the policy of the government." Ultimately Islam must be left free for spiritual progress, but it was probably one of the many necessary evils of the dictatorship to shatter some of the superstition, bigotry and petrifaction of the old system. Such iconoclasm, however, is always dangerous in its destructive phases and young Turkey has been deprived of the inspiration and steadying influence of needed spiritual guidance by the secular iconoclasm of the dictatorship.

The Constitution makes the neutral declaration: "Every adult Turkish citizen is free to adopt the religion he or she wishes to adopt." But many of the old religious institutions have been abolished and the government schools give almost no religious instruction, while at the same time attendance at the mosques is steadily declining. The government has not encouraged nor even permitted some needed reforms proposed within Islam. Religion has been taken out of the state, but not the state out of the control of religion. A complete and consistent separation is needed on both sides at this point. Political influence and interference have been the bane of religion in Turkey in the past. It should be completely removed for the future.

The Gazi is a soldier and a political statesman with apparently little personal interest in either religion or morality. It is possible that he and some of his associates, rather cynically contemptuous of religion as a reactionary force, would have preferred an atheistic secular régime like the Communists of Russia, had they deemed it possible or politically expedient. As it is, they seem to have gone as far as they dared in crippling or handicapping reactionary Islam. The Constitution only six years ago declared the Moslem religion to be that of the Turkish state. In 1928 this article was repealed with apparently complete indifference to the feelings of, or the possibility of challenge from, the more fanatical adherents of Islam. It is to be hoped that the present destructive phase in the government's attitude to religion will pass and that the Gazi, dissatisfied as he well may be with the manifestations of religion that he has seen in the past, may look for something better both for himself and the nation.

In the struggle during the last eight years between nationalism and Islam, the former has won every encounter and the latter has steadily given way. This would have been impossible if religion in Turkey had been modernized or socialized or had a strong hold upon the intelligent portion of the community. The separation of church and state has also failed to afford more tolerance for non-Moslems. Although the government is officially pledged to freedom of religion and of speech, and to permit the following of all professions without distinction of race, creed or language, yet these provisions seem to be increasingly disregarded in practice. All important offices are reserved for Moslem Turks, and pressure has been brought to bear for the use of the Turkish language in the streets and public places.

The Turks have prohibited by law all proselytizing among minors and they require the tacit acceptance of this principle by the foreign missionaries who choose to remain in the coun-

try under these conditions. A real attempt to convert a boy
or girl student to Christianity would bring the missionary
under the penalty of the law and probably lead to the punishing
of the offender and the closing of the school, as happened in
Brusa where four pupils became personally interested in Christianity and a light legal sentence was imposed upon the missionary. The press is quickly aroused over even the rumor of
a case or two of the conversion of adherents of Islam to
Christianity. It is strange that in the growing indifference
to and neglect of their own religion there should be such deep
hostility to any change of faith on the part of the individual
and as yet so little genuine tolerance in public opinion. This
will doubtless be a matter of slow growth. Both the spiritual
and educational mission of Christianity and of a future reformed Islam should be allowed to make their full contribution
to the national life of Turkey if the nation is to develop its
latent possibilities or to build the strong moral character which
the youth and the new leadership of the country so deeply need.
Though more modified and tolerant, something of the same
tendency to secularization and hostility to religion are observable in the new Turkey that were to be found after the French
and Russian revolutions. Turkey is still living in the negative
period of the tearing down of the old order. Anything in the
nature of religious discussion is still considered out of order.
Religion has a bad name throughout the country and it is
fashionable for educated men to profess disbelief in it.

It is significant, however, that at the personal request of the
Gazi the Department of Education recently printed for use in
the Turkish schools Ludwig's *Son of Man* and also Dermeng-
hem's *Life of Mohammed* which treats of the Prophet as one
who was never opposed to Orthodox Christianity of the Western churches.

It is a sign of the times also that the old weekly magazine
Ictihat,[1] while printing a poem addressed to Jesus as the
Prophet of Love, begins a series of articles on the *Life of
Mohammed* quoted from the formerly condemned volume of
Dozy's *History of Islam*. The articles describe how Moham-

---

[1] June 15, 1930.

med, after the death of Khadijah married Suda, then Ayisha,
"a child of ten years who still played with her toys," then
Hafsa, Zenhab, and Ummi Salma. "But Mohammed did not
suffice with these five wives." Upon visiting Zaid, a former
slave, now his adopted son, he became enamored of his wife.
Zaid divorced her to accommodate the Prophet. Mohammed
soon had "a revelation from Allah in which he was allowed
to marry the wife of Zaid. . . . This revelation was simply
the result of his own personal wish, but faith in him had
become so strong and deep that his followers accepted this
revelation to be as good and genuine as other revelations."

Such articles are not only permitted but welcomed in the
new Turkey. They show that a cast iron system that bears
the mold of Arabia of the seventh century, with its obsolete
attitude to women, to war, to slavery and other social issues,
presents a very real spiritual problem to Turkey and the Mohammedan world, for "Islam is a spiritual problem even to
itself." Without the stern social discipline of Communism,
or the dynamic of the Sermon on the Mount, where is Turkey
to find the power for its moral reformation and spiritual
regeneration?

The new attitude of the government to religion is strikingly
shown in three textbooks recently issued by the Department
of Public Instruction entitled *Religious Lessons for the
Children of the Republic.* It is an attempt to interpret Islam
in terms of nationalism. Since the Prophet enjoined alms-
giving Turkish children are urged to be religious by contributing to the Airplane Society: "The fatherland cannot be
protected by prayers, as the old blind fanatic leaders thought,
it is protected by arms, by strength, by soldiers. . . . A few
aeroplanes can devastate with five or ten bombs a great city.
. . . Therefore we ought to give alms to the Aviation Society."

Instead of the angels, demons, heaven and hell, or a holy
war to exterminate the infidels, as found in the Koran, we
have a modern religion of science and of toleration: "Islam
is the religion of science and civilization. . . . There is no
room in Islam for the queer stories about angels . . . nor for
such a prophet as the Christians have. . . . In Islam there are

no foolish ideas which do not appeal to the mind." The first fundamental of their religion is not "Islam, tribute or the sword," but now it is "not to interfere with the religion, the belief or the work of anyone. . . . The religion of Islam forbids fanaticism. It leads toward new ideas and civilization. . . . Islam is the easiest and truest religion. . . . The Mohammedan religion is a perfect way for human beings. . . . The character of the Prophet was absolutely perfect. . . . Children, you know that Christians have priests and that without them they cannot worship. However, a Moslem may worship either at home or, if he wishes, in the mosque."

"Our country will always go forward, and will always conquer our enemies. When the name Turk is spoken my chest swells with pride, my head goes up. . . . The greatest worship of God is to love Him, to be a good man, to serve our government, our fatherland, our nation, and afterwards all mankind. . . . Religion is goodness of character. One who serves his nation, fatherland and government is also a religious man of faith. . . . Long live the Turkish nation and the Republic."

Such is the religion that has been recently taught in some of the schools for two hours a week instead of the instruction once given in the old mosque schools.

The old Turkish Empire occupied the heart of the Near East which has always been regarded as the early homestead of our Western civilization. It included the sacred places of the great monotheisms of Judaism, Christianity and Islam, and the great battlefields of the ancient world. Here Joshua at Hazor left "not any to breathe." Here the Emperor Basil II caused all of his 15,000 Bulgar captives to be blinded and sent home. Here were the scenes of the Armenian massacres. Yet in these regions the American Red Cross spent $2,000,000 in ministering to the civil population during and after the war. And here in modern Turkey, that was once ancient Asia Minor, American colleges have been making a notable contribution to the training of the new leadership for the whole Near East.

The American Board of Commissioners for Foreign Missions began missionary operations in Turkey in 1819, more than a hundred years ago. The Turks were naturally hostile to their work in the beginning. The Armenians were the first to respond, followed by the Greeks. No attempt was made to proselytize among these ancient churches. American missions and indigenous Protestant bodies in Turkey long maintained nearly five hundred institutions from the kindergarten to university grade, with some 25,000 pupils and students in attendance.

Robert College is still the most important foreign institution in Turkey. It occupies a splendid location on the outskirts of Constantinople, fronting the blue Bosphorus, with its imposing buildings and assets valued at more than three and a quarter million dollars. Its 750 students represent twenty-five nationalities. Before the war it trained the Bulgarian, Armenian and Greek leaders. At present about half the students are Turks. The college was founded by an enterprising young American missionary, Cyrus Hamlin, who went out to Turkey in 1829, over a century ago. During the Crimean War he built a steam flour mill and sold hundreds of thousands of loaves of American white bread and roasted coffee to the English army and to the hospital made famous by the work of Florence Nightingale. More than $25,000 of his profits he invested in new buildings. With the wise financial backing of Christopher Robert, a far-sighted merchant of New York, he founded the institution which is now named Robert College, and remained for seventeen years as its president. Such early and obscure investments of life and money on the part of a few discerning pioneers from Great Britain and America have raised up a significant leadership in all the seven countries of Asia which we are considering in this volume, and there is no need to belittle or ignore this leadership, whatever may be the fad or fashion of the moment among us.

Constantinople Women's College, with nearly five hundred students in attendance, is training many of the future women leaders of Turkey. These colleges are typical of smaller institutions whose influence will be incalculable.

In the nine schools of the American Board in Turkey ninety per cent of the enrollment is Turkish. The Gazi's adopted daughter has been a student at one of the schools, and another daughter has attended Constantinople College. Other high officials have sent their children to the American schools which are working loyally in training the leadership of the new Turkey.

The American missions, in addition to their effective educational and medical work, are rendering valuable service in agricultural and village work, in the development of playgrounds, reading rooms and wholesome literature. Books like Booker Washington's *Up From Slavery* and Barton's *Life of Lincoln* have been used extensively by the Department of Education.

The Friends of Turkey are also rendering valuable aid. A group called The Society for the Helping of Benevolent Projects has been organized in Angora with twenty-one representative Turkish men and women as members. Cooperating with Mr. Asa Jennings and other Americans they are launching new projects in the way of supervised playgrounds, athletics, reading rooms, the publication of literature, etc., where Americans assist with half of the cost and the Turkish cooperating organization with the other half. Such wholesome cooperation is most promising for the future.

Next in importance to the American educational work, but outnumbering the American institutions, are those of French origin. Before the War there were over a million pupils in the Turkish Empire in schools under French management, while over two million persons secured relief or assistance in French hospitals, clinics or charitable institutions which were subsidized liberally by French government funds. Even now the French government pays the salaries of teachers of the French language.

America, with no territorial ambitions, with no memory of imperialism and intrigue from the past to live down, and with a good record in education, philanthropy and friendship, is in a peculiar position of opportunity and responsibility to aid the Turkish people in their worthy efforts to create and build a new national life. This is part of the challenge of the East.

CHAPTER VII

Palestine was an ancient battleground and meeting point of three continents, Asia, Africa, and Europe. It is today the center where the three great monotheisms of the world impinge upon one another, Judaism, Christianity and Islam—a "Holy Land" to all three religions. The Wailing Wall at the western base of Solomon's Temple has become a bone of contention between Moslem and Jew in their bitter conflict over the holy places sacrosanct to both. Jerusalem, the sacred city of the Jews, containing the Holy Sepulchre as a place of pilgrimage for Christians, and a place of conflict between the Roman and Greek Churches, is, next to Mecca and Medina, a revered city also to Moslems. It contains one of their three or four most sacred mosques. It marks the traditional site of Abraham's sacrifice, the scene of Christ's crucifixion, and of Mohammed's traditional ascent to heaven. In modern times Palestine was designated by Great Britain's promise in the Balfour Declaration as the National Home for the long-persecuted Jewish people. Yet according to the Arabs, it was previously promised by the British through Sir Henry McMahon, when he was High Commissioner for Egypt, to the Sherif Hussein of Mecca, as included in the Arab lands that were guaranteed independence, contingent upon their entering the War on the side of the Allies against Turkey. Under a mandate of the League of Nations, supported by international public opinion, all the world has a stake in Palestine. In the midst of the present controversy we have need sympathetically and objectively to evaluate the various factors in the situation.

Sometimes called the "least of all lands," the average length of Palestine from north to south is but 160 miles and can be traversed in a few hours by automobile, and its extreme width from east to west is only about 70 miles. As defined by the

British mandate, Palestine covers some 10,170 square miles in extent. It is about equal in area and resources to the state of Vermont, and less than one twenty-fifth of the area of Texas.

Apart from its rich coastal plain, widening from two hundred yards to twenty miles in extent, the hot Jordan Valley and the Plain of Esdraelon, it is chiefly a mountainous plateau of barren hills, "desolate to the last degree of desolation." Once seeming to a desert folk a land "flowing with milk and honey," its hills have now been denuded of much of their former soil, and have suffered from centuries of foreign conquest and Turkish neglect. Of its 6,500,000 acres only about two-fifths is now cultivable. Of some 4,000 square miles that can be cultivated Jewish individuals or organizations now possess 400 square miles or about one-tenth of the available land.[1] There are now 135 Jewish agricultural settlements with a total population of approximately 35,000.[2] The story of the heroic struggle of some of these colonies is a romantic one but almost none of them has as yet reached the point of economic self-support.[3]

Palestine is a poor country with slender natural resources.[4]

---

[1] *Shaw Report,* p. 23.

[2] The colonies are of three types: first, the older individualistic or bourgeois colonies on the right, second the cooperative colonies in the center, third, the communistic or communal colonies of mutual sharing on the left. These are Tolstoyan rather Bolshevist. The few political Communists in Palestine are foes of Zionism. *Palestine Today and Tomorrow,* John Haynes Holmes, p. 176.

[3] The budget of the Zionist Organization has been about five million dollars a year. The Joint Palestine Survey Commission found that the cost of settling a Jewish family on the land varies from $5,000 to $7,000, as compared to $600, exclusive of the grant of land, required to establish a Greek refugee family. Sir John Campbell, one of the experts of the Joint Palestine Survey Commission, wrote: "The broad fact which emerges is that no single colony is at present on sound economic ground, irrespective of the date of its establishment. No repayments have been made. . . . From the time the work in Palestine commenced, there has been continuous and heavy over-expenditure, relative to income."

[4] The area of Palestine is 10,170 square miles. The unit division of land there is the dunam, which is about a quarter of an acre. The 27,000,000 dunams of land in Palestine may be thus divided:

10,000,000 dunams already cultivated
2,500,000 more are cultivable

Before the War there was no industrial development, but through Jewish enterprise many small industries are now being developed. There are already some 3500 small industrial establishments, employing only 18,000 workmen, with a total capital investment of some $17,000,000.[1] An important hydro-electric concession has been granted to Pinhas Rutenberg for the Palestine Electric Corporation, to utilize the water power of the upper Jordan; and power is already being supplied to several cities and towns. The potash deposits of the Dead Sea may also prove commercially valuable. George Adam Smith maintained that the total population of the country "is much less than that of the Province of Galilee alone in the time of Christ."

The small annual budget of the Government of a little over ten million dollars shows an occasional deficit and it is difficult to make ends meet.[2] The trade balance has been of late increasingly adverse, the imports being from three to four times the exports. Equilibrium has been partially adjusted by immigration, tourists and charity. After 1926 Palestine experienced a severe economic depression and Jewish immigration had to be curtailed.

The officially estimated population in 1929 was 898,000, incuding 660,000 Moslems, 150,000 Jews and 79,000 Christians; but excluding about 103,000 nomads.[3] The Arabic-

---

[1] Industries consist of brick making, the manufacture of vegetable oil, cement, soap, flour, salt, textiles, furniture, chocolates, matches and smaller cottage industries. The principal exports are wine, soap, olive oil, oranges and lemons.

[2] The average annual budget has been $11,375,000, of which $2,683,565 is devoted to defense. Taxation averages $9.25 per capita. *Shaw Report*, p. 19.

[3] *The Shaw Report*, p. 8, 1929. The population at the time of the census in 1922 was 757,182, of whom 590,890 were Moslems, 83,794 Jews and 73,024 Christians. Mr. Maurice Samuel in his *On the Rim of the Wilderness* estimates the present population at about 910,000 of whom about 170,000 are Jews and over 700,000 Arabs. Of the Arabs, the Moslems outnumber

    7,500,000 pasture, forest or urban land
    7,500,000 uncultivable.

The Commissioner of Lands estimated the total cultivable area as 12,233,000 dunams, while the Director of Surveys, followed by Sir J. Hope Simpson, places it at only 8,044,000.

speaking Arabs include both Moslems and Christians. Together they constitute about five-sixths of the population and are united in the present controversy. The hundred thousand Arab nomads who have always settled the Arabian peninsula still dwell in their portable tents of black goat's hair. The settled Arabs may be divided into the privileged class of landlords, and the working class, peasantry, or fellaheen whose position has, on the whole, been improved under the mandate.

Throughout much of its checkered history of over 4,000 years, Palestine has been the prey of surrounding nations and a center of strife. Jerusalem was the scene of more than forty sieges and battles, and has been almost destroyed some thirty times. Armies from Syria, Assyria, Babylon, Egypt, Macedonia, Rome, Byzantium, Arabia, the Crusaders of Europe, the Turks in the sixteenth and seventeenth centuries [1] and under Napoleon in 1799 had trampled over Palestine in turn.

The British occupation of Palestine was based upon the conquest of the country in 1917 by the forces under General Allenby. Five weeks before Lord Allenby's entrance into Jerusalem, Mr. Arthur Balfour, then Foreign Secretary, made on behalf of the British Government this historic declaration over which there has been such fierce controversy between the Jewish and Arab population. [2] *"His Majesty's Government view with favor the establishment in Palestine of a National Home for the Jewish People, and will use their best endeavours to facilitate the achievement of this object, it being clearly understood that nothing shall be done which may prejudice the civil and religious rights of existing non-Jewish communities in Palestine or the rights and political status enjoyed by Jews in any other country."*

[1] The Turkish domination of Palestine lasted from 1516 to 1831 and again from 1840 to 1917.
[2] Declaration of November 2, 1917, indorsed by the Allied Powers, and embodied in the Treaty of Sèvres, which made provision that the country should be placed under a mandate to be approved by the League of Nations.

the Christians about eight to one. Of the 16,000,000 Jews in the world about 4,000,000 are in Russia, 2,000,000 in Poland, 1,000,000 in former Hungary. New York has the largest Jewish city population with some 1,750,000.

Ever since it was issued this Declaration, in the words of Sir Herbert Samuel, "has dominated the situation in Palestine." After the Balfour Declaration the Zionist organization sent a commission to Palestine to act as a link between the British authorities and the Jewish population and to look after Jewish interests of colonization, education, etc.

On July 1, 1920, a civil government was established under the able Jewish High Commissioner, Sir Herbert Samuel. Arab national sentiment, mindful of the promises that had been made to the Arabs during the War, was inflamed against the Zionist Jews and alarmed at what seemed to them their aggressive and tactless propaganda. Riots began in Jerusalem in April, 1920, and these were followed the next year by the outbreaks in Jaffa and later by fresh disturbances in Jerusalem on the fourth anniversary of the Balfour Declaration.[1] In 1922 the policy of Mr. Winston Churchill, the Colonial Secretary, which was welcomed by the Zionist organization, disclaimed the intention of creating a Jewish Palestine, or of subordinating the Arabs, but maintained the necessity of internationally guaranteeing a Jewish National Home in Palestine. This statement was rejected by the Palestine Arab delegation then in London, alarmed over what seemed to them the prospective loss of their country. They maintained a boycott against a proposed legislative council.[2]

The Government of Palestine is administered by Great Britain under a mandate from the League of Nations according to the constitution of 1922. It provides for the appointment of a High Commissioner, Commander-in-Chief and Executive Council. The High Commissioner appoints an Advisory Council. The Government recognizes the Jewish Agency which is the organ of the Palestine Zionist Executive, for the upbuilding of the Jewish National Home. It is unfortunate that the Government, in the words of Dr. Magnes, the

[1] In April, 1920, 9 persons were killed, 22 dangerously and some 200 seriously wounded. In May, 1921, 95 were killed, and 219 wounded. *Shaw Report*, pp. 12–13.

[2] The legislative council was to consist of the High Commissioner and 22 other members of whom 10 were to be officials, 8 Moslems, 2 Jews and 2 Christians.

head of the Jewish University, is "an absolutist colonial régime," and that the people of the land, both Arabs and Jews in proportion to their numbers, should not have a "voice in their own government." [1]

Jerusalem is a place of pilgrimage alike for Jew, Christian and Moslem. From 326 A. D., when the Mother of Constantine visited Palestine in order to locate the places of the birth, crucifixion and burial of Christ, Christians became interested and began to visit the Holy Sepulchre. From the fourth century onward multitudes of Christian pilgrims visited the shrines. The Crusades, whose pathetic record of superstition and slaughter from 1096 to 1291, did so much to inflame western Europe for the recovery of the empty tomb and the Holy Land, and to embitter Moslems by their atrocities, tended to accentuate the importance of these shrines for Christians. Up to the time of the war, multitudes of simple pilgrims from Russia and other lands could be seen on the roads leading to Jerusalem. There has been an age-long controversy between Greek and Latin Christians in Jerusalem focused in the feuds over the Church of the Holy Sepulchre.

Although there is much genuine piety to be found in all three communities, religion in Palestine is sometimes fanatical, fetishistic in the sense of being associated with inanimate objects and places, and political. This is true at times of the Jewish, Christian and Moslem communities alike. The clash between Moslem and Jew for the political and economic supremacy of the land is localized at the base of the western wall of the Jewish Temple, known as the Wailing Wall, where the Jews for centuries have met to commemorate the destruction of the Temple and the loss of their land.

The Wailing Wall and the pavement facing it is the absolute property of the Moslem community and next to Mecca and Medina the site is an object of veneration to their coreligionists.[2] The jealously watched and rigidly maintained

[1] *Like All the Nations,* J. L. Magnes, 1930, p. 13.
[2] *Shaw Report,* p. 27. Here Mohammed is supposed to have kept his charger when from the Dome of the Rock above he ascended to heaven on the occasion of his celestial journey. The Commission appointed by the

status quo of the place was infringed in 1929 by the introduction of a screen, benches, and other appurtenances of worship by the Jews.   Upon the protest of the Moslems the British District Commissioner visited the spot and explained to the Jewish beadle that the screen must be removed.   The beadle agreed but on the following day when this had not been done the British police forcibly removed it, to the great indignation of the Jews who claimed it was a violation of their service on the Day of Atonement.   The Moslems, angered by the encroachment of the Jews, retaliated by intruding upon the Jewish worship.

On August 15, 1929, a procession of patriotic young Jews to the Wailing Wall was conducted as an offensive demonstration, accompanied by the raising of the Zionist flag with cries of "the Wall is ours," "shame on those who profane the Holy Places" and "shame on the Government." [1]   Some 2000 Moslems conducted a violent counter-demonstration.   A few days later during a quarrel a Jewish youth was stabbed and his funeral "became in effect a political demonstration of the Jews against the Government and the Arabs," breaking through the cordon of the British police. [2]   Fanatical feeling was now rapidly fanned to flame on both sides.   To a neutral observer it would seem that neither party was free from blame, nor was the provocative press of both sides.   The British authorities, although striving to be fair, were not always as wise nor as firm as they might have been.

On August 23rd the Arabs surged out of their mosques and violent and destructive mobs attacked the Jews in Jerusalem, with but forty British police vainly attempting to maintain

---

[1] *Shaw Report,* pp. 52-57.   August 14th and 15th were the days of the Jewish Fast connected with the Day of Atonement, while the next day, August 16th, was the Moslem Sabbath and the eve of the Feast of the Birthday of the Prophet.   "The incident which in our view most contributed to the outbreak was the Jewish demonstration at the Wailing Wall on the 15th of August."   *Shaw Report,* p. 164.

[2] *Shaw Report,* pp. 52-57.

British Government with the approval of the League of Nations reported on June 8, 1931, that the Moslems have the sole ownership of the property. Both parties are to have free access for purposes of devotions.   No political speeches or demonstrations are to be permitted to either.

order. During the week that followed, in the riots and massacre on the part of the Arabs in Jerusalem, Hebron, Safed
and other centers, 133 Jews, 83 Moslems and 4 Christians
were killed.[1] Martial law was enforced and order was restored by British troops called in from Egypt and elsewhere.

The Arab Case

The Arab case, if stated alone, seems unanswerable. The
Arab points to the Balfour Declaration as the whole source of
the trouble. He maintains that there is a fundamental contradiction between the two clauses of the Declaration itself. A
small land with slender resources, how can it be handed over
as a National Home for another people drawn from all over
the world, without the consent of the inhabitants who have
been in possession for a thousand years, without doing these
inhabitants injustice?

Suppose, without consulting those in possession, and in complete violation of the principle of self-determination, someone
should from a distance make a "declaration" to provide a
national home for the Red Indians in Vermont. What would
the inhabitants of that state say to such a proposal? The Arabs
claim that much of the crime of recent years [2] was due to these
now landless and unemployed men, and that Jewish immigration has been more rapid than the country could absorb, which
has added to Arab unemployment and economic depression.
They had no difficulty in getting along with the Jewish settlers
and colonists before the War, but since the Balfour Declaration
it seems to them that, backed by Jewish wealth and British
bayonets and airplanes, a new type of young Jew, often arrogant and offensive, is entering the land. They object that
immigration which "should not exceed in numbers the economic capacity of the country to absorb new arrivals" has
been permitted beyond that capacity.

---

[1] Report of Mr. Arthur Henderson, Foreign Minister to the Council of
the League, Sept. 6, 1929. There were also wounded 339 Jews and 181
Arabs. Many of the Arab casualties were caused by rifle fire of the police
and soldiers. *Shaw Report,* p. 65.

[2] In 1920 the number of crimes was approximately 11,000; in 1924, 20,000;
in 1928, 27,000.

The Arabs have no quarrel with the Jews on racial grounds. The two peoples are Semitic cousins and lived together in prevailing peace here and throughout the Near East until the Arabs were alarmed and threatened with the dispossession of their own land. The Arabs remind the Jews that, for more than a thousand years before the latter entered and took possession, it has belonged to the Arab. The Palestine Arab Executive is an unofficial political organization claiming to represent the opinions of 80,000 Christian Arabs as well as 660,000 Moslems.

The Arabs know only too well that they are no match for the Jews, who are shrewder business men, better educated and backed by their world-wide organization. It seems to them that they also, sons of Abraham through Ishmael, are now being sent out into the wilderness away from their possessions. The Arabs claim that pressure has been brought to bear upon their simple peasant proprietors to sell their land. Like Esau they may be selling their birthright, but they feel that craftier Jacob is everywhere outwitting them and coming into possession. Even though a fair price is offered the improvident, individual Arab, they think they see their land slipping from them. Their lands, their suburbs, their banking and business, the water-power and natural resources, the wealth and education, and above all the whole power of government, including all the higher offices without exception have been held by the British or Jewish foreigner. Granted that they sold their barren land for what it was worth a decade ago, and now see it irrigated and raising its golden crop of oranges through the superior intelligence and enterprise of the Jew, still they seem to see themselves increasingly dispossessed and the Jew dominating the situation. A decade ago the Jews were one-ninth of the population, today they are a sixth, but their plans and propaganda point toward an inevitable majority.

As against the Balfour Declaration the Arabs point to previous promises that were made to them. They claim that in 1915 the British Government pledged itself to recognize the independence of the Arab countries, with the exclusion of Lebanon in which France was said to have certain interests.

Colonel Lawrence has told the world how the Arab peoples were persuaded to join in the War against the Turks, their fellow Moslems. The official correspondence is contained in letters exchanged between Sir Henry McMahon, then High Commissioner of Egypt, and the Sherif Hussein of Mecca. As the British have thus far declined to publish the whole of this correspondence, it is not yet certain whether Palestine was included in the area that was promised Arab independence, conditional upon their revolt to enter the War against the Turks.[1] Although the negotiations may not have reached final agreement, they certainly induced the Arabs to revolt against Turkey and stimulated the hope of Arab independence throughout the Near East. Subsequently the Sherif was recognized as King of an independent Hedjaz and Feisal, his son, King of Iraq.

The Arabs also quote Lord Allenby's proclamation of 1918 in their favor: "The object aimed at by France and Great Britain . . . is the complete and definite emancipation of the peoples so long oppressed by the Turks, and the establishment of national governments deriving their authority from the initiative and free choice of the indigenous population."

The Arabs claim that, although before the War they enjoyed wide powers of self-government and were on the same footing as the Turks themselves, since the Balfour Declaration, their former democratic system has been replaced by an autocratic British and Jewish administration in which they do not hold a single significant office,[2] and that they have been offered no democratic representation in the government in proportion to their numbers. They accordingly unanimously rejected the Constitution offered in 1922 and have ever since maintained a boycott against the Government. The Arabs maintain that

[1] According to the best available authority, however, Palestine was always excluded from the promises made to King Hussein by Sir Henry McMahon.

[2] "The Arab majority, then of 93 per cent of the population, was completely excluded from high posts of the government. . . . It is hardly realized amongst British people that the Attorney General and Legal Secretary, the Director of the Immigration Department, the officer in charge of Publicity, the Government Land Advocate, the Assistant Chief Secretary, besides many others, are ardent Zionist Jews." *Arab Statement on Palestine* to the British People, p. 3.

they are being heavily over-taxed in comparison to their position before the War, or compared with conditions in Syria and Egypt.

All about Palestine are peoples, including other Arabs, awakening with the demand for self-determination, in Arabia, Syria, Iraq, Egypt and India.   They feel that they have something of the solidarity and sympathy of the whole Moslem world behind them.   And Great Britain, which rules over some seventy million Moslems in India alone, is not unmindful of this sentiment.

The British Commission of Inquiry reports: "It appears to us obvious that the Arab attitude, the result of a dangerous combination of anger and fear, is a potential cause of future disturbance unless . . . the Arab people are satisfied that they will be adequately protected from either subordination or expropriation." [1]

The Grand Mufti

We sat with his eminence the Grand Mufti, civil and religious head of the Moslem Arabs of Palestine, and discussed the deadlock in the relations between Arabs and Jews in Jerusalem and throughout the Holy Land.   It was a striking scene. A fine-featured Arab of the desert, a lineal descendant of Mohammed, he appeared to be a man of quiet dignity and high intelligence.   We were sitting over a corner of the castle of Antonia, the former residence of Pontius Pilate and the Roman governors of the land.   Just below our window were the stairs of the castle where Paul made his defense before the infuriated Jews who had dragged him from the Temple to kill him. To the right lay the broad white limestone platform where once rose the sacred Temple itself.   In the center stands the Dome of the Rock, on the summit of Mount Moriah, where tradition holds that Abraham prepared to offer Isaac.   Farther to the right in Solomon's porch the early church was founded, and across the city is the Church of the Holy Sepulchre, held sacred by Christian pilgrims as the spot of Christ's crucifixion.

Far below the Temple area is a narrow alley way where

---

[1] *Shaw Report,* p. 98.

still stand the huge stones known as the Wailing Wall, that are supposed to have lain at the foundation of Solomon's Temple. Here, weekly or daily, pious Jews read the penitential psalms and the Lamentations of Jeremiah under their Temple of which there is now left not one stone upon another. Since he dare not enter the Temple area lest unwittingly he tread upon the ancient holy of holies, this wall is now the most sacred spot in Jerusalem, or the world, to the orthodox Jew.

We had talked with representative Jews and British officials. We were now anxious to hear the official statement of the Arab case from the Grand Mufti himself. During an interview lasting an hour and a half His Eminence spoke quite freely. We submitted the following written account of his own statement for his correction and authentication. The Grand Mufti said:

"We deplore all bloodshed and violence. We ask justice alone as the only possible means to peace in a land which is sacred to all three religions. During the War we fought on the side of the Allies and against Turkey. In 1915 we were promised independence for the Arab states, including Palestine. This promise was made to King Hussein by the High Commissioner of Egypt on behalf of the British Government. We understood that it was confirmed by the proclamations of General Maude in Bagdad on March 19, 1917 and by Lord Allenby in Jerusalem on December 2, 1917. President Wilson's fourteen points including self-determination further aroused our hopes of complete independence after the War.

"When the British under Lord Allenby entered Jerusalem they were received with joy. Then like a thunderbolt came the Balfour Declaration of November 2, 1917. This was to be our reward for winning the War—to hand over our country, which had been ours for the last thirteen centuries, as a 'National Home for the Jewish people'! Let us suppose that legislation were enacted in Washington, London or Geneva handing over, say California, as a home for the Japanese, or because of our occupation of Spain centuries ago, offering that land as a home for the Arabs. How would California or Spain feel about it? Whose are these countries that they could be given away by others to whom they do not belong and without their own consent?

"There have been events and encroachments on the part of the Jews at the Wailing Wall, but the root of the trouble is not in these occasional or surface happenings, but in the fundamental contradiction that lies in the Balfour Declaration itself, a document that we regard as unjust, unnatural and impossible. We have tried to keep the peace and be friendly to the British, but after a fair trial of twelve years we regard this Declaration as a complete failure and the cause of all the present trouble and friction in Palestine. We had no objection to the Jews who lived peaceably in Palestine before the War, and who had visited the Wailing Wall without molestation for some centuries. It should be remembered, however, that it is one of our sacred places also and that it is our property. We shall never accept the proposal to hand over our country as a national home for others. According to an Arab proverb: 'You cannot put two swords in one sheath.'

"Notice the fundamental contradiction between the two clauses of this Declaration. In a small land of such slender resources it is impossible to hand over our homeland as a National Home for an alien people, without prejudice to the civil and religious rights of existing non-Jewish communities. Again notice the contradiction and injustice in the last clause of the Declaration. While the 'political status enjoyed by Jews in any other country' is carefully preserved, so that every Jew from Britain or America or any other country is backed by his consul or representative and the wealth of the Zionist organization throughout the world, nothing whatever is said about the *political* rights of the vast majority of the population in our own land.[1]

"Here is the source of all the trouble in Palestine in the out-

---

[1] The Balfour Declaration reads: "His majesty's government view with favor the establishment in Palestine of a national home for the Jewish people and will use their best endeavors to facilitate the achievement of that object, it being understood that nothing shall be done which may prejudice the civil and religious rights of existing non-Jewish communities, in Palestine, or the rights and political status enjoyed by the Jews in any other country."

breaks of 1920, 1921 and 1929. The two promises are absolutely and diametrically contradictory. You cannot at once
provide in the same limited area independence for the Arabs
and a National Home for the Jews of the world. Because of
the financial assistance of rich Jews during the War the Balfour
Declaration was made. But after a dozen years of fair trial
the civil and religious rights of the Arabs have not been protected as promised. The Arabs constitute the overwhelming
majority of the population and our 700,000 people pay the bulk
of the taxes, yet we have not a single representative on the
Executive Council and have no voice whatever in the making
of the laws of the land. These are drafted by the Attorney
General, who is a Jew and naturally in favor of the Balfour
Declaration, and passed by the Executive Council, which is composed exclusively of Englishmen. Indeed, there is not a single
one of the highest officials who represents the Arab majority and we have no voice in the making of laws or in voting
for the disposal of the taxes which we pay.

"It is not only that the impossible Balfour Declaration is
invidious and unjust to the Arabs; it places the Jews themselves in danger. Remember that Jerusalem is also our sacred
city. By the declaration of many Zionists and political Jews
in various parts of the world, they ultimately want the Temple
area, the sacred places and all Palestine as a national home.
This arouses every sect and the entire population of this land
that is sacred to all three religions. This will raise the menace
of racial conflict with the whole Moslem world.

"Notice these large pictures which the Jews have prepared
as 'souvenirs' for their people—a part of the world-wide propaganda of which they are masters, with large control of the
news agencies, the press and the financial and political centers
of the world. Here in this large placard you see the pictures
of all the Jewish sacred places of Palestine, including the
Mosque of Omar, the Temple area, the Western Wall, the
Mount of Olives, and a dozen more. Above these are the Ten
Commandments, and above them all is the crown of the restored Jewish kingdom. What can such a picture mean but the
possession of all our holy places and the entire land? Or, take

this other picture which has been broadcast throughout the world, of the Zionist flag placed on the Mosque of Omar and the Zionist leader calling this vast multitude of Jews from the ends of the earth to go up and possess the land. What can such propaganda mean?

"We ask no special favor for ourselves. But we do ask justice. We ask for the formation of a democratic, representative, elective government, with representation for Arabs and Jews in proportion to their respective numbers, with a careful safeguarding of the Jewish minority. Only by a just democratic government can peace be secured for all three religions. And it is peace through justice that we seek."

The above represents the official statement of the position of the Arabs in Palestine today.

The Jewish Case

The Jewish case in Palestine also seems unanswerable. First of all in reply to the Arabs it should be said that, as between the Arabs and Jews, the latter are by far the more modern and efficient community. The Arabs are more backward, medieval and feudal. They are divided between the gentry or effendi and the peasants or fellaheen. The latter are ignorant, poor and as tenants or laborers are kept at the mercy of the privileged class. The two hundred and fifty leading effendi families own approximately 1,000,000 acres of land, or an average of 4,000 acres per family. In this small country the Husseini family of the Grand Mufti owns some 12,500 acres, the Tajji family an equal amount, the Abdul Hadi family about 15,000 acres. The former corrupt Turkish administration and the absence of reliable land records gave the intelligent effendi the opportunity for "adding of field to field" against which the prophets of Israel thundered.

The Arabs of the privileged class commonly charge the poor fellah a rent of a third of the crop, and half the gross yield is not unknown.[1] On short term loans the interest charged the

[1] Thus the Arab paper *El Jezira* writes: "There is no injustice when the fellah who leases his land from the owner pays one-third of the crop as rent." Quoted from Maurice Samuel *On The Rim of the Wilderness*, p. 23, to whom we are indebted in this section.

peasants by the merchants of Nazareth is 30 per cent for six months, with the right of foreclosure by the usurer if the debt is not paid. The Arab press protested violently when the government reduced the term of imprisonment for debt from the maximum of 91 to 21 days, fearing that the helpless fellah would get out of the effendis' control.

Jewish labor is powerfully and democratically organized, but their effendi masters speak for the Arab peasants. No Arab paper speaks for its own peasants or for labor. Out of 143 municipal councilors, not one represents Arab labor. While the Jews have some 200 cooperative societies with 3500 members and deposits and savings of $3,500,000, the Arabs have not a single successful cooperative. Such societies would be opposed by their feudal effendi. One of their bitterest complaints against the Jews is in reality that their own peasantry is getting out of hand. Any genuine national movement among the Arab masses would be opposed to the death by their own leaders. The advance of the fellaheen will be promoted by the presence of Jewish labor and colonies providing examples in method and stimulus, but under the protection of the British Government. Their worst enemies will be their own feudal families.

A proverbial weakness of all Arabs, from the days of Mohammed to the present, is family rivalries. The Arabs seem never able to combine or cooperate save for a short time in the face of a common foe. All Arab writers and their best friends deplore their internal dissensions. Palestine is no exception to this rule. The political, economic and social power of the community is held by a handful of families divided into jealous and quarreling factions. The Supreme Moslem Council, which is more powerful than the Arab Executive, controls the funds of the Wakf, or Moslem religious foundations, consisting of some $300,000. The Council is now largely in control of the Husseini family of the Grand Mufti, with two rival factions contending for the power and privilege. The party in power is always accused of tyranny and misappropriation of funds by the factions in opposition.

252   THE CHALLENGE OF THE EAST

Any parliament or executive body elected in proportion to population, would inevitably be controlled, not by the Arab majority, but by the small section of the quarreling effendi who had been able by any means to secure or seize power. The whole habit of thought of these privileged feudal families is one of tyranny over their serfs. The Jews point out that only one-tenth of the land purchased by the Zionist Organization was bought from the independent peasantry; the rest was sold by the large Arab landholders, and half of this was waste when it was obtained.[1] The Jews claim that they have brought into the country in public and private funds some $200,000,000, of which $17,000,000 was paid to the Arabs for land, and that the Arabs derive an annual revenue from the Jews of not less than $5,000,000. "Of all the mandated territories taken over from the ruined Turkish Empire, Palestine is the only one that has managed to pay the whole of its allotted pre-war debts, refund the home government for the expenses incurred during the occupation, and make good the cost of property taken over from the military administration. . . . In ten years $20,000,000 have flowed out of the country for the payment of debts and for purchases. It is an extraordinary achievement."[2]

In regard to the Jews themselves, centuries of persecution and race prejudice, especially in eastern Europe, culminating in the pogroms of Russia, drove the Jews to cherish the recovery of their ancient homeland which pious Israel believed was promised by Jehovah to Abraham.[3] From the pressure of the crowded ghettoes where the Jews had been oppressed for centuries, many of them turned with longing hearts to the cradle of their race and faith.

Modern Zionism revived the spirit of Israel which existed among the Babylonian exiles in captivity and after the destruction of the Temple by the Romans in 70 A. D. Since the latter date the Jews have never ruled in Palestine. Less than forty years ago, in 1896, Theodor Herzl, a then unknown

[1] *On the Rim of the Wilderness,* Samuel, p. 207–209.
[2] Ibid, p. 222.
[3] Genesis 13:14, 15. "And the Lord said unto Abraham. . . . All the land which thou seest, to thee will I give it, and to thy seed forever."

Jewish journalist from Vienna, returned from the Dreyfus case in France, almost as an inspired prophet of fresh hope for the national resurrection of his people. Zionism began as a spiritual movement awakening the national consciousness of the Jews to a renaissance of Jewish life, literature and culture. Herzl's pamphlet on *The Jewish State* advocated an autonomous Jewish commonwealth in Palestine, which was at that time under the Sultan of Turkey.

The first International Zionist Congress in Basle declared as its aim: "Zionism strives to create for the Jewish people a home in Palestine secured by public law." Up to the outbreak of the War some 60,000 Jews had returned to Palestine. During the War, in recognition of the powerful financial assistance of Jewish financiers and of the services of Dr. Weizmann of Manchester University, influential Hebrews secured the Balfour Declaration promising them a National Home for the Jewish people. It was like Lincoln's Emancipation Proclamation for an oppressed people. The declaration of the British Government was confirmed by the Allied Powers, endorsed by President Wilson and the American Congress and officially recognized by the League of Nations.

Wealthy Jews from all over the world generously responded with their gifts and over $50,000,000 have been invested in the enterprise in Palestine. Today there are some 170,000 Jews settled there. "Palestine became for the Jews more than a mere country; it became a symbol of regeneration, of a return to the days of its youthful vigor, to health bodily and spiritual." [1]

At the Sixteenth Zionist Congress in Zurich in 1929 the old political Zionist Organization for the establishment of the National Home in Palestine gave way to a new international body called the Jewish Agency. Control passed from the nationalistic, socialistic Jewish idealists of eastern Europe to conservative Jewish business men of wealth in the United States, many of them non-Zionists.

In a poor country, against heavy odds, Palestine has witnessed a heroic record of Jewish achievements. Agriculture

---

[1] *Joint Palestine Survey Commission.*

and industry have been promoted, waste land has been reclaimed, hills afforested, tracts of wilderness have been turned into irrigated gardens, and swamps have been drained. Hebrew culture has been revived, and education, sanitation and social service extended. "In brief, wealth, prosperity, culture, civilization, sacrifice to an idea—all these have been brought into Palestine by the new Jewish settlers."

Practically all the land held by Jews has been acquired by purchase and often at high prices. The Jews own or cultivate some 225,000 acres of land. While the Jews constitute about one-sixth of the population they still own less than one-twelfth of the 2,750,000 acres of cultivable land.

The beneficial economic development of the country has on the whole often improved the condition of the working-class Arab, although the Arab landlord class has lost influence and power.

Zionism is an evolving and complex phenomenon and the Jews in Palestine are made up of many diverse elements, religious and secular, orthodox and atheist, capitalist and Communist, laborer and peasant. Mr. Maurice Samuel finds their chief component elements as follows: The dominant group is found in the labor movement both in numbers and initiative. Over all classes towers the Jewish Federation of Labor, the most significant force in the country. The Federation numbers 27,000 out of a Jewish population that is approximately 170,000. An older group was the conservative middle class element on the land. They represent the more prosperous colonists who have been overshadowed by the more aggressive labor group. There is a third element in the pre-Zionist Jews, orthodox, religious, medieval, reactionary. Finally there is a chauvinistic group, fortunately small because Zionism did not tempt many chauvinists. "Palestine Jewry therefore contains everything that is to be found elsewhere: a tiny group of jingoes, a tiny group of sentimental pacifists, anti-laborites, liberals, clericals, socialists and Communists. The last, however, are a smaller proportion than in other countries." [1]

---

[1] *On the Rim of the Wilderness,* pp. 137–139.

Russian Communism is inevitably against both the nationalist and the religious element in Zionism. Zionism drew during the last decade 100,000 Jews to Palestine from all over the world from the most enterprising and earnest pioneer elements of this virile race.

The creation of a National Home for the most persecuted race in the world will be a unique achievement of modern history. It has come not by the orthodox hope of miraculous divine intervention, but by the people themselves undertaking their own deliverance.[1] John Haynes Holmes makes an excellent statement of the Jewish case in his *Palestine Today and Tomorrow*. He shows that three waves or impulses carried the Jews back to their land. The first was the movement of individual pilgrims. The second was that of the refugees in the last quarter of the nineteenth century driven thither by the pogroms of the Czars and other persecutions which expelled two and a half million Jews out of eastern and southeastern Europe. The third was the real return of the Jews in the self-conscious movement of Zionism. This was backed at first by the generous millions of Baron Edmond de Rothschild, and later by wealthy Hebrews of America and Britain.

The recovery of their own land means all that the restoration of Ireland or Poland did to those peoples, and more. The Jews of the world need no longer be wanderers or aliens without a country, for they now have, as the modern prophet of Zionism says, "a natural spiritual center of Judaism, to which all Jews will turn with affection, and which will bind all Jews together; a center of study and learning, of language and literature, of bodily work and spiritual purification; a true miniature of the people of Israel as it ought to be." [2]

---

[1] The justification for Jewish rights in Palestine is based on the occupation of the land by the Jewish Kingdom from about 1000 B. C. to 597 B. C. and from 536 B. C. to 4 B. C. In the Preamble to the Mandate for Palestine, The Council of the League of Nations says: "Recognition has thereby (in the Balfour Declaration) been given to the historical connection of the Jewish people with Palestine and to the grounds for reconstituting their national home in that country."

[2] *Summa Summarum*, by Achad Ha-Am.

Palestine is thus both a country and an idea of racial and individual self-fulfillment. The Jew is seeking in Zion not only his country but his soul.[1] He is "translating religion into terms of a better social order." These heroic settlers suggest "the Pilgrim Fathers of Palestine." They are making these barren, malarial lands once more to blossom as the rose. When Dr. Holmes objected that to restore the soil now washed away from the once-terraced and fertile hills would take a hundred years of toil, his Jewish companion replied, "What is a hundred years to a Jew." The Jew remembers the Mandate of the League of Nations to "encourage the close settlement of Jews on the land, including State lands and waste lands acquired for public purposes."[2] But in his heart he believes he holds a higher mandate of the need of his people for the promised land of which they have been deprived for nearly nineteen centuries.[3]

Reliance on force aroused by the violence of the War and the infection of the war fever awakened an alarm in the Arab, and a temporary exultation and at times even arrogance in some of the young Jews, which was answered by the violence of the Arab outbreaks. But this spirit must subside and be cast out if the high destiny of the land is to be fulfilled for the Jew, for the Arab and for all concerned. It must indeed be the welfare of all or none in the Zion of the future. Surely enough blood and bitter tears have been shed, enough mistakes have been made in this Holy Land in the past by Jew, Moslem and Christian to warn all with the living voice of the prophets that deliverance will not come by might or by power. "The only hope is from moderates who can see that both races may live together in a land which is their mutual heritage, and can co-operate in working out a relationship of peace. . . . Deep down is the social idealism of the Jew which is the spiritual substance of his life. His one vast achievement in the world, his one unique contribution to humanity, is his prophet's dream

---

[1] *Palestine Today and Tomorrow,* p. 81.

[2] Article VI of Mandate of the League for Palestine.

[3] "They shall build the old wastes, they shall raise up the former desolations, and they shall repair the waste cities, the desolations of many generations." Isaiah 61:4.

of righteousness and peace upon the earth." [1] In the noble words of the Twelfth Zionist Congress: "Our determination (is) to live with the Arab people on terms of concord and mutual respect, and together with them make the common home into a flourishing commonwealth, the upbuilding of which may assure to each of its peoples undisturbed national development. The two great Semitic peoples united of yore by the bonds of common creative civilization will not fail in the hour of their national regeneration to comprehend the need of combining their vital interests in a common endeavor."

The story of their achievements against terrific odds forms an epic of which every Jew may well be proud, and which would require volumes to record. Their title to a National Home in Palestine is backed by strong international guarantees. The treatment which the jews of eastern Europe still receive would seem to make such a home a necessity.

As between the conflicting claims of these two peoples how then is this problem to be solved? A Commission of Enquiry was appointed by the British Government under the chairmanship of Sir Walter Shaw with three members of Parliament representing the three political parties in Great Britain.[2] After conducting its sessions in Jerusalem, the Shaw Commission presented its report to Parliament in March, 1930. The findings of the commission may be briefly summarized as follows:

1. The outbreak of 1929 was not premeditated, and "not intended to be a revolt against British authority in Palestine," but "was from the beginning an attack by Arabs on Jews for which no excuse in the form of earlier murders by Jews has been established." [3]

2. The Mufti of Jerusalem "must accept a share in the responsibility for the disturbances."

3. "The complaint that the Palestine Government have consistently shown a lack of sympathy towards the establishment

---

[1] *Palestine Today and Tomorrow*, pp. 132, 141.

[2] Its terms of reference were: "To inquire into the immediate causes which led to the recent outbreak in Palestine and to make recommendations as to the steps necessary to avoid a recurrence."

[3] See *Shaw Report*, pp. 158-171. Also the *Palestine Mandate*, League of Nations Association of the U. S., p. 13.

of the Jewish National Home and that their policy has been one of weakness is, in large measure, due to the difficulties inherent in the Mandate and to a failure to appreciate the dual nature of the policy which the Government have to administer. It is our view that the Government did discharge to the best of their ability the difficult task of maintaining a neutral and impartial attitude between two peoples whose leaders have shown little capacity for compromise."

4. Jewish immigration has conferred material benefits upon Palestine in which the Arabs share, but "there is incontestable evidence that in the matter of immigration there has been a serious departure by the Jewish authorities from the doctrine accepted by the Zionist Organization in 1922, that immigration should be regulated by the economic capacity of Palestine to absorb new arrivals." The feeling of Arab apprehension caused by Jewish immigration "was a factor which contributed to the outbreak."

5. The land policy, as pursued under the Protection of Cultivators Ordinance of 1929, while giving compensation for disturbance "does nothing to check the tendency towards the dispossession of cultivators from their holdings . . ." "There is no alternative land to which persons evicted can remove. In consequence a landless class is being created which is a potential danger to the country." "Palestine cannot support a larger population than it at present carries unless methods of farming undergo a radical change."

6. It is believed "that a feeling of resentment among the Arabs of Palestine consequent upon their disappointment at continued failure to obtain any measure of self-government is greatly aggravating the difficulties of the local administration."

7. The inherent difficulties "in the Balfour Declaration and in the Mandate for Palestine are factors of supreme importance in the consideration of the Palestine problem." A clear definition of policy "backed by a statement that it is the firm intention of His Majesty's Government to implement that policy to the full, would be of the greatest assistance in securing the good government of the country."

8. The fundamental cause of disturbances in Palestine is believed to be "the Arab feeling of animosity and hostility towards the Jews consequent upon the disappointment of their political and national aspirations and fear for their economic future."

The Report concludes with the recommendations that the Government shall issue "with the least possible delay" a statement of policy which "will clearly state that the rights and position of non-Jewish communities in Palestine are to be fully safeguarded," the regulation of immigration "with the object of preventing a repetition of the excessive immigration of 1925 and 1926," [1] the introduction of improved methods of agriculture, an *"ad hoc* Commission to determine the rights and claims in connection with the Wailing Wall," etc.

Taken as a whole the Report of the Commission is rather favorable to the Arab cause and recommends the greater protection of the interests of the majority of the population. Mr. Snell, the Labor member of the Commission, added a special note placing a greater share of responsibility for the disturbances upon the Arab religious authorities, differing from his colleagues in certain matters regarding immigration and the constitutional grievances of the Arabs, and on the whole favoring the Jewish cause.

In October, 1930, the British Government issued a statement of its policy on Palestine in a White Paper "to convince both Arabs and Jews of their firm intention to promote the essential interests of both races to the utmost of their power, and to work consistently for the development, in Palestine, of a prosperous community. . . . To the difficulties created by the mutual suspicions and hostilities of the two races has been added a further grave obstacle, namely, an attitude of mistrust towards His Majesty's Government fostered by a press campaign in which the true facts of the situation have become obscured and distorted." "It must be realised, once and for all, that it is useless for Jewish leaders on the one hand to press

---

[1] The net Jewish immigration in 1925 was 31,650, in 1926, 13,081 entered but 7,365 emigrated. The net total of immigration during the decade 1919–1928 was 77,751. *Shaw Report,* p. 101.

His Majesty's Government to conform their policy in regard, for example, to immigration and land, to the aspirations of the more uncompromising sections of Zionist opinion. That would be to ignore the equally important duty of the Mandatory Power towards the non-Jewish inhabitants of Palestine. On the other hand, it is equally useless for Arab leaders to maintain their demands for a form of Constitution which would render it impossible for His Majesty's Government to carry out, in the fullest sense, the double undertaking already referred to."

The White Paper states that the two sections of the population are of equal weight. In defense of the Arab claims it is said: "At the present time and with the present methods of Arab cultivation there remains no margin of land available for agricultural settlement by new immigrants. . . . It also appears that of the 86,980 rural Arab families in the villages, 29.4 per cent are landless. . . . There is at present a serious degree of Arab unemployment, and Jewish unemployment likewise exists. . . . Both races should consent to live together and to respect each other's needs and claims. . . . The general developments of the country shall be carried out in such a way that the interests of the Arabs and Jews may each receive adequate consideration."

The White Paper states that the time has now come for the establishment of a measure of self-government in Palestine and proposes a Legislative Council of the High Commissioner and 22 members of whom ten will be official members appointed by the government, and 12 unofficial, elected members.

This White Paper met with a storm of protest from the Jews. The Arabs also were, as previously, unwilling to cooperate in any plan which would give the balance of power to the Government and not to them as the majority section of the population.[1]

---

[1] In October, 1920, there was set up an Advisory Council in equal parts of official and nominated unofficial members. Of the latter four were to be Moslems, three Christians and three Jews. The Arabs refused to cooperate, as they did later in September, 1922, when a Legislative Council was proposed.

So effective and influential was the protest of the Jews that the British Government had to change its policy in certain matters and on February 13, 1931, Ramsay MacDonald stated that the White Paper "did not imply a prohibition of the acquisition of additional land by Jews" and that the Government did not contemplate any stoppage or prohibition of Jewish immigration. Dr. Weizmann, the former Zionist leader, felt that the statement of the Prime Minister had restored Jewish rights which had been seriously infringed by the White Paper. However strained the relations may be between the three parties in the dispute, it is fortunate for all concerned that the Jews and Arabs are dealing with the British Government which is the most experienced and the most impartial in the world for handling such a delicate and difficult situation. However thankless the task of the British may seem, we may confidently hope that all three parties will in time work out a solution that shall do justice to all and commend itself to world public opinion.

A solution could be found for this unsolved problem, this chronic impasse, if Moslem, Jew and Christian had the spirit shown by Dr. J. L. Magnes, president of the Hebrew University in Jerusalem. His words that follow might have been written by Woodrow Wilson; they might have been written by Abraham Lincoln; or by Amos or Isaiah. In his book *Like All the Nations,* Dr. Magnes asks for his Jewish people in Palestine, in reasonable proportion, three things: "Immigration, settlement on the land, Hebrew life and culture. If you can guarantee these for me I should be willing to yield the Jewish 'State' and the Jewish 'majority,' and on the other hand I would agree to a Legislative Assembly together with a democratic political régime. . . . A former Administrator of Palestine reckoned that, with agriculture remaining the chief industry, the land . . . could accommodate roughly 3,000,000 people. As for myself, if I could know that in the course of a long, long period a Jewish community of 1,000,000 souls— one-third of the population—was possible here, I should be well content.

"The Holy Land is no place for an Arab National State or Government, or for a Jewish National State or Government, but for a bi-national country with a mandate as nearly permanent as possible held by Great Britain from the League of Nations. It should be clear that the official and equal status of the Hebrew language must be removed constitutionally from the competence of the Legislative Assembly to interfere with . . . I am heartily in favor of including within this régime, a Legislative Assembly in which the two nationalities shall participate upon the basis of a carefully worked out system of suffrage. It is right in morals, that the people of this and every other country should have a voice in their own government; and it is not possible, even though it were desirable, to maintain the present status quo—an absolutest colonial régime. . . .

"I am asked must we do that now? My answer is, Yes, now, and the pity is we did not do it before Hebron and Safed. . . . We must face this problem not because of the pogroms but despite them, not as a result of violence, but as an attempt to remove excuses for violence, not because of pressure from without but because of spiritual pressure from within ourselves. . . . The question is, can we establish our life here not on a basis of force and power, but upon that of human solidarity and understanding . . .

"Palestine should not be a place of political domination at all on anyone's part. It is of much more importance to mankind than that. It does not 'belong' to Jew, Christian or Moslem, but to all of them together, to humanity. It does not belong, even in the narrower sense of that term, to its actual inhabitants, but to Jews and Christians and Moslems everywhere, for whom their brothers in the Holy Land have the privilege of acting as trustees. This making of Palestine the football of politics—Jewish, Arab, European—ought to be brought to an end. Unless Palestine can be built up upon a high ethical basis it is not worthy anyone's having. . . . The Joshua method is not the way for us of entering the Promised Land. The retention of bayonets in the land against the will of the majority of the population is repugnant to men of good will, and the Eternal People should rather continue its long wait than attempt to establish a home in the Holy Land, except on terms of understanding and peace." [1]

It must be recognized that the situation in Palestine is at best one of grave difficulty. Its solution will require wisdom, forbearance, patience and courage. The nineteenth century might have flung it with the spoils of war to either Arabs or Jews, fulfilling the promises and hopes of one or the other, and might have maintained it by military force. But that cannot be done in the twentieth century. Palestine is an international, sensitive nerve.

Both reasonable and fanatical adherents of three great monotheisms impinge upon one another there. The Christians are not so immediately concerned. After the disgrace of the Crusades and their long-standing quarrels over the Holy Sepulchre and other places they are not at the moment looking for more trouble. The Jews, the Arabs and the British Government are all in difficulty over the situation.

The Jews have a large stake in Palestine. It is not only for the protection of the present handful of the hundred and seventy thousand Jews there, but the land has become a national symbol, a creative hope for all patriotic or nationalistic Jews. After the treatment they have received, all the world should desire that they should have a genuine National Home in Palestine so long as it can be provided without injustice to the Arabs who constitute the majority of the population. But if their policy is political and aggressive, demanding their pound of flesh without regard to the majority, backed by Jewish finance and British bayonets and led by the arrogant young local Jews who have provoked the Moslems to riot and bloodshed, then there will inevitably follow further outbreaks and manifestations of the growing bitterness of the Arabs. In such an event world public opinion would not support them whatever their influential press connections and propaganda. The world should be ashamed of its historic treatment of the Jew and its attitude toward him. But the Jew should remember that there are sometimes causes for his unpopularity and for

---

[1] *Like All the Nations*, by J. L. Magnes, Jerusalem, 1930, pp. 6–40.

existing prejudice for which he is not altogether blameless. Whatever these may be they appear at their worst in Palestine. The Arab is not opposed to the Jew as such but has lived with him in peace for centuries. He is opposed to the aggressive predominance of *political* Zionism which he believes menaces his national existence in Palestine. There is a certain aggressive arrogance in the worst of the Jewish race in Palestine whose action is such that it turns almost all neutral observers against them. In our opinion a whole series of impartial commissions would only endorse the findings of the Shaw Commission. And the Jew will naturally conclude that they are prejudiced against him. He will blame the British for not being more firm and giving him more protection. But the time must come when he will learn that the solution of the problem lies not in British bayonets but in Jewish and Arab attitudes.

Tagore has remarked: "The success of Zionism depends entirely upon Arab-Jewish cooperation. This can be obtained in Palestine only by means of a direct understanding between the Arabs and the Jews." Professor Albert Einstein now urges that Jews and Arabs establish direct contact, and thus diminish the Palestine Government's function as the arbiter of their joint interests.

Syud Hossain, a Moslem publicist and editor of the *New Orient,* writing in the San Francisco Chronicle, September 9, 1929, declared: "The time has come for the Jews to take stock of the situation. They must choose one of two foundations or sanctions for their national home—either British military support or Arab moral acceptance. Recent events have shown that it cannot be both for any measurable period of time in the near future. I have indicated that in my opinion Jewish and Arab aspirations in Palestine are not irreconcilable, provided both can be cleansed of ulterior or extraneous motives."

Rabbi Louis Newman writes: "Amid the babel of voices, one clear and imperative call is emerging at last regarding the future of Zionism. It speaks in terms of an Arab-Jewish concordat, negotiated between the leaders of both races, without the mediation of any third party. . . . The fundamental factor involved must never be ignored; Jews and Arabs need each other; neither can achieve the redemption of Palestine single-handed."

If, in the spirit of Dr. Magnes, the Jew will build up in Palestine a spiritual and cultural home and a rallying center for the Jewish people of the world, but consent to such restriction of immigration and of political control that it shall make possible the ultimate democratic government of Palestine equally in the interests of Jews and Arabs, the problem can be solved. Such a solution world public opinion will probably demand in the end.

DATE DUE

GAYLORD			PRINTED IN U.S.A.